"*Ghost in the Ranks* offers an impo:
It weaves veterans' stories and up-tc
narrative that challenges dominant ι   ....ι y ιrauma and its
treatment. Dr. Whelan moves our focus from individual medical diagnosis
and specific traumatic events to the broader context of military culture and
workplace relations. Provocatively, Whelan asks whether central aspects of
military culture—such as a tough version of military masculinity that relies
on emotional avoidance—may be one of the reasons behind mental health
problems among serving and retired military personnel. He does not offer
simple answers or solutions, but opens new avenues for empathetic dialogue
and deeper understanding. Military trauma, as the book shows so well, is
profoundly personal, relational, and political."

Dr. Maya Eichler,
Canada Research Chair in Social Innovation and Community Engagement,
Mount Saint Vincent University

"In this text that intertwines commentary with autobiography and true
soldier stories, Dr. Whelan delves into the problem of mental injuries in the
Canadian Forces. The narration outlines how the deepest values underlying military commitment—valour, honour, brotherhood—can become the
ground for disturbance when elements of the system fail to be supportive.
The pain and alienation of the psychologically injured and abandoned
military members is poignantly depicted in this compelling book. Equally
important are Dr. Whelan's insights into how these men and women could
be buttressed. As a psychologist who treats those who serve as well as veterans, I recommend *Ghost in the Ranks* to anyone seeking to truly understand
the hardship and the hope that exists for our best and bravest Canadians."

Dr. Robin McGee,
Clinical Psychologist

"Well written, *Ghost in the Ranks* is an explosive look at the inner workings of
the Canadian Armed Forces. Dr. Whelan offers an open and straightforward
message to the men and women who serve and Canadian society about the
lingering effects of an acquired military identity on mental health struggles.
The book captures what it means for these men and women to become mentally broken and then face being turned out of the military. Dr. Whelan has
captured the very fabric of the men and women who serve. A must read!"

Michael Hobson,
Veteran and R2MR Mental Health Educator

"The insights within Dr. Whelan's newest offering—*Ghost in the Ranks*—once again demonstrates his unique understanding and vantage point into the world of PTSD and those who are supposed to be there to provide support. A must read for anyone ever touched by PTSD!"

Derrick Nearing, PO1 (Ret), MMM, CD2

Ghost
in the Ranks

Forgotten Voices & Military Mental Health

by DR. JOHN J. WHELAN

*For the military men and women who silently bear
the costs of serving as our protectors. May you continue
to find the courage to speak out and be heard.*

 FriesenPress

Suite 300 - 990 Fort St
Victoria, BC, V8V 3K2
Canada

www.friesenpress.com

The people described in this book represent composite characters,
even though the events are factual as reported by serving and retired
military personnel. All names and identifying information reported
herein have been altered to protect the anonymity of actual people.

ISBN
978-1-4602-8529-9 (Hardcover)
978-1-4602-8530-5 (Paperback)
978-1-4602-8531-2 (eBook)

1. PSYCHOLOGY, PSYCHOPATHOLOGY, POST-TRAUMATIC STRESS DISORDER (PTSD)

Distributed to the trade by The Ingram Book Company

Table of Contents

Introduction

Shrouded in darkness, it travels on the breeze, steady and silent on its deadly journey towards unsuspecting soldiers huddled in their trenches. An unseen enemy, it invades their world, blanketing them, choking out life—chlorine gas; its victims, soldiers during the First World War. An invisible enemy against which strength of arms is no defence, it is a fitting description of another modern day enemy—mental illness. It too threatens to invade the Canadian military, having already ended the careers and the lives of soldiers and veterans prematurely, forcing the leadership to take it seriously. This new enemy comes by various names—depression, panic, addiction, and suicide—but it is post-traumatic stress disorder, or PTSD, that stirs the same fear and confusion created by that other 100-year-old foe.

Many members sneer in feigned bravado to ward off this invader even as it moves through steel walls and body armour to infect their senses directly. It has been called insidious, leaving no trace of its approach as it settles in the brains of unsuspecting victims. It may lay dormant for years, growing, festering, infecting thoughts and perceptions of reality and then erupting without warning. It requires members to become vigilant of themselves and others for any signs of affliction. Its origins tantalize observers; maybe this germ, this *infection*, was there all along to be activated on the battlefield, or maybe it crept in during the time away from home only to be fertilized on familiar soil. Make no mistake, PTSD is a serious foe, and the Canadian Armed Forces (CAF) has engaged it in the form of overlapping programs and a complex mental health network in hopes of shedding light on this intruder and rooting it out.

Operational stress injuries (or OSIs) have slashed across the heart of our military like a sabre, cutting into men and women of all ranks across the three service elements. The past twenty-five years have seen the CAF deployed on the ground, across oceans, and in the sky over many troubled places. The Canadian Armed Forces has navigated the eras of downsizing, right sizing, the pursuit of efficiencies, and the preoccupation with information control demanded by its civil leaders. Throughout all this, many of the foreign deployments that have drawn our Canadian soldiers have left them suffering with OSI issues. Ghostlike casualties.

Our recent decade of war has produced many more of them, ranging from Privates to Generals, who also quietly seek out help. We have preoccupied ourselves with efforts to solve individual cases, but absent from discussion are meaningful conversations to better understand this newly recognized phenomenon. Alongside the many efforts to address concerns about mental health within the military, there is also a deafening silence. There are no venues, either in the public sphere or privately, through which the institution can truly understand how it has been changed by the full impact of recent wars. Many veterans tell me that the institution has become tougher and more bureaucratic even as it labours to be more accepting of mental health concerns. It can be confusing to unravel their concerns and the challenges they face as mentally wounded military veterans.

Who am I to be commenting on mental health within our military institution?

This is a question I often ask myself, for I have been out of uniform for many years. Even so, I have never been far from the military in terms of offering help, both professionally and personally, to those people who have been somehow broken or compromised by their experience. Many of these men and women have come to see themselves as a consumable resource despite everything they were taught about brotherhood, commitment, and loyalty to one another. It is extremely challenging to reconcile their stories with my continuing gratitude to the military for offering me the opportunities for a different life. I grew up in the military, and a part of my identity will likely always remain tied to the Canadian Armed Forces. Even so, I believe I hold a responsibility—maybe even a duty—to ensure that the voices of those men and women emotionally wounded by their service are heard and not forgotten.

For many serving in our military, mental health is of little concern; their work and family lives are all they wish them to be. And when it comes to the benefits of comradeship, shared purpose, and representing Canada on the world stage, there is no equal anywhere. For other members, however, mental declines follow on the heels of overseas deployments as they try to forget their experiences and come back to routine military life. Forgetting is often preferable to trying to thaw out emotionally because it has no place in routine military life, and privately it is often too scary and too painful to consider. My belief is that, if we continue to look only at those veterans with diagnosable mental health problems, we risk neglecting the broader military experience and its relationship with mental health in general.

When it comes to the well-publicized issue of PTSD, almost every person seems to struggle with unresolved emotional dilemmas related to the ideals of military service. Members have few opportunities to reconcile these struggles in a population that prizes stoicism and denigrates emotionality as weakness. In the absence of places or adequate time within the organization to unravel these experiences with other members or their leadership, many of them manage by shutting down emotionally—while others become too difficult to handle. However, common among people who have been released medically are reactions of disorientation, disillusionment, and unfinished business. Many of them also face concurrent pain from physical injuries that are life-changing; their lives are often centred on medication regimes or they drink or use other substances to manage daily living.

My central goal for writing this book is to highlight mental life within the military and possible reasons for the ongoing distress and disorientation reported by medically released veterans. *Ghost in the Ranks* is a follow-up to *Going Crazy in the Green Machine* (2014)[1] and serves as a continuation of the discussion on mental health

---

1   J.J. Whelan, *Going Crazy in the Green Machine* (Victoria, BC: FriesenPress, 2014).

and trauma among military members and veterans. Previously, I spoke about the central role of military identity in understanding and developing more effective ways to respond to operational stress and PTSD.

Many readers of *Going Crazy in the Green Machine* asked that I expand the discussion of issues that were addressed peripherally. Many of them also challenged me and reminded me of the many silent stories that needed to be told. Indeed, the upsurge in military men and women being released medically because of mental health problems over the past fifteen years ought to serve as a harbinger for the effects of multiple and overlapping deployments on our military institution as a whole. These mental casualties also raise fundamental questions about the meaning of brotherhood / sisterhood within the military family.

A word about the title

The mental health of our military personnel and veterans continues to be the subject of a national conversation. Missing from these discussions are the voices of forgotten men and women who have drifted into the unknown. *Ghost in the Ranks* aims to capture the reverberation of those voices as a response to the noticeable silence within the CAF over the human costs it has paid and which it continues to pay in the wake of its commitments to Canada. The title is emblematic of the anxiety-provoking acknowledgment of mental illness within the military. It is a notion that is centuries old. Only in recent years, however, has it been accepted by the military leadership as a workplace reality even as other first response organizations continue to debate its existence. Mental illness challenges the myth of invincibility within the military and among young soldiers and their leaders. It exposes the fragility of human beings, and it gets in the way of established training and the usual ways of operating because it undermines the sense of safety and community created through ideals of loyalty, sacrifice, brotherhood, and family. The spectre of unseen mentally injured members in the ranks also threatens to shake the bond of military brotherhood where men and women are required to display unwavering commitment to each other through their actions.

As I think about the issues presented in the book, the reference to *ghosts* also conjures up the general view of mental illness as an unseen attacker capable of hitting anybody regardless of physical strength or abilities, age, or rank. Publicly, at least, it is portrayed as a faceless enemy that can strike at any time. For those people who are afflicted, they describe being haunted by mental pictures and upsetting images of particular people from the past who died or who were seriously injured. From my perspective, when military men and women decline psychologically within the military, they often view themselves as diminished versions of their former *soldier*-selves. In essence, these men and women become phantoms or ghosts among their peers when compared to their established reputations and identity. One proposition throughout the book is that military membership at home and during deployments may require people to unwittingly misplace aspects of their humanity—as it pertains to their sense of themselves and each other—in order to carry out the things required of them.

Ghost in the Ranks focuses on the role of group life in the military as an important emotional regulator for its membership. I suggest that many operational injuries centre on disavowed emotional reactions to real and perceived breaches in these relationships and that symptoms of distress often reflect the loss of their connection to the group as central elements of emotional stability within the military and beyond. Soldiers and veterans can become disoriented and disheartened in a military family that has been stressed and hardened by the demands placed upon it.

Traditionally, the term *in the ranks* refers to any collection or group of non-commissioned officers. It provides an image of people living in close quarters, knit together into a coordinated brotherhood as a component of the larger military family. Those members who struggle privately with mental health issues often do not stand out from other people and appear just like any other soldier within their sections and units. I use the term more broadly to include groups of officers and men and women that comprise our military institution.

One

Understanding Mental Health in a Military Context

It is Sunday morning. I have been writing for nearly three hours, and it's time to head outside for some air. The sun's rays are warm and welcoming, and the sights and smells of wild flowers surround me. Birds chirp and squawk at each other in the background. Summer has finally announced its arrival to Canada's east coast, but I am elsewhere.

My head spins on a scene from the movie *Thin Red Line,* and a line of dialogue haunts me.

"Where is it that we were together, who were you that I lived with? The brother, the friend...."

I have just ended working with another group of military veterans who bear the mental scars from various deployments—Somalia, Rwanda, Bosnia, Peggy's Cove, and Afghanistan; each place is someone's purgatory, and all are forgotten in the public discourse. These men have taken a leap to begin a journey back towards something they believed was all but lost to them—their humanness.

It is time for me to begin a trek to reflect on the things they continue to teach me. It is a daunting journey because of the many voices I am left to reconcile—a continued loyalty to our military institution and to those who have been injured that comes from having served in uniform myself; an appreciation for what it means to be a soldier as a relative of still-serving members; and a professional responsibility to demystify mental health based on my clinical experiences and relevant research. In the end, this journey has taken me to a landscape that reveals the central importance of relationships in understanding issues of mental health and trauma, the *social–relational* context of military life, if you will.

Some readers will remember the movie *Full Metal Jacket*. Over the years I have seen it many times, and each time I have mixed reactions. Giddy nostalgia for sure, when I try to describe those days and many of the funny things to our children, but I also feel something else that is much more difficult for me to put into words. The best way to describe it is something like a *tightness* somewhere deep in my chest. It is not because of the scenes of war; it is much deeper than this. It is the sense of connection and compassion for those recruits—young men who had no clue what was happening as they were exposed to the rawness of that environment. I watch them as they become tougher over the course of their training, and I can't avoid a reaction of sadness for the things they were trading away. It reminds me of when I also willingly participated in my own transformation from a naïve youngster into an idealistic and accepted member.

In my case, excelling at almost everything that was thrown at me turned into cockiness and probably even arrogance. But I was also a cheerleader and morale booster for the group, and yes, I also teased people and participated in so-called *blanket parties* (a practice of restraining a recruit with their bedsheets for non-sanctioned discipline—blows on the body with objects contained in socks—by other recruits) to bring sub-standard guys in-line.

I think that, in the process, something was given up, other values perhaps or the loss of gentleness or kindness towards other people. I think I became a little less human—maybe I had too much to prove to myself and to everybody else. I'm not really sure anymore, but I know that it was not done in the interests of simply *fitting in* (an overused phrase as far as I am concerned). I could already fit in anywhere I wanted. What I lacked was direction; I had all kinds of potential, but no compass. I wanted to succeed at anything and everything they threw at me, and being accepted by other people was just something coincidental along the way. I wanted a new beginning to forget about the past, and I just wanted to see where it would all lead me. But an odd thing happened along the way.

Many of these strangers really *did* turn into my brothers, and some of them are still my closest friends today. For the first time in my life, I knew exactly where I stood with other people. I came to recognize what shortcomings I had but also my strengths, which were respected by other people. We were a society onto ourselves. I knew that I belonged. I was called a natural leader. It was a weird trade-off

It has taken years to realize the things that I put aside in the interests of competence and self-discipline in order to co-exist alongside other people who wore the same uniform. I had learned, just like everyone else, to perform as a calculated machine when required, a bit crazy at times but also a grown-up (or so I thought). But I could never get past the thoughts in the back recesses of my mind that I was somehow *cheating*, that who I was in uniform wasn't really me. I had side-stepped life and put it on hold to do this other thing—a kind of abdication from myself for a while until I was ready to step back into my own life. I earned the respect of others and learned the lessons of pride, confidence, and competence. Nobody could have warned me that it would take many years and a lot of hard work to find *the box* I had put safely away on the shelf in my mind.

I also have to say that I was not interested in sentimental talk about brothers and family. I had enough of those in my biological family, and I was not interested in having any more of them. In fact, the mental and emotional needs of my family were among the very things that drove me to the military. I secretly felt that I had walked away and abandoned my siblings—part of my private box. The truth was that I could not make room within my family to stake my own place in the world.

Life with this new band of people was like a breath of fresh air. I also realize that many of the young men and women leaving military service also face incredible challenges in coming to terms with the things they also put aside for the sake of their brothers and sisters in uniform. Even though many of them are older than their years in world experiences, they still have to find a way to mature as emotionally healthy men and women—because, in uniform, emotionality was something to be consigned to their secret selves and thus unimportant.

When it comes to the phenomenon of operational stress and the present focus on fight–flight reactions, military people know that we exist in some version of these modes all of the time. I think this is part of the reason why soldiers often appear perplexed when they are asked about a specific event that created their reactions—this mode often started the first day most of us put on the uniform! The problem is learning to *stop* living in this mode when it turns into emptiness and becomes too exhausting. When people are taught to push their physical and mental limits continually, the other mode of slowing down can feel like being dead inside. When other emotions start to surface, many people have no idea of what to do about them. They don't know how to trust them, and it can really feel like going crazy. This is the downside of a life in adrenaline mode; it is a life in an altered state of being, an altered mode of relating to other people.

Military life affects many of us deeply, but most people do not recognize it while they are still in uniform. I am not suggesting for a moment that these effects are necessarily negative, just that these qualities often go unnoticed until life circumstances require us to have other abilities. Put simply, the skills that are necessary for deployments and routine military life are often at odds with the requirements of family life and other civilian encounters.

To give you an idea of the depth of this training, when I was released from the military, I remained in Halifax to attend university and lived several miles away from the Navy shipyard. In retrospect, the only thing different about me during those initial years was that I did not wear a uniform. I was still a 'type-A pinball' lost in a sea of civilians. It was a confusing and lonely time. Apart from my wife, I had virtually no other relationships, and I was as regimented and self-disciplined as I ever was before leaving. It helped me manage the constant sense of anxiety. I remember that when a ship's action alarm would go off during the night, even though it was barely audible, I would awake on alert, ready to act. This reaction continued for several years until we eventually moved further inland.

Many years later, when I would run past the naval dockyard, I would still feel the goosebumps and the adrenaline surge and sometimes even tears when a ship's action alarm was activated—it meant that something bad was happening. This heightened state would often stay with me for the remainder of the day and was usually followed by dreams of being at sea again. These types of automatic reactions were so hard-wired that it was a real challenge to relearn spontaneity and to just let go of the need to be prepared all of the time, to let my mind and emotions drift—like I saw from our children. It took many years to come out of prepared alertness and to realize that internal calm, gentleness, and wonder had been put aside. It takes real work to find these things again.

Several years ago, I was on a training program with civilian clinicians where I tried to explain to them the process of taking on a military identity. The best analogy I could give was that I had to hide any signs of vulnerability in order to make room for this new identity—to package these qualities in a sort of mental box and secret them away in a private closet. The problem was that, during the intervening years, I just seemed to misplace those other qualities. They were simply unimportant. When I did begin to search for them again, to my surprise, I also realized that I had to open a lot of other boxes as well. The experience is like thawing out after experiencing frostbite. Sure, coming inside to the warmth feels great, but it is also incredibly painful as blood circulation returns to the damaged area. This same challenge of having to traverse a psychological no-man's land also faces many military veterans trying to make the mental leap into civilian life. It can take a long time to learn to decompress. As many veterans have told me, they have to learn how to regain some of their humanity.

I don't think any of us realized what we were trading during this life-altering transformation. I am not blaming the military, for this is just the way it is and probably the way it has to be. Wide-eyed and testosterone-filled, we were ready for anything new. Whether we were all a bit antisocial—sensation-seeking types—to begin with, I am not sure. But even if anyone did realize these internal changes, it is unfathomable to think that it could ever be discussed. We were like the band of street kids from *Oliver Twist*—renegades and lost sheep within our real families under the watchful eyes of demanding surrogate fathers.

We were also looking for something to believe in; we were willing to take a journey to find better versions of ourselves. Our non-commissioned officers (NCOs) hammered and honed us into something useful for the military: "We will make you or we will break you." And we all saw people who were broken along the way and sometimes, with the encouragement of our instructors, we participated in helping to root out those who did not quite fit. There were always those people who were just too naïve or quietly rebelling by holding onto some aspects of their individuality—the ones marching to their own drums. I am not sure why we treated them so roughly.

For my part, it was to avoid being punished for their shortcomings and a desire to protect them at the same time. In some cases, we became like older brothers, and the best we could offer was to advise them to get out. Maybe there existed some element of envy that these people could resist the tyranny of this new family and the brotherhood, but there was also the knowledge that eventually they would be crushed by the process—nothing personal. Some of them found their place eventually, while other people became casualties and decided that they had to leave. Such was the military life that I remember.

Beginning in the late 1990s, Canada underwent a dramatic shift with the rise of the modern-day veteran—the adoption of an identity once reserved for those who served in the Great Wars. All who have served Canada honourably are now identified as veterans. This change in status appears to reflect a societal recognition of our military efforts, and at the same time, it has been echoed among groups of ex-military men and women who have been injured in various ways. The term denotes self-sacrifice and pride in one's service. Veteran status also serves as a recognition of the costs of service in terms of physical and mental injuries. The latter can lead us down a rocky path. It comes with the risk of creating permanent victimhood among those ex-military men and women who are left to seek support for mental wounds following release.

At an institutional level, there are no answers to profound questions facing the CAF. *Who are we now that we've shifted from peacekeepers to peace-making warriors? Where do we go from here? How do we go about reconciling our losses?*

The military institution does not have the time nor the luxury to engage in self-reflective efforts to regroup and to recalibrate in the face of new issues and ongoing deployments. It is simply not built that way. The priority is on action and, apart from periodic 'lessons learned' reviews, it recoils at the notion of such navel-gazing. Instead, these other places and times, along with their casualties, are necessarily erased from the corporate memory as the military marches forward. Maybe civil society has done the same thing; maybe they are also weary from having been toughened and they too just want to forget. What it boils down to is this: There is no place to entertain the most fundamental of questions. *Did we ask too much of them?*

My observation is that mental and emotional fatigue may be directly influencing our entire military membership, which challenges our usual way of defining mental health as a private concern for individual members to manage. The ongoing stories from medically released men and women, however, underscores a deafening silence over the effects of military ideals and culture on its membership as they struggle to begin the task of repairing themselves as human beings. They are left to re-evaluate the inherent disconnections between their expectations in terms of masculine military life and notions of good mental health, brotherhood and family, and the operational imperatives and the consequences of training and deployments. They are left to reconcile the costs of stoic pride and shutting off emotionally in order to meet the expectations of life in uniform. There are lingering costs from living an idealized, compartmentalized existence in service of others where members may unwittingly and necessarily trade pieces of their humanness along the way.

Over the past fifteen years, the CAF has committed to a massive undertaking to identify and offer help to individual members who have been affected by operational stress injuries, including PTSD, depression, and suicide. Some have argued that these changes were a matter of catching up with a major shift in public health policy that began in the mid-nineties. It goes without saying that, as a public institution, our military is intensely sensitive about its image—brand protection is of paramount concern.

In retrospect, media attention and the public outcry in the aftermath of the Somalia Affair and several publicized articles on sexual abuse within the military led to the creation of a Department of National Defence/Canadian Armed Forces Ombudsman's office in 1998. One year later, the CAF created the first specialized centre to begin addressing the issue of PTSD for distressed soldiers who had served in the Balkans. Several reports and recommendations by the CAF Ombudsman to improve mental health services to military members also contributed to a mental health initiative known as "Rx2000"—a complete overhaul and modernization of the mental health system within the Canadian Armed Forces.

In a relatively short time, the CAF responded by establishing additional Operational Stress Injury Social Support Centres across the country, instituting a national Operational Stress Injury Social Support program (OSISS) for serving and retired members with operational PTSD, and later establishing a network of Joint Personnel Support Units (or JPSUs) across the country focused on helping members deal with mental and physical injuries. In the past several years, it has also rolled out a military-wide educational program dubbed "Road to Mental Readiness" (R2MR) designed to provide mental health education and resiliency skill training to the entire membership from young recruits to senior leadership. These overlapping efforts within the CAF reflect a cultural shift that acknowledges mental health problems within its membership. These combined efforts are ongoing and seem designed to address and possibly to head-off the intrusion of mental illness within the military.

Behind the scenes, many distressed members are also managed in the community through confidential counselling services, specialized treatment centres, emergency hotlines, and countless hospital emergency room medical staff and private clinicians who work to support members of the Canadian Armed Forces. All of these efforts hold the promise of helping individual members, but none are designed to address the needs of the institution. The mental well-being of the organization and the implications of institutional-ized beliefs, values, and inherent contradictions are excluded from these well-intentioned efforts.

For those members released medically, the introduction of the New Veterans Charter in 2006 has been a continual source of aggra-vation, and veteran complaints contributed to the establishment of the Office of Veterans Ombudsman or OVO in 2007. Many of the issues continue to centre on disability coverage and concerns over levels of care. Again, numerous studies and reports produced a long list of recommendations concerning the care of military veterans. Veterans Affairs Canada responded by expanding its network of OSI (Operational Stress Injury) clinics across the country staffed by medical personnel of all types. This expansion continues.

Despite these combined efforts, reports about persistent distress and suicides among veterans continue to capture public attention. There remains much that we still do not know about the causes of mental declines among serving and retired members or how these relate to their difficulties in transitioning to civilian life. In the case of military PTSD, much of what we were taught was based on the American experience in Vietnam and subsequent combat opera-tions. This means that, in Canada, we are only now beginning to systematically gather information on the nature and prevalence of mental health struggles among serving members, the long-term out-comes for those who seek help, and the career trajectories for those members who silently manage on their own. Further complicating this mental health picture is the tendency to decontextualize these *illnesses* as a reflection of individual susceptibility; something that I propose is sorely inadequate.

"Mental health" is a term used in everyday language, but ironically it seems to serve as a type of code to refer to its opposite—mental illness—which means that, as a useful diagnostic construct, it has limited utility. We assume that we know good mental health when we see it among family members or among other people whom we encounter. Rachel Dodge and her colleagues[2] presented a cogent discussion of the complexities of defining mental well-being as

2   R. Dodge et al., "The challenge of defining wellbeing," *International Journal of Wellbeing*, 2(3) (2012): 222–235; doi:10.5502/ijw.v2i3.

much more than the absence of illness. They concluded that professional disagreements have ended in a simplistic definition as *a state
of equilibrium or balance that can be affected by life events or challenges.*
This cryptic definition does not provide much help in identifying
when mental well-being is present or when it is challenged. By contrast, however, when it comes to formally defining mental illness, a
term I reject professionally and dislike personally, in North America
we have a wealth of descriptions as outlined in the *Diagnostic and
Statistical Manual of Mental Disorders.* The most recent iteration, the
DSM-5, is an expansive document based on the assumption of a
biological basis of mental illness and a vague notion of the average
reasonably well-adjusted person. However, when it comes to diagnosing military personnel, I am still unsure how we can compare
military traits and behaviours against everyday notions of what it
means to be normal.

In fact, it seems a bit paradoxical to me that, in the formal mental
health world, many of the characteristics acquired through military
training are easily seen as mental health issues. For example, take the
issue of depression, a longstanding concern for the military. This so-
called disease is characterized by behaviours like black-and-white
thinking, perfectionistic standards and mental rigidity, an over-
developed sense of responsibility and self-blame, a generally negative focus, emotional avoidance, and intolerance for ambiguity. What
is notable about this is that it describes routine life within military
culture almost perfectly. Therefore, it is probably not by accident that
the rates of depression within the military are estimated to be twice
the rates for civilians.

This raises an issue for members who seek out mental healthcare
when they lose their mental stamina. While all the above traits are
normal within the military, in everyday citizens these beliefs and
behaviours are easily recast as abnormal. I also wonder whether the
same may hold true for the diagnosis of PTSD, particularly when it
comes to the cardinal feature of emotional avoidance. There is little
doubt that these members are distressed, but obsessively reviewing
specific negative events is often unhelpful for them unless these
efforts are positioned within the broader context of their training
and their military relationships.

For the most part, mental illness is poorly understood. Our understanding has been obscured by sensationalized reports through the
popular media and complicated by the involvement of the pharma-
ceutical industry. Many of these outdated myths easily portray mental
declines as an invisible enemy. This is due in part to our inability to

discuss the context of mental-emotional distress and in part due to a lack of consensus within our professional communities. Instead, we judge those who report problems as being different from the rest of us in our efforts to protect ourselves from being afflicted. It is also equated with older notions of madness, insanity—losing control of one's faculties and being rendered helpless in a bottomless abyss.

These longstanding misconceptions are a leftover from the Freudian concepts of biological and moral degeneration, which work to maintain our collective silence and possibly even our reliance on experts. And whether we realize it or not, our notions of psychological trauma are interwoven with the history of psychoanalysis and psychodynamic psychotherapy.[3] Then, as now, degeneration implies moral as well as biological weakness, a matter of chicken and egg, since weak people were expected to be prone to immoral acts just as immoral acts were expected to weaken both character and the brain.

While clinicians do not use the word *degenerate*, many people still hold strong convictions that these people were fundamentally compromised before the traumatic event either because of their biology or because of their character. These same concerns pervade Canadian society and contribute to the stigma associated with deployment stress problems; probably the biggest barrier for veterans to receive care.

The reality is that most people travel back and forth along a mental health continuum throughout their lives. Some people remain on the healthy end of this spectrum for the majority of the time but at other times move or slip along a continuum into what is generally termed mental illness. However, considerable research into psychological stress tells us that one's mental health status usually coincides with the waxing and waning of life challenges and is influenced, more than most people may realize, by our social context and by our relationships. By constructing mental distress as an enemy to be struck down and slain, we also create an unnecessary ghost to be feared. Instead, if we discuss mental health—good or bad—as a reflection and consequence of social context and relationships, this enemy can be seen for what it is, which is to say a normal and expected part of the human condition.

3   H. Kudler, "A psychodynamic conceptualization of retraumatization," in *Retraumatization: Assessment, treatment, and prevention*, eds. M. P. Duckworth and V. M. Follette (New York: Routledge, 2012), 33–60.

Mental distress often serves as a mirror reflecting the ways in which we organize modern life and how we go about the business of navigating day-to-day challenges along with other fellow travellers. In terms of our military then, increasing reports of mental health problems may be signalling fundamental shifts in the nature of relatedness within the organization—a shift towards impersonal, bureaucratic practices and away from the personal. When the promises of brotherhood and family begin to collapse, mental distress may be the mirror for these relational ruptures. In the aftermath of combat and other deployments, soldiers seem to be searching for people and places within the institution where they can safely decompress and regroup. They want to know that they are valued as people and that their commitment to duty meant something to the organization. They want opportunities to restore their belief in military ideals. A question worth consideration is whether patient symptoms reflect particular things about military service, including the phenomenon of emotional numbness and exhaustion—the personal price to be paid for stoic adherence to a well-established military ethos and confusion about finding a new place to be in the world. In other words, the very process of turning young men and women into soldiers may dramatically reshape both their perceptions and their responses to mental distress.

It is not accidental that, despite the military event that spurs soldiers to seek mental healthcare, it is often on the heels of some personal emotional event and a realization that they feel deadened inside. They become upset for having no feelings of sadness or compassion over the death of a parent or a friend, being unable to feel joy or pride over the birth of a child, or being unable to have loving feelings for their spouses or children. No emotion at all, save for anger and spiralling negativity, cynical thoughts, and impulses to hurt other people or to destroy themselves. It can be experienced as a profound emptiness. They aspire to meet their military ideals, which leaves no room for the complexities of personal vulnerability. It is only at this point that many of them realize the person they have become. The risk in trying to connect these reactions to specific traumas is that it can miss the point entirely. Maybe they took their military persona too seriously or traded away too much of themselves for the new version of themselves—those people like me in search of a new identity. Many people tell me that their issues are not only about specific bad events. They talk about it as something more insidious, something that crept into their souls over time and just wore them down mentally. At the same time, it is important to recognize that the circumstances surrounding specific critical events can plant the seeds of distress for these men and women.

Without an external goal or an internal sense of purpose in life, individuals unable to face themselves desperately try to hang onto their military ideals and values. I see the need for veterans to face these issues head-on before they can transition mentally and emotionally to civilian life. They need to come to terms with themselves. The people I grew up with said that I was brainwashed, which to my mind is a bit of a strong term. That being said, I do think that many members may benefit from formal retraining, a type of reprogramming when leaving the military that is conducted just like any other training. Here, people can be taught how to take the uniform off—to leave behind what they don't need and learn to be re-humanized again. This need to find a way back to humanity was underscored recently by a soldier as he choked through sobs trying to tell me about the killing of an armed youth overseas:

You don't fuckin' get it at all, do you? How am I supposed to live with this? I shot a kid in the head because I was a gung-ho asshole.

We need to be warned about the after-effects of moral dilemmas and culture shock and what to do about them. We need venues where anger and even bitterness towards the military can be aired out and taken seriously. We need to be told that the things done in uniform—and many of our military qualities themselves—were meant to serve specific needs of military operations and that some of these qualities are not relevant in the civilian world. We need to know that our concerns are not ours alone. We need to be taught the true costs of living a depersonalized and compartmentalized life.

As young impressionable men and women, nobody considered the cost of entering the blood brotherhood. I am close to my youngest brother who still serves, but I have a different relationship with my other two brothers. I do not mean this disparagingly. In fact, I may even have a level of envy, but they seem somehow innocent, less cynical, softer, easier going, and less focused on planning and details compared to my youngest brother and I. They can occupy themselves with minor things and absent-mindedness, but we just always seem to be a little bit wary, scanning, thinking, and observing. Situational awareness just seems to be automatic. We carry it without even realizing, but other people pick it up almost instantly.

We try to hide it to fit in, look relaxed, try to be absorbed in whatever is happening, but another part of the mind is always busy watching and calculating risks. For me, this was particularly true when our children were young. No matter what I was doing, I knew intuitively where they were at all times and seemed to know instinctively when they were in danger of being hurt.

My youngest brother and I are testier, rougher versions of our other two brothers. I think it came from passing the tests of training, by learning how to take crap only when you had no other choice, knowing when to play along but also when to give out as good as we got by resorting to threats and violence when needed. It gets to a point where you put on the uniform and the transformation is immediate.

For me, I also learned to use humour and to appear just a bit crazy as weapons to protect myself. Show no signs of fear and always give off the signals that you have the potential for violence or risk being someone else's victim—running in the wolf pack meant checking each other out continually. I became good at this, and these things earned me respect among my peers, but this wasn't really me, at least not the *private* me. But this was a better existence than the guys who were picked on and ridiculed and still others who were ignored completely because they were just too weird. Within this arena, we continually had to show that we could be counted on to do our jobs, to follow orders, and to not make trouble for the system. In a weird way, these things became sources of confidence and a shared understanding and connection with my buddies and fellow sailors.

In many respects, I grew up in the military in terms of self-assurance and pride, but moving into manhood, as I now understand it, was an entirely different and difficult transition. While self-reliance and initiative were reinforced in the military, many times following orders was the objective. I don't think that we learned emotional maturity, compassion, independent thought, forgiveness, or how to navigate contradictions and inconsistencies; all the other important things that are necessary for good men and women. Like many other people, I had to spend time, years after leaving the service, sorting out these things, deciding the lessons and the personal qualities to keep from the military and the other things that had to be discarded. The most difficult ones to negotiate were cynicism and self-reliance because they were so central for me and many of the people that I knew. We all had to be a bit prickly, but we were united in our commitment to duty. These were part of our primary shields to help us get by in the military—everyone had roles to play, but I believe that some of us got lost in those roles.

Beyond the world of our immediate buddies, the system can be incredibly bureaucratic and rife with inconsistencies and contradictions that cannot be acknowledged in this black-and-white world. The reality, of course, is that the world is mostly grey, requiring negotiation and cooperation, especially when it comes to human relationships and one's mental and emotional life. In fact, I think we hang onto the notion of brotherhood as a refuge—a kind of antidote to the dehumanizing and maddening aspects of the bureaucracy. There are specific things that happen in people's careers that erode their sense of pride and enthusiasm to be replaced by bitterness and cynicism and even lingering mental health struggles. Some become disheartened about life in general and about their roles in the world. If we are to truly understand military operational stress injuries, including depression, anxiety, and traumatic stress, I believe we must also account for the structure of relatedness within the 'military family' system.

The stereotypical image of the strong military man or woman excludes sensitivity, emotional expressiveness, humility, genuine connections to other people, or admission of personal vulnerability. Instead, embedded within the notion of masculinity in the military, which applies equally to males and females, are well-established clichés of things like sucking it up, winning at all costs, and strength and reliability. As said to me somewhat graphically, "They think that strutting around with your dick in your hand means that you're a man." Whether this is through displays of physical or sexual prowess or through one's ability to handle military weaponry, masculinity often comes down to the ability to contain oneself under pressure and to exercise power over other people when needed. Unfortunately, it continues to be the case that sensitive people and those who display overt signs of vulnerability are not considered to be the stuff of real soldiers, and maybe this is how it has to be. However, in my experience, it is this stoicism and adherence to an outdated version of prideful masculinity that may be contributing to the problems of emotional exhaustion and mental health declines including the phenomenon of chronic PTSD.

The stories that follow centre around actual events described to me by men and women of the Canadian Armed Forces and the RCMP. Individual stories are presented to highlight key issues and the relevant research, even though readers may note that several issues are often reflected simultaneously. These stories may be interpreted as an attempt to climb onboard a bad news wagon in search of villains. Not so. Instead, it represents a continued commitment to the ideals of military service and a responsibility to alert members and the organization about the things that can be done to foster better mental health. It is aimed at moving past simplistic good-bad dichotomies in order to uproot issues common to people who serve and especially for those people who have been released because of impaired mental health. It is my belief that the forgotten voices on the fringes need to be included in our understanding of military mental health if we are to move forward.

Two

A Brother in Need

Over the phone, his cousin's voice was dark and brooding, and it scared Ron. The winter of 2011 was the beginning of a tough year. There had already been a wave of suicides among soldiers returning home from the sandbox, and another one had taken his weapon and killed himself on the base in the past week. Ron's guts were churning. He knew what had to be done.

Up early the next morning, he packed his car and headed off for central Ontario to spend time with his cousin and make sure he was okay. His oldest daughter was eager for a road trip, especially since she was old enough to drink in Ontario. The sun was just starting to shine as they headed out for the fourteen-hour drive. They made an overnight stop at the halfway point in northern New Brunswick and arrived mid-afternoon next day.

Brad was still at work, but Jean was home with their infant son Joey and two-year-old Brandon playing on the floor. Jean looked tired and worried but seemed relieved to see them. She told Ron that she was not sure what was going on or where to turn but that they needed help. She had done what military wives are supposed to do—keep most of her concerns to herself and only called the base when she was really upset or worried about her husband who was now being treated for depression.

Ron caught sight of Brad as he entered the house. His cousin looked haggard, an older version of the bright man he remembered.

"What's goin' on? Good to see you." Ron grabbed his cousin for a quick man hug.

Brad shrugged him off after a second and motioned him out of the room with his chin. On the back deck, away from the kids and his wife, Brad lit his first cigarette of many. He was still dressed in his combats.

"I am getting screwed over," he said, his voice was flat and distant.

"Yeah," said Ron leaning against the deck rail. "How so?"

Ron was an ex-military social worker, and his concerns shifted to frustration and thinking about options as he began to hear a familiar story—bureaucracy playing out through another chain of command, another soldier powerless to protect himself in the system. His anger grew as his cousin talked in detail about what was unfolding on the base. It was hard to hear. Still, it was better to see Brad annoyed and animated than the beaten man Ron had seen come through the front door.

Brad believed that, behind the voiced support from his higher ups, they blamed him for what went wrong during his deployment. Nobody wanted to entertain the idea that he should not have been deployed in the first place. He had been selected as a last minute replacement for another senior non-commissioned officer; a reservist. Brad already had a couple of deployments to Bosnia under his belt, but he felt duty-bound to tell this new Regimental Sergeant-Major (RSM) that he did not have one key qualification and had not completed the pre-deployment training with the battle group. The RSM had told him not to worry because he would not be "outside the wire" and would not need that stuff for his security detail in Kandahar with the International Security Assistance Force (ISAF).

"Might have been fine for the RSM to tell me this back in Canada," said Brad. "But on the ground under ISAF, six weeks later I got reassigned as a replacement for one of the LAV commanders tasked for convey escort." He shook his head, pitched his butt into a Tim Horton's coffee cup, and lit another. "I had no idea what I was doing."

Brad's deployment had lasted for about a month once he'd been reassigned, and then he'd been sent home—humiliated. Brad was so preoccupied with what had happened and trying to give his leaders the benefit of the doubt that Ron found it almost painful to watch. His cousin was still reeling from Afghanistan. He felt hurt and discounted by their response to him. Though Brad was told that they had his back, it sure as hell didn't feel that way to him.

"What about your buddies?" Ron asked. "Any of them drop by or..."

But Brad was already shaking his head.

"Nah, it's not like that. I mean, sure, I got one buddy, I guess. He's okay, but even he, well... fuck it. I don't need to be handed around like a goddamned head case. Too much time on the base spent talking about folks."

He shot Ron a sour glance. "You know what we're like."

Ron listened to him for several hours until he could not contain his anger any longer.

"These people are not your family, man! Those two little boys, your wife and us, we are family! These people are only concerned about themselves and making sure that nothing sticks to them or the system over their screw-up in sending you to that shithole in the first place."

It had come out a little rougher around the edges than he had planned, but Ron couldn't help it, his cousin needed a reality check.

"You are an example of the system not working, man. They simply can't have you around telling a different story. They will bury you."

Behind the scenes, they were questioning Brad and what voiced support there'd been initially was shifting incrementally and predictably to subtle accusations from his higher ups. Before long, there were duty restrictions coming Brad's way. The game was underway to have him gone because he was raising embarrassing questions about the system. In fact, his cousin was even considering release and just heading back home.

Ron had seen too many people leave the military, disgusted and ashamed—and he'd seen the long-term consequences for these men and women. He told his cousin that it was certainly fine to pack it in and simply move on, but that it was important that he leave on his own terms, otherwise, this could haunt him long after he was out of uniform.

Ron looked at him squarely.

"Don't make it easy for them. You don't owe them a goddamned thing."

Brad talked then about having been drinking during a mess dinner and how the RSM had sauntered over. How he'd stood up and told him exactly what he thought about the lack of support he'd received and about the RSM's failure to follow through with his promises to call his wife and to look into things. To Brad, he'd received little more than lip service from the folks who claimed to have his back, and he made sure other people heard what he had to say. The RSM had simply walked away and waited until the next morning to retaliate.

Brad's bitterness was obvious.

"Sonuvabitch sent me to a mental health nurse, and all she wanted to do was talk about my father's drinking. Man, I lost it on her. What the Christ did my father have to do with Afghanistan? They wait and just brush shit under the carpet while they squeeze and push, and when you explode, they can point their fingers and say, 'See there, what a fuck-up he is. He's the problem, not us!' That's how the game is played in this family!"

In Ron's mind, the Regimental Sergeant Major could have admitted to his oversight and met privately with Brad and, yes, cautioned or even sanctioned him for unbecoming conduct in public. He could have also acknowledged that the actual grievance had merit. It might have gone a long way in helping Brad come to terms with his own sense of failure over the mission.

Instead, the RSM managed the situation as a bureaucrat to avoid facing his own shortcomings or having them aired in front of his commanding officer. Not exactly the type of leadership that fosters notions of brotherhood and the military family. These were the kinds of things that soldiers had told Ron over the years, but they had to keep this knowledge to themselves for self-protection and, ironically, to protect the image of the CAF—after all, almost everyone is loyal to a fault.

· ■ ⬥

It is quite easy to look for villains and to blame the system for the predicament described by Ron's cousin. Apart from the leadership shortcomings in this case, however, Brad's knowledge of the military as a Sergeant meant that he could have refused the deployment on safety grounds, and he could have pushed the issue up his chain of command. Admittedly, yes, there could have been career ramifications for refusing a deployment. He agreed to go, in part, to be seen as a competent team player and to have this deployment experience along with his buddies.

Upon returning home, in his efforts to protect his wife from the truth—that he was ashamed and believed that he was a failure—he simply shut down. All she heard were periodic bouts of anger and bitterness resulting from his wounded pride as a soldier. Technically, this emotional shut-down can easily be translated into a mental health diagnosis of depression. However, the alternative of displaying signs of emotionality within the military is equated with loss of control; it runs counter to military discipline—persevere, adapt, overcome. This requirement to keep oneself in-check emotionally has been described to me as constantly living in a pressure cooker. While the context of these behaviours may become important later for treatment considerations, this military context is not relevant for the purpose of diagnosis. This distinction is crucial, and I highlight the consequences of this artificial separation of symptoms and context throughout the book.

As far as Brad's chain of command was concerned, it seemed to be a straightforward issue of re-assigning a Sergeant to other duties since there were no reported critical events or physical injuries from his deployment overseas. Yet they were privately discussing the Afghanistan debacle in terms of his performance deficiencies, for the alternative of suggesting an investigation into a completed deployment would have been too risky for his Major.

Ron's reactions, apart from his training and experience in the military, came from the fact that it was close to home personally—he wanted to protect his relative from the risk of becoming another post-war statistic. Secondly, it came from his experiences under strong leaders from his past who, in his mind, would have taken the time to listen and then done the right thing. It came also from his loyalty to the idea of military family and from witnessing veterans who carried baggage that ultimately wore them down, ending their careers prematurely. It forced him to face inconsistencies, contradictions, and the seeming inability and absence of compassion within the military bureaucracy to appreciate the tremendous impact it has on the psyches of its members which begins in the earliest days of basic training.

Young people join the military for various reasons—a search for change or excitement, family tradition, idealism, and even patriotism, but a common motive seems to be the search for meaning and connections in their lives on the road to adulthood. Many of the people I know personally and professionally joined to rewrite personal stories of failure in search of a new beginning. Some people just wanted a secure job, and their previous lives were marked by a lack of clear direction, or perhaps they were uninterested in the usual paths to life success. The military provided the promise of a different life, one that could remake them into special people with national pride attached. For new recruits, the military provides channels for youthful physicality, idealism, and a desire to belong in groups, and it feeds their belief in personal invincibility. For their part, parents want to know that the military will look out for their children and not harm them. They want to be reassured that military training will transform their sons and daughters into competent and confident men and women.

Understandably, for the military, young recruits represent its lifeblood, replenishing the annual turnover of personnel who leave the military for various reasons. The Canadian Armed Forces has to reassure the public—and especially parents—that they are a caring and high standard employer, or they risk losing support for sons and daughters who are considering joining. The military understands that many potential recruits will consult their parents, and in the case of very young recruits and cadets, they may even need parental permission. For its part, the general public wants to protect itself. It wants to hear good stories, plausible stories about the value of particular missions around the world—they want heroes.

Canada's role in the Afghanistan War put the spotlight on the military in the wake of returning dead and injured soldiers from communities across the country. This national focus also brought many other stories into the public sphere, and the military has had to manage a series of public affairs nightmares amid reports of administrative bungling, harassment, abuse, and sexual violence. Other stories also hit the public airways, questioning the level of care for wounded soldiers and veterans. The military bureaucracy was criticized for obfuscating legal proceedings and for punishing parents who challenged it publicly.

Unfortunately, they reacted as per their training and closed ranks; sometimes responding by criticizing individuals and news agencies, accusing them of sensationalizing anomalous cases and for failing to provide fair coverage of the many good news stories—they were pushed back on their heels. As an institution, the military is vulnerable to public opinion and has to convince parents that, should their sons and daughters be injured or killed, their sacrifices were for the greater good in pursuit of something honourable, a source of national pride, and not forgotten.

I recently treated an Afghanistan veteran who summed up something important in a couple of sentences:

We don't tell our families or our parents what it is really like in the military, and I am not sure why we do this. Maybe embarrassment or because they wouldn't understand.... we don't want them to worry or to tell us that we should get out.... I don't know why.

For the military, at the level of personnel resources, there is much at stake if the recruit supply dwindles or if politicians are forced to defend their decisions and are held accountable for the financial toll of lingering mental and physical injuries among young men and women. Military leadership is also under constant pressure to convince politicians and its members that the chain of command and the divisional systems operate effectively and that it can manage its own affairs independent of outside influence.

Among other things, the military is a place that is necessarily secretive, and the reality is that it is also an institution that teaches people how to kill other people on behalf of the country when needed, to bear witness to inhuman things as required, and to carry out deadly and clandestine operations around the world. It has had to become tougher and arguably more secretive. Civil society has a difficult time with these realities, relegating the military institution and its members to an ambiguous position in society. Why wouldn't there be two different faces, one for within the organization and the other poised at the public eye?

The reality of military life is that people and deployments are forgotten—though mantras about honour, sacrifice, brotherhood, and protecting our way of life go a long way in soothing public reactions to tragedies that happen during foreign deployments and domestically. Duty, honour, loyalty, integrity, and sacrifice; these are powerful ideals meant to capture the best of Canadian society and unite a warrior brotherhood and forever set them apart from everyone else. With such powerful words, I think we need to understand why people like Ron's cousin report being crushed by bitterness and a sense of betrayal.

In my experience, the 'true believers' (and I counted myself among them) seem to have the toughest time with reactions of betrayal because many of us join as teenagers and form intimate identity attachments to the organization. For many people, the military family ideal comes with the promise of a new life; a structure that will protect us and where loyalty and commitment will be reciprocated. When our connection to others is strained or severed, in order to manage the mental stress of confronting competing beliefs, ideas, values, and damaged pride—we often blame the organization, ourselves, or both in order to reduce these conflicts.

This may partially explain why many of the veterans I know are intensely angry about their service and want nothing to do with the military after retirement. While this may help them avoid reminders of how other people failed them, or conversely how they may have failed other people, they end up completely cut-off in the outside world. They seem to be caught up within themselves, wrestling with the interplay between damaged pride and shame. Through avoidance, they hope to forget about the conflict between how they believe they should have acted, or been treated, and the situations surrounding the actual end of their careers.

A sad reality is that many military veterans are not interested in learning how to fit into the larger society, so they are left in a perpetual limbo, convinced that they are permanent victims. And the truth for most of us is that we never do really fit within civil society following military service—there is no reset to one's pre-military identity. Whether we describe it as a loss of naivety or innocence, for better and worse, when it is disrupted, the effects are often permanent.

Many people who are discharged medically because of injuries reconstruct their military service as a game about performances and perceptions where it was difficult to know what to believe. They can become incredibly cynical in order to protect themselves, but they also carry grudges from damaged pride and beliefs about personal failure. They believe that they were duped and that their loyalty and commitment to their duty and military ideals were the very things that wore them out.

In the overall scheme of things, many believe that their service was meaningless in terms of their personal worth within the system—that they were just a number. Another hard reality—in the military and in most workplaces for that matter—employees are skill sets, ranks, and positions that serve operational requirements that are replaced as needed. A rather cold prospect of existence for any employee, and most of us expect more than a paycheque from high personal investments—when we have skin in the game. We all need to feel valued and supported, and we seem biologically driven, as social creatures, to develop relationships and friendships.[4] It is this awareness that drives most organizations to draw on the family narrative to create and maintain institutional bonds and connections—it is a compelling metaphor for young men and women. This is particularly relevant in the military where people live and work in groups divorced from general society and where one's life is literally in the hands of other people.

4   M. Lieberman, *Social: Why our brains are wired to connect.* Crown Publishers, NY, USA (2013).

In Canada, the Vanier Institute defines family as any combination of two or more persons who are bound together over time by ties of mutual consent, birth and/or adoption, or placement and who, together, assume responsibilities for the physical maintenance and care of group members. New members are added through procreation or adoption with responsibilities for the socialization of children, social control of members, the consumption and distribution of goods and services, and affective nurturance.[5] This notion of family also exists as an archetype insofar as there is a loosely defined but generally agreed upon understanding of what it means. In reality, however, it is a highly complex notion—blended, extended, divorced, single parent, dual parent, adoptive, same sex, and grandparent families to name some of the current permutations. Even so, when politicians and senior leadership within the military, RCMP, local police, or first responder organizations use the term, it is often in the aftermath of a tragic event involving their members. There is an intuitively held understanding of what they mean by 'we are family'. It evokes strong sentiments of caring, concern, mutual commitment, and images of a standing, unseen collective ready to support the person and their biological family.

---

5   R. Glossop, "Family definitions: What's it to me?" *Transition Magazine* (1992).

Three

*We Were a Commodity to Be
Used and Forgotten*

Jim is in a talkative mood on this day with his therapist.

"We were used to go, go, go. Then hurry up and wait, y'know? And then go, go, go again. A generation of military people who did not have the luxury of human rights. We were loud and proud and operated under strict discipline and the threat of swift punishment from our higher ups. And we would *never* admit to needing help from anybody."

"Man, in our eyes, we shone as bright as the sun. I mean we had egos, you understand?"

He blows out a long, slow breath. His smile is hard to read.

"And y'know what? We expected nothing from the military when we left. Expected nothing from society either because we had nothing in common with them. And so many of us simply vanished into the wind."

After eleven years, and at the rank of Sergeant, Jim left the military and considered himself lucky to be hired as weekend security in a men's shelter—since nobody was interested in his leadership skills or his technical training. Within a year of this, his organizational abilities were noticed by the owners, and he was offered a management position; it was a task he took on willingly and with the same commitment he had learned in the military. His focus on protocols, rules, and procedures quickly earned him the title of 'Little Hitler'.

He had been trained to figure things out on his own, to put his head down and get things done, and to never admit to not having an answer to a problem. Jim's favourite saying, learned from the military, was that there was no such thing as a problem—only opportunities to create solutions.

Eighteen months after his promotion, he was on a stretcher with wires and tubes hanging off him because of a suspected heart attack. He was thirty-one years old. Multiple investigations and trips to hospital emergency departments would eventually end with a doctor suggesting that it might be a stress problem because they could not find anything wrong with him physically.

Jim, of course, had no idea what the hell the doctor was talking about; he was ex-military and working in a men's shelter. A stress problem? In retrospect, however, managing a staff of six, working with a volunteer board of directors, handling a budget and the needs of ten clients had been too much to handle. He simply put on his sneakers and started running again, and a year later he resigned from his position. Problem solved. Never once did he think that leftovers from his time in the military could be related to his problems.

Jim had entered the military as a naïve, nineteen-year-old kid from small town nowhere and had left the military as a driven, angry thirty-year-old in a city that was not his, and where the only real family he had ever known was now behind the locked gates of the base. He was lost and disoriented, trying to fit into trade school with kids who were ten years his junior and with whom he had absolutely nothing in common.

Even after all these years, he still doesn't have words that can describe what it was like to come out of a tightly knit, regimented system where competence and dependability were the order of the day into a world with vague structure and unclear directions. Maybe a combination of words such as lost, bitter, anxious, confused, or invisible captures what it felt like. Wandering in a sea of young faces down hallways and trying to figure out what he was doing there, he felt adrift, so he did what he had been trained to do, learn by watching, ask questions—but keep his doubts to himself—and just fake it to get along.

Jim forgot about the military, or so he thought. He needed to chill out, but he had no idea about the things that he needed to relinquish. First among these things was his lingering anger and humiliation surrounding his decision to leave the military—a subsequent investigation by the military had ended the career of an officer because of his misconduct in Jim's case.

There were other things that he had simply discounted as meaningless—the death of a young sailor in a car driven by his closest friend from basic training when he was the one who was supposed to be in the car. And then there was the suicide of one of his friends from basic training barely four months later—and how that had never been discussed. Being overseas and watching the effects of starvation were similarly packed away as another meaningless event to be forgotten.

Jim ends today's session somewhat philosophically.

"So Doc, when I left, I was done with them. And as far as I was concerned, they had forgotten about me even before the ink was dry on my release papers."

■ ⬛

For generations, new recruits in the Canadian Armed Forces have been told that they are now part of the military family—a welcoming message that evokes sentiments of acceptance within the group, being cared for and caring for others, and which also speaks to commitment and responsibility. There is no feeling in the world like being so closely connected to other people that it seems like you share one mind and knowing that you would do whatever it takes to protect them rather than let any of them down—that your existence as an individual matters little when compared to the importance of being a vital part of a collective of brothers and sisters.

It is an unspoken understanding and, dare I say, a type of intimate bond that is shared but rarely spoken aloud. It comes with tremendous responsibilities and a freedom to be 'all-in' no matter what. And just like many others who have served in our military, I willingly traded one family for the promise of this new family without even realizing it.

Of course the flip side of being part of the military family is that you are no longer an individual. This equally important message is quickly emphasized to new recruits and has far-reaching implications. It underpins the central importance of uniformity, which is meant to serve vital goals such as replaceability and unquestioning loyalty to the group. But alongside the remarkable sense of group identity and connection honed through shared challenges comes the risk of neglecting our private worlds—our autonomy and emotional selves—along the way.

The requirement of uniformity within the group teaches members to separate or compartmentalize their internal thoughts and emotions and keep their personal reactions from interfering with the overall goals of training. One's private world is necessarily traded, maybe even rejected, in the interests of adopting a common military identity—an identity that I believe is best described as the *reconstituted collective self.*

In essence, one's newly acquired identity hinges on the internalization of military ideals and connections to the military group. Whether this is recognized by members during their service, through normal retirement, or abruptly because of career-ending injuries, many people are left to contend with an unforgiving emptiness and a continual search for ways to resolve the loss of their unspoken emotional connections to the military. Many people who leave the military are also left to reconcile the aftermath of two parallel but contradictory worlds—alongside the strong military brotherhood, in the form of surrogate fathers and siblings, lies a bureaucratic reality which can be demanding and unforgiving in its responses to new and seasoned members alike.

A longtime friend of mine drove this point home to me over a coffee recently:

After thirty-three years in the Navy, when I asked to stay for an extra couple of months to get ready for retirement, the answer was an immediate no. That's when it finally hit me. I was just a number, and that did me in. I was put on pills and told that I had mental issues, but I know it's because I finally have to face everything I put my family through and all the times I put my wife and children second.

There is another military maxim that gets drilled into the heads of new recruits early: This is not a democracy. It emphasizes the central importance of discipline, rules, and orders as driving imperatives that support and reinforce a clear, black-and-white world. To do otherwise is to risk confusion and chaos—a toxic mix for any military. In a hierarchical system, these imperatives serve as the basis for coordinated collective action under decisive leadership. It is the foundation for assured action, which simultaneously removes contradictions and inconsistencies and silences dissent. This socially constituted reality is devoid of the grey because grey leads to hesitation, which can get people killed. In this environment, the opinions or personal sensibilities of individual members have no place. Leaders have to be clear, decisive, pragmatic, and self-assured where the emphasis is on one's ability to make decisions—right or wrong—and then deal with the consequences later.

Over the years, many soldiers deployed to faraway places and different cultures described being placed squarely in a world of grey. This means that reactions to the things that they witness, including cultural shock and disorientation, had to be packed away. It is easier to become robotic, stay in mission mode, and just ignore these other things as irrelevant or *not our job*. The starving child, the corrupt official, the wildly differing cultural values, the unclear mission objectives all have to be ignored in order to remain focused and to stay on task. If the rules don't apply, then you *make* them apply.

A sailor from the first Gulf War in the early 1990s told me about the experience of entering that warzone.

We had to make things up as we went. It was just chaos because we had no ROEs or even SOPs [rules of engagement, standard operating procedures] for that situation.

Unclear direction is deadly to a military force.

Apart from the effects of these operational stressors, when it comes to mental declines among military people, I wonder about the downside of pride and its relationship to the notion of stigma. I also wonder about the combined effects of group allegiance, the loss of individuality, and the continual submission to authority. As I think about my work over the years, I have seen very few people with less than five or six years of service who are diagnosed with chronic mental health problems, including PTSD.

Admittedly, the early years are designed to weed out those people who are not suited to military life. This timeframe is also focused on preparation and training before being deployed, but even so, large numbers of young reservists and regular members have always been deployed on various missions. This was especially true for our recent war in Afghanistan. This raises an interesting question about the role of *specific* events in the development of PTSD and other mental declines versus the role of *cumulative* experiences that may lead to emotional exhaustion and burnout.

There can be a mounting tension between one's inner world and the demands of the black-and-white operational world. Put another way, the personal costs of living behind a mask of stoic toughness and bravado may simply become too much to manage. Combine this need to appear unflappable with the risks that come with asking for help during one's career, and it is understandable how people can feel trapped and helps account for why they remain silent. The Canadian Armed Forces universality of service doctrine[6] continues to send a chill throughout the military when it comes to personnel asking for help. Among the men and women I see, it is interpreted as being thrown away—a disregard for their loyalty and an assault on their dignity.

In terms of the normal range of healthy mental and physical functioning, uniformed service challenges members to get used to being in a continual state of prepared alertness; even eating a meal at home, sleeping, or taking a shower comes with an urgency to not waste time and to remain alert to one's surroundings. During post-deployment or release, soldiers and veterans are often disoriented by the loss of this heightened state and miss the sense of internal readiness, which they equate to purpose and feeling alive. Many veterans report doing all kinds of things to maintain these heightened states and their self-image—bar-fights, extreme sports, fits of road rage, use of stimulant drugs such as cocaine, starting arguments with their spouses, or prowling dangerous neighbourhoods at night just to see if someone will challenge them. It's as if they continually have

6   Universality of Service has existed since at least 1985. It is imposed by section 33(1) of the *National Defence Act*, which states that all Regular Force members are "at all times liable to perform any lawful duty." This legislative imperative means that a member who cannot "at all times... perform any lawful duty" may not serve in the Regular Force except during a limited period of recovery from injury or illness. This is to allow for transition back into military service for those whose impairment is only temporary, or out of the military and into civilian life for those permanently unable to meet the liability imposed by the Act. Section 33(2) of the *National Defence Act* states that Reserve Force members "may be called out on service to perform any lawful duty other than training at such times and in such manner as any regulations or otherwise are prescribed by the Governor in Council." Since the Primary Reserve is given the role of directly supporting the Regular Force, operational effectiveness requires these Reservists to meet the same Universality of Service standards as their Regular Force counterparts, *[http://news.gc.ca/web/article-en.do?nid=848259]*.

something to prove to themselves, perhaps in the service of pride and self-confidence.

The alternative is a deadening emptiness, and the prospect of looking inward to understand this void is often rejected outright. Without pathologizing this search for excitement and purpose, these people seem bored with their lives—the idea of putting out the garbage or clearing the supper table like other people pales in comparison to these other experiences. These things are not the stuff of real men! They are continually searching for ways to feel focused and charged up because it is so intimately connected with their self-worth and identity. The military provided a ready mix of external sources of focus for them, and boredom was just something to be endured until the next thing happened. There was no need to find other constructive or creative interests to occupy them.

If we ask the average person to describe the military, they will often make references to military equipment like aircraft, tanks, uniforms, and even references to Afghanistan or Iraq. Ask a military person and, depending on the audience, they may describe exciting aspects of particular deployments, the things they saw overseas, or they may comment on the political nature of life in the military—a reflection of their direct experiences which are often wildly divergent from public perceptions. Similarly, ask people about military trauma, and they will talk about battle scenes, firefights, and maybe a reference to their relatives who served in WWII or in Korea. Ask military people who have been identified as being traumatized, and they will usually describe personal demons, being broken and worn out, or having enduring mental wounds. Even among different generations of veterans, their struggles are quite different even though the issue of damaged pride seems to be a constant struggle.

There are noticeable differences between the issues facing the veterans from the Cold War years up to the 1990s and those facing soldiers and veterans from Afghanistan. Among the first group, who were primarily tasked in so-called peace-keeping roles—veterans will quickly remind me that active combat and death also occurred in the name of peace—their struggles came primarily from operating under unclear and restrictive rules of engagement. They were forced to bear witness to atrocities, which led to incredible frustration and a crushing disillusionment with humanity and their military values. Among the second group, the rise of the warrior metaphor and our peace-making role in the regional insurgency in Afghanistan means that their primary struggles are often about trying to live up to this image alongside disillusionment from unmet expectations. In fact, our role in Afghanistan may have provided the military a means of excising the effects of former peacekeeping roles, allowing it to reconstitute its historical image in the public's eye. However, our newest generation of veterans seem to be struggling to continue to maintain this all-or-nothing warrior mentality in a society which can be fragmented and mundane and which has no place for such people. The grey is everywhere. Many of them have been diagnosed with PTSD, cutting short their military careers.

I believe it is important to remember that many Canadians objected to the decision for a combat role in Afghanistan, and they made a distinction in the well-publicized 'support the troops' campaign. This provided a way for average people to respect the efforts of the military while decrying the mission itself. We have not had a national conversation about the costs and benefits of our involvement since traditional notions of victory have seemed irrelevant in the ongoing proclaimed war on terror. In fact, the lack of discussion does not hide continued public anger about the actual war that is expressed in calls for better care for soldiers returning from this conflict. The serving soldiers I speak with, for the most part, want to forget that Afghanistan ever existed. If they do talk about it, it is only within the context of specific deployment experiences but not about the meaning of the war itself or its outcome.

In terms of lingering effects from deployments, traumatic stress reactions are identified by the things that people have in common—intrusive thoughts and images, avoidance of thinking or feeling about specific events, a hyperaroused nervous system, and emotional exhaustion. However, a closer look at their specific concerns shows major differences, which can be sub-grouped. In my experience, PTSD-diagnosed veterans are separable into different groups through their disavowed emotional reactions: guilt, shame, outrage over failed ideals, boredom and loss of excitement, or a continual search for identity and recognition.

This means that a PTSD diagnosis can miss the particular struggle for veterans—some people believe they have lost parts of themselves that they want to have back while others have taken on things from the military that they need to unload. Many traumatized veterans replay events because there are things they need to get off their chest with their buddies or with their leadership, but there are few places for their voices to be acknowledged. In a number of cases, they have been sworn to secrecy over their operational experiences. Other people avoid facing their own emotions over the loss of close buddies, some replay mental scenarios from the past out of boredom and lost self-worth, some people contend with self-recriminations over the things they did while in uniform, and still others believe that the military owes them for taking away their dignity and self-image. Since none of these things can be addressed directly, veterans rehash the past and are disoriented by the humdrum of daily life—it seems insufferable to them.

This disorientation, which is often equated to the notion of transitional stress these days, applies not only to our recent generation of veterans but also for those who left the military in previous decades. Several years ago, a Canadian study reported on the issue of veteran homelessness. Ray and Forchuk[7] found that these men had served during the 1970s up to the early nineties; a cohort of lost vagabonds in their mid-fifties who had served for less than ten years in the military. These were ex-military men from my generation. Almost all of them had lost contact with parents, wives, and children, were perpetually unemployed, and had become drifters with serious addiction problems. Jim's story above captures this experience of disorientation and the struggle to find a place in civil society—we don't quite fit.

I believe we are left to consider an unsettling question about the disjuncture between the legacy of an acquired military identity and the realities of civilian life—maybe it was not such a good idea after all to continually tell us that we were different and better than undisciplined, 'flat-faced civvies.' In other words, civil society is somehow beneath us, so why would a veteran want to fit into this world? As one soldier commented sarcastically, "I had a mother once upon a time until I realized she was a civvie."

A question worth serious discussion is whether the military institution bears a responsibility to undo some of the idealistic messaging and effects of training—its emphasis on emotional suppression in particular—to better equip veterans to make the mental transition back to civilian life. It is one thing to make a physical transition out of uniform, but it is an entirely different matter to make a mental shift back to civilian life, especially for those people who are medically released because of operational stress injuries.

---

7   S.L. Ray and C. Forchuk, "The experience of homelessness among Canadian and allied forces veterans," paper presented at the 2011 CIMVHR Conference, Kingston, ON.

When it comes to the phenomenon of military PTSD, when I am asked about my personal thoughts, the first thing I usually say is that they have changed considerably over the years. Initially I believed, as did many clinicians, that the answers were to be found under a microscope or from sophisticated brain imaging scans. My answer today is quite different and probably difficult for some people to accept.

In the case of military PTSD, I believe it rests on the shoulders of parents of soldiers, on soldiers and their military leadership, and on all the rest of us. We allow and encourage our military institution to operate in particular ways, and we support, even in our silence or indifference, the incredible weight of expectations that we place squarely on the backs of idealistic young men and women. It seems to serve Canadian society to uphold and to recreate notions of manhood that were forged into the national identity from the Great Wars. However, just like those older warriors, today's wounded veterans also present Canadians with an unsettling reality—that these ideals may simply be necessary illusions to quiet our preoccupation with national identity. There are few places for these wounded veterans, these failed warriors, to be fully accepted back into society. So, when it comes to addressing the ghost of mental anguish related to military service, I am not sure if we really do have the stomach to face it head-on.

What is trauma to a soldier or first-responder? Most often it means that, when he finally has no choice but to slow down, he is left to grapple with unwanted emotions and a recognition that he and the organization may have changed in ways that he does not like and he does not know what to do about it. He has to come to terms with inconsistencies and contradictions and unmet expectations of the warrior ideal such as the belief in enduring respect and a special status among others. He learns firsthand that ideals, no matter how noble, often fail to be realized. Instead, he has unwanted knowledge gained through his direct experience that capsizes everything he was taught about life and about himself. As a result, his life can turn into a crushing emptiness. He has no place, while in uniform, to put this knowledge into words and hence no way to unravel its meaning or to find alternative meaning for his life. For the most part, he wanders in silence, erupting now and again when the humdrum gets to be too much. In uniform, he had assurances and clear directives and the fleeting experience of real power. He has lost the ability to simply settle back into sleepwalking through a life preoccupied with trivialities—normal life can be a meaningless chore. He can also be an unwelcome mirror to friends and family and especially to other people in uniform. In sum, among these groups, he has to go!

In an unfortunate twist, I think that much of our mental health efforts amount to trying to convince them to come back to the rest of us, back into the fold with other people and to forget about these other things because they are too upsetting to hear—they shatter our beliefs about the world. We fail to recognize their central struggle of repairing their military identity, and we go about well-intended efforts to access their emotional worlds. These people must be fixed! Our efforts can become additional sources of hypocrisy for veterans, and many of them resist our work to bring them back to civil society because it means having to deny what they know to be true.

In my experience, many soldiers simply want an opportunity to tell their full stories in their own words. While this may sound somewhat 'unmanly', I believe they need to find their own voices and to have their experiences acknowledged. When we know a thing, we can never return to not knowing it. This is the blessing and the curse of experience.

Four

Left by the Side of the Road

There was comfort in the dark. The solitude around him was broken only by the rumble of the engine as he rolled down the empty road. It gave him an immense peace of mind. This was independence and freedom; freedom from his own mind and the day-to-day drudgery of civilian life. A faint reminder of what it meant to feel focused and alive.

Alone with full control over his fate through a throttle and handlebars, there was no room for thoughts of other things. Cool air rushing past his face and the tingling briskness on his lower legs kept his body alert. Twin cylinders echoed in the blackness as he accelerated down the next hill, the reverberation catching his ears, and the valley groaning in acknowledgment of his presence. Two hours alone before the first glimmers of dawn broke off to his east.

He had needed this.

The spell was broken by a set of car lights approaching. His resentment over this intrusion was immediate. It was time to think about getting off the road, heading home and maybe getting some sleep. The road always put him in a different frame of mind, reminding him of who he had been in the past, distancing him from the prospect of another day without purpose or connection to things around him. All those things that seemed to be important to other people were of little concern to him.

At fifty-one, Roger was many things—a father, husband, son, friend, and veteran. None of these grabbed his attention, even though most of these roles required things from him. *Veteran* still meant something, but it felt like a stab in his guts whenever he thought about it. The word simply reminded him of the things that he would never do again. It was a hole in his centre that the wind could blow through.

Where had all those places and people from that time in his life gone? They had been so important. At the time, they seemed larger than life and had been emblazoned on his soul, but it meant nothing in his life these days. Faraway places that most people didn't even know existed, places where he watched his brothers spill their blood and where he spilled some of his own in the name of Queen and Country.

He hated the outsiders for not knowing what he had done, and it was beneath him to even try to tell them. It was all forgotten. What had it meant? Were his boyhood friends right when they told him he had been brainwashed believing in the military? While he and his buddies had been overseas doing their jobs, the rest of the country had carried on, oblivious to their struggles and sacrifices on behalf of Canada.

His friends had finished school, had girlfriends, gotten married, and lucked into nine-to-five jobs to pay their bills. They had been nowhere, but maybe they had been the smart ones. He could not give them the right to comment about the military because they had not earned it. But he wondered about it himself. He had no idea how to go about adjusting to civilian life when he did not even know who he was anymore. Part of him had been left back there.

As a young man, Roger had rejected the life of his father, a hard-driving man who grew old too fast from running a farm from dawn to dusk. He had wanted more, and he got it—and then some. There were things he had taken on without question, and other things he had placed on hold without even knowing it. Decisions, some of which hadn't seemed like decisions at the time, which could not be undone.

He was not the kid who had joined up a lifetime ago. He would never be that person again. In fact, he could not even think about himself as that wide-eyed boy without feeling anxious. He grew up the oldest of four brothers in a family where men did not talk about themselves and where value rested squarely on their ability to work. He learned to be a hard worker, and it had gained him the respect of older men, including his father. Hard work was also valued in the military, but he quickly learned to develop a thicker skin, a shield to protect himself. He became a tougher, rougher version of himself.

His inner world changed the day he ran into a minefield to rescue an injured four-year-old boy. He had cradled the child in his arms, leg covered below the knee and bleeding badly; one minute he was watching helplessly as life drained from a foreign child, the next minute he was staring into the pleading eyes of his own son back in Canada. He had lost it. In that instant his shield had sundered and an unseen crack had run down into his very core. No matter what he did, the shield would never be the same. All of his training, every exercise and deployment where he had gained the respect of subordinates and superiors alike meant that this could never be known to others—never, ever talked about.

They had shown their worth and pledged their loyalty through actions, and they had backed each other up when their lives were at risk. They had been taught to watch over each other as brothers in those places because they had no choice. These had been environments where everything had to be put on the line. It had been the closest feeling of family and belonging that he had ever known. Looking back, it hurt to remember when this began to evaporate. Maybe it began after he missed out on a couple of exercises with the guys because of his knees. Or maybe because he had become too serious, he couldn't be sure. But the guys who had been like brothers to him just seemed to slowly exit from his life. It was beyond him to admit to the loneliness that he felt every day.

Out here in the real world, there was no place for a soldier to find a connection to people. He had done strange things since leaving the military, trying to find that part of himself—working in a soup kitchen, roaming the streets to help forgotten vets. He'd tried desperately to find some new mission to fill the hole and repair his invisible cracks. His two attempts at a steady job ended badly. They called him a perfectionist, a loner, a person that was simply too difficult to have around their workplaces. In Roger's mind, they were incompetents without standards, and he was not about to lower his for the sake of keeping the peace. He did not need them.

His bike gave him life again on his own terms, but it also meant pushing his wife away when she got too close by asking questions. Standing toe-to-toe with armed 'one-percenters' to prove to them and to himself that he was a man and that he feared nothing. He was not going to be pushed around by anybody else. His standards, whether he lived or died, were just black-and-white issues to him.

Fifteen years of marriage ended abruptly the night he thought about hitting his wife to stop the continual questioning. She had become too pushy, but the truth was that he had no answers to explain why he was doing these things. Maybe he was trying to fill the hole of utter uselessness. He had something to prove to himself. It was still hard to accept that his body had let him down, worn down over years from the continual grind. He was not needed anymore, and that had been the only value that ever mattered to him.

■ ⬛

Roger's story is a common one among seasoned military veterans. They live by a value system that is non-negotiable, and despite the personal costs, I think there is a kind of nobility in living as an uncompromising man or woman. However, their narratives also point to a fundamental loss of what they were as soldiers along-side reactions of loneliness and disorientation—*from hero to zero in the blink of an eye.* They remain loyal to their training, and they are also trapped by it. They continue to search for the heroic act or the personal sacrifice that will give value and meaning to their lives once again.

While civil society appears to hold our military personnel in high regard, I am not sure how well they understand these ideals. Some people view honour, sacrifice, or even chivalry as naïve, old-fashioned, or even entertaining. When employers or family members ask for compromises in these basic values, however, they are often taken aback by strong reactions and brutal honesty from serving or retired military people. These same ideals which served them well in the military become problems which can separate veterans from the larger society.

If these values were compromised while they were serving, they may be left with baggage—emotional baggage—that had to be contained and ignored while they were in uniform. And among the strongest emotions they work to contain are anger and outrage over lost identity and the things they witnessed but kept tucked away in the interests of mission and loyalty. Some of them work to contain unspoken disheartenment over deployments where they were help-less but caught in a system where they had little choice but to suck it up—to keep their reactions under wraps.

As an emotional reaction, intense anger or rage is scary for most people to experience. Many of us have been taught to equate it with going berserk, having a complete loss of control and somehow embarrassing and self-indulgent. But it is also an incredible source of power when it can be understood, harnessed, and directed towards re-establishing personal integrity and self-worth. Roger was taught to control it by denying it. There are few venues where these strong reactions can be safely acknowledged or expressed openly, but it is a reality for many of the people I know. It lies beneath their cynicism, social avoidance, and even apathy towards life in general. They struggle to continue to live a stoic life based on their military training while trying to come to terms with the reality that it is over.

Separation from the group, for whatever reason, can be an intensely emotional but unspoken experience for many veterans. It is a loss that cannot be put into words because of the inherent shame in admitting to vulnerability or feeling out of control. This is especially true when it comes to admitting to intimate feelings of any type or love for other men and women—it remains a taboo topic that is often confused with sexual interest or being a gay man or woman. These sorts of admissions, in other words, would be equated with men and women who do not fit with the notion of being a real man or a real soldier. Many veterans describe their emotional lives as being caged up internally; smothered in a windowless closet. They become depressed. The challenges of a lifetime of focusing on training and mission requirements meant that keeping an eye on their emotional health and their humanness was a contradiction in terms. It can become even more confusing when soldiers are encouraged (or directed) to go for help. It feels like, as one patient put it, "being handed a shovel and told to go dig your own grave". Unfortunately, members of the military often interpret offers of mental help as personal insults.

Even in these mental health settings, there are certain things that can be discussed and other things that are strictly off limits. Clinicians struggle with the possibility that our theories about mental health in the military may be inadequate because we do not have theoretical or practical means of accounting for the centrality of this social-relational context. We are also caught up in vague notions of biological causation and our professional obligations regarding safety and the expectation of keeping them under control. In the meantime, soldiers and veterans become separated from their groups—the brotherhood—and by extension they can become strangers unto themselves.

When it comes to understanding mental health problems among soldiers and veterans, there are various theories and even sophisticated gadgetry that attempt to provide global explanations of mental health functioning. Interventions are imported from the outside and adapted to fit within a military context. Absent from these theories and interventions are considerations of the impact of soldiers' attachment to their established military identities and to their units and how they learn to manage each other on a routine basis. For better and worse, these military groups are their families, and their emotional lives are intricately interwoven within these relationships and shared experiences. Most researchers and clinicians march past these relationships in their search for the real roots of distress and proposed solutions to resolve mental health problems.

Many caregivers, including myself, are increasingly aware that a large number of military members who ask for help because of mental health problems also have challenged histories, especially in cases of persistent PTSD and depression. Even here, we need to avoid drawing conclusions prematurely since we do not know how many men and women with stressful pre-military lives end up in the military. For example, we do not conduct the type of psychological screening that is completed for RCMP applicants.

The risks in looking for developmental causes for adult distress is that we can usually find them since many people have mental-emotional leftovers from their childhoods and unresolved relationship issues with their parents. It could be that developmental adversity is simply an artifact of other causes of mental distress. For instance, learning to devalue emotional needs early in life and having it further reinforced as part of military training. In fact, the most common lingering after-effect of developmental abuse of any type seems to be shame, which is the fundamental rejection of oneself as a worthy person.

These men and women often blame themselves for not being able to prevent abuse or for not protecting siblings or other adults even though they may have been children at the time. Some of them even believe that they deserved their mistreatment. These struggles with secretly held shame, in my experience, often contribute to a variety of behaviours, including addiction, persistent anger, infidelity, emotional avoidance, and even arrogance and the preoccupation with self-image as adults. If these men and women happen to be in the military, any failures on their part or negative attention through criticism or ridicule can easily resurrect these older reactions. Of course, the most common strategy to manage this reaction is avoidance.

It may also be the case that people with troubled backgrounds are more likely to seek help, or perhaps they are identified as having performance issues at higher rates compared to other personnel. Even when there is a direct developmental component in military trauma cases, we have no place to connect this knowledge within the context of organizational factors. It is tempting to explain military mental health declines as a consequence of a single horrific event, the fault of childhood, or the sole responsibility of individual soldiers to solve. In my experience, it is usually the intersection of the member's personal history, features of specific events and interactions, and how they have been taught to deal with emotional health in the military that often results in mental health declines.

When events occur within the military that trigger intense emotional reactions, training and operational imperatives direct them to compartmentalize these experiences, to ignore them, and remain focused and in control. In the case of Roger, he experienced an intense emotional response to the sights, smells, and sounds of a dying child in a warzone—a very human reaction—but he needed to remain task-focused and judged himself in the aftermath for being weak. The intensity of this event crystallized his worries about his family back in Canada; yes, we do worry about them when we are away.

Roger was worried about his son's welfare because of his ongoing medical problems. His disorientation and reaction of shame separated him from people around him while a conversation with his immediate supervisor or even a phone call home to talk with his son could have made all the difference for him. Instead of talking about his emotional upset with anybody on the patrol or anybody else for that matter, Roger withdrew and over time secretly committed to becoming a tougher soldier. In the years afterward, it is my impression that this event and Roger's toughness got in the way of his relationship with his son for many years. It was simply too painful to be reminded of his fear of losing his son.

Young soldiers look up to their leaders as surrogate brothers and fathers to guide them through the demands of military service. Leaders become role models who can sometimes have even more impact on their charges than their parents had. Subordinates learn by watching how their superiors manage stressors and how they treat other people in the workplace, and they adopt these same behaviours. In so doing, they internalize their social-relational environments. Over-arching messages to suck it up and push through physical and mental challenges become a central feature of their identity as a reliable soldier. While supervisors may accept their educational roles, they often do not grasp the tremendous responsibility that goes with their positions. Indeed, leaders often deny its very implications: "It's not my job to be a babysitter."

Many soldiers have the experience of wonderful leaders who are remembered as good men and women years, even decades after leaving the military: "He was tough, but he was fair and always looked out for us, and I would have done anything he asked." On the other end of the leadership spectrum, the reality for some serving members is that inconsistent or self-serving leadership, indifference, and in some cases manipulation and outright abuse have tremendous impact. Young men and women have been taught to trust their leadership without question: "I was an eighteen-year-old kid when I joined. They could have told me anything, and I would have believed them."

When we look closely at the specifics of mental health injuries, there are often themes from the past that are played out with leaders and peers who may also be replaying unfinished business from their own past—their own relationships with parents, their own struggles for worth, and their own struggles for power and authority.

For instance, consider the young soldier who grew up in a critical and unsupportive environment who is eager to please her boss. Her supervisor is a husband and father and feels increasingly neglected in his marriage but having grown up in a strict military family he never learned to communicate his emotional needs to other people. The attention he receives from his subordinate because of his rank and work abilities are distorted as signs of affection and sexual interest in him. He ignores the reality of military power relationships. Meanwhile, the subordinate, who feels special because of his attention, is easily drawn into an entirely different workplace relationship.

The point in providing this example is that getting to the roots of mental health abuses within the military is a much more complicated enterprise than most people can accept. They reflect many of the same issues plaguing our understanding of mental health within Canadian society but with one major difference: The military value system dictates that abuses should never occur. The legacy of our British ancestry, the medicalization of mental issues, and the secrecy around interpersonal relationships means that we live by codes of stoicism, silence, and keeping our emotional worlds to ourselves under umbrellas of politeness and political correctness. In fact, in my travels and discussions with people from other countries, they sometimes believe us to be two-faced, with surface pleasantries that belie a darker emotional side to our national character.

The usual manner of responding to abusive behaviours is to increase sanctions and punishments against the perpetrators in ways that are mandatory and predictable. However, focussing only on tighter controls may contribute to other less desirable ways for potentially abusive members to manage themselves within the system. As in any family, there is a need for mechanisms and safety valves for members to understand and to manage their reactions. For the military, the management of controlled aggression alongside the personal frustrations of members is an important reality.

What we know from experts in developmental psychology is that it is often not safe for people with less power to vent strong anger directly. These people can be tagged as not being on the team or out of control, but it is often impossible for them to annihilate the felt urgency to be acknowledged. In fact, left ignored or suppressed, angry thoughts and emotions often get stronger over time.[8] Periodically, most of us need to find ways of alleviating negative emotional build-up without causing serious damage to relationships. We begin to act out. We lie to ourselves about not being angry but our behaviours often give us away and betray us. We find ways to sabotage, undermine, and deceive.[9]

"Sorry Sergeant, I didn't understand," or "it was just an accident."

I know many veterans who show all of the physical signs of intense anger, but they deny it outright or tell me that they feel nothing. These same people are often engaged in endless submissions of grievances and rebuttals towards anyone and everyone within their chain of command. And often, their grievances have little to do with the real basis of their anger. Sometimes these actions seem to serve as avenues to rebel and to retaliate against powerlessness and damaged pride. If these men and women are to evolve into emotionally mature and compassionate human beings, they do need to acknowledge personal vulnerability and develop empathy and

---

8   L. Campbell-Sills and D.H. Barlow, "Incorporating emotion regulation into conceptualizations and treatment of anxiety disorders," in *Handbook of Emotion Regulation*, ed. J.J. Gross (New York: Guilford Press, 2007), 542–559.

9   L.F. Seltzer, "How unresolved fear and anger can lead to passive-aggression," *Psychology Today*, Jun 15, 2008.

understanding towards others even though they may not ever have received these things previously.

The nature of the military, with regard to both its organizational mission and its training procedures, inherently involves anger and aggression. While this is obvious, there is no existing delineation of the forms that these phenomena take in military organizations, and there is little systematic work on the environmental determinants of anger and aggression among military personnel outside of combat.[10]

Various conditions of the training regimens, role strain, and interpersonal conflict within this authoritarian organizational structure can create strong emotions and result in either direct or displaced hostility. Veterans have told me about instances where aggression was directed at peers and superiors in the form of physical assaults, destruction of property, and much worse things like going outside the wire to do what had to be done.

10   R. W. Novaco and G. L. Robinson, "Aggression in children and youth: Anger and aggression among military personnel," *NATO ASI Series* (1984) 17: 209–247.

Five

I Loved the Army

The blackness of the Kandahar night erupted into blazing fireballs and ear-splitting blasts from the two 500-pounders. Concussions could be heard and felt miles from where the aircraft had mistakenly taken out the Canadian patrol—four killed instantly, many more wounded.

At first they thought it had been an IED (improvised explosive device) or a nighttime ambush by the Taliban fighters, but when the first casualties and the dead began to arrive back at camp, Gerry and the others knew from the gruesome injuries what had caused them. Gerry was a section leader and immediately started applying battlefield first aid to the injured. It was utter chaos. Guys were screaming, crying. Disoriented and in shock, he moved through the ranks to check on his guys. He was up most of the night with them trying to do the impossible, to eradicate the terrible impact on his guys. Young wide-eyed faces, none of whom, himself included, would ever be the same.

Two years later, Master Corporal Gerry Hynes from the 3rd Battalion, Princess Patricia's Canadian Light Infantry was released because of PTSD. He had gone back to school on his own dime and managed to complete training to become a paramedic. He was not interested in talking about Afghanistan or taking any more medications. No one understood how utterly heartbroken he felt or how his pride had been kicked around during those two years since that night. He knew he worked too hard. The other paramedics called him a perfectionist. These people had no idea of how much effort it had taken to overcome being thrown away by the military and the struggle to study and pass the tests to become registered. He knew how to care for people, and that is what drove him. But something else drove him like a fire inside, a volcano that could erupt if he lost control. On other days, he felt emptiness in the place that used to be filled with the pride of being a soldier with his own section that had been taken from him.

Gerry's eyes avoid mine as he speaks.

"As far back as I can remember, all I ever wanted was to be a soldier. I loved the army and my guys, and I would have done anything for them."

A couple of days after the friendly-fire incident, Gerry had been tasked to the mountains on a search and destroy mission. Three days later, with his left leg severely busted up, he was on a medevac flight to Germany and then home to Canada. During physical rehab, Gerry was also diagnosed with severe PTSD and kept back by his unit. Instead of being given a new section or responsibilities, he was assigned to a job in regimental stores, which told him that he was now broken and useless. This was the beginning of the darkest days of his life.

"The thing that hurt the most was that everybody scattered like I had leprosy. Nobody and I mean *nobody* called me to even ask how I was doing."

To him, the word had been passed: *Hands off*. Gerry volunteered for various jobs, anything and everything to stay in the Army; he even took university classes at night in the hopes of remustering to Medic. Nobody wanted to hear about his alternatives. He was deemed unfit for military service, and that's how his career would end. He despised the uniform. They had betrayed him.

Beneath Gerry's anger is obvious heartbreak. Apart from not having a chance within his section to resolve the horror and grief of losing his friends, his biggest struggle since his release is trying to keep his anger under control.

"I don't fit anywhere."

In spite of all of his counselling and therapy, he could still lose control without warning. The physical toll of his leg injury and the mental toll of constant anger, shift work, and sleepless nights had worn him down. The thing that angers him constantly is that his role in taking care of other soldiers—*his* soldiers—had been dismissed and that any acknowledgment of his commitment to his guys had been taken by superiors who had not been there as he watched his buddies fall apart. Instead, he felt ignored, and when he was injured, in his mind, he became just another useless liability overnight. All his efforts to get better in the medical system were meant to show them that he was still a good soldier and salvageable, but it was discounted, leaving him little choice but to play along. Gerry wanted to be recognized for what he had done to help that night, but he was also embarrassed for wanting this recognition. The importance of these acknowledgments, formally and informally, from people who matter cannot be overstated.

■ ⬛

Gerry's problems were not a by-product of a damaged childhood. Instead, he described being raised in a close family, and he remembered having many cousins, aunts, and uncles who were always nearby. As a kid he was athletic. He did well in school, but all he ever wanted was to be a soldier, something that may have been a leftover from the long talks with his grandfather who had served in WWII.

When thinking about his identity as a soldier, it is important to note what may seem obvious about military identity. A soldier is the embodiment of a code of values and ideals based in our national history, and he is the end product of a demanding set of training experiences. He exists as part of a collective and the embodiment of our national narrative about masculinity—pride, bravery, courage, winning at all costs, and self-sacrifice—a belief about manhood that is held with incredible esteem in this country. But he is also an enigma and the personification of lethality that forces us to acknowledge the terrible things that human beings do to each other. He is history unfolding among the rest of us. When his identity is called into question or taken away, devastation hardly seems to capture the resulting sense of loss. He is left to contain himself and pack away his acquired warrior mentality and instincts because they have no place in civil society.

Having said this, I can also understand the view that Gerry's reaction for not being recognized seems to be an extreme one. I think his reactions go much deeper than damaged pride and a superficial desire for glory. He wanted to be remembered as a man who truly cared for his fellow soldiers whom he counted as brothers. They were his sources of worth and confidence as a man. His story also reflects a silent sadness among military people over the loss of friends and comrades over the years. Apart from formal ceremonies, there are few places to come to terms with lingering grief and loss. In his own words, he "loved and missed them, but in the military we do not know how to say goodbye." Somewhat in keeping with Roger's story, Gerry also wanted people to understand his level of commitment and loyalty and to be seen as a cut above the rest. Even though they are embarrassed to say it, they want to be remembered, to know that they were valued and that others were proud of them.

We all wish to be recognized in our workplaces, and for various reasons, many of us do not receive this feedback about our performances. In fact, those people who become upset by these oversights are often deemed to be over-invested in their work roles. In Gerry's case, the importance of being recognized as an exemplary soldier by other people seemed to highlight many of the things that simply could not be said out loud. He lived by his ideals and would have willingly died in the name of loyalty and love for these other men. The only thing that mattered to him was being a soldier; being a husband, father, and son paled in comparison to the importance of being a 'go-to' soldier in terms of his self-worth. With so much invested in this identity, then, any slight or oversight by key members of his military family takes on tremendous significance. It truly can be heartbreaking for them.

Our military institution, once championed as the place for rough and ready men, has morphed itself publicly into a culturally diverse, caring, and respectful family. At the same time, it appears to have become more rational and bureaucratic and less personal in its efforts to shake off the ghosts from Afghanistan and other places. Put simply, those members who do not or cannot shift out of deployment mode and adapt to the military's post-conflict realities may have to go. An Airborne veteran put it this way: "In time of war simply break glass, otherwise keep him locked away."

Soldiers often struggle with these two realities—when directed they can be aggressive combatants, and when they return home they are expected to contain this potential for violence and lethality in order to fit as husbands and fathers and as agreeable co-workers within the larger military family. For the most part, they are expected to navigate these emotional transitions on their own unless they signal mental distress to those in authority.

The notion of a *military family* has been around for decades, and it was stated frequently on the heels of the Afghanistan War. The lingering effects of war-related deaths and physical injuries, the ongoing issue of suicides at home, and the growing number of people being released because of PTSD all contributed to the need for this family metaphor. Historically, this was not the case after WWII since the vast majority of war veterans were short-timers and simply returned to civilian life. In contrast, most of our men and women returning from Afghanistan and other deployments are career soldiers, meaning that they have an entirely different level of connection and set of expectations from the military. The military is their workplace and their family, and they seem to be demanding the same level of loyalty in return. Unlimited liability is much more than a political phrase for them.

But even here, there is a disconnection. Soldiers often describe their military service in terms of employment contracts, which may or may not be extended or renewed. One may ask, then, about the origins of these expectations and their sense of entitlement since most of us in the civilian world have no such expectations from our employer.

I think it comes back directly to the notion of military family and the commitment to sacrifice oneself for the continuance of that family. There are few modern-day equivalents to this type of commitment and loyalty. The disjuncture between expectations of reciprocated loyalty and the reality of being "handed an envelope during release and offered good luck" creates an incredible level of separation and bitterness over perceived betrayal. I have to admit that it is challenging for me to put into words this experience of betrayal since soldiers like Gerry may be pointing to a profound dilemma: Namely that they traded their innocence and their youth for the promise of something greater and are devastated by the loss of this belief. The reality of universality of service legislation introduced in the mid-eighties, however, emphasizes the fact that we serve at the pleasure of the Crown, which in turn has limited obligations to us. This is a stark contradiction to notions of brotherhood and family.

This notion of military family is based on a shared, largely unspoken Canadian ideal—a pattern of thoughts and images that are held within the minds of individual citizens. Many organizations including the military draw from this archetype to help wide-eyed youngsters accept the process they are to undergo to become part of the system. Over the years, I have learned that this family metaphor is much more than a tool for recruiters and drill instructors; it is referenced openly among senior leadership and seasoned soldiers and reflected in recent efforts to address the mental well-being of our military members. There are a considerable number of serving military people and veterans who simply cannot accept the instances where military leadership does not live up to its values and standards.

Many military members vehemently defend the military's reputation, and it is challenging in this all-or-nothing world to accept that competing realities can coexist. Unfortunately, there are instances where errors and failures are all too real, and for those members who took the military at its word, they expected to be treated as a family member. They are unforgiving when it comes to mistakes made by the larger organization. It is within the notion of the caring family and brotherhood that reports of betrayal, neglect, and abandonment by some members can be understood. Part of the problem, as I see it, is that many of these men and women cannot seem to put into words what they want or need from their buddies and their leadership without seeming unmanly or disloyal. Predictably, for many of the soldiers who are directed to leave their surrogate family because of physical or mental injuries, brotherhood and family are words that ring hollow.

When we envision typically healthy relationships, including those that occur between family members, we often think about things like empathy, genuine concern, compassion, and open dialogue that allows for the exchange of ideas and sentiments. Adult children will often seek open conversations with parents to understand them as people and to clarify their relationships. For many, they want to know if their parents are proud of them. These typical interactions can apply to some situations within the military, for example, when talking with a same-ranked buddy or even to one's immediate superior, but in most cases interactions are mediated through rank and position. The things said to another Private or Sergeant would never be said to an RSM or to an officer, and if they are voiced, they are highly censured. The possibility of being reprimanded for speaking disrespectfully in anger can be a syllable away: "Keep it up and you will be charged."

These highly mediated relationships mean that most members understand that they live within a complex interpersonal structure. When supervisors feel that they are being challenged or when they have to engage in genuine exchanges with their charges, they can resort to rank and bureaucratic protocols. In many respects this is quite understandable in a hierarchical system. However, supervisors often fail to realize that their subordinates are not simply challenging their authority; instead, they are often looking for direction and mentorship, to be heard, or to have their struggles or grievances taken seriously. Less confident people in leadership roles seem preoccupied with the need to protect their self-image and career aspirations.

A number of retired Master Warrant Officers, Chief Warrant Officers, and commissioned officers have told me very similar things:

> There are two types of leaders in the military, the ones who look down and the others who are always looking up. The first group are the leaders who are constantly looking out for the welfare of their men and women while the second group are preoccupied with impressing their bosses and their career advancement.... Part of the problem is that the promotion system can be a popularity contest where like-minded, black-and-white thinkers look out for each other's career advancement.... They want the rank but not the responsibilities that go with real leadership.

I have often wondered why annual performance evaluations do not also include ratings from subordinates. They are in key positions as stakeholders to evaluate the effects of particular leader qualities that are often not seen by superiors or career managers.

In this environment, an open conversation with a buddy about a legitimate grievance can be altered abruptly by the appearance of a superior. It requires members to develop two different personas—the private one that few people get to see and the mask one puts forth at work. It is akin to always being on stage because one is always unsure in the military of one's audience—seen and unseen. Even among their brothers, soldiers talk about their fears of being 'bladed' by assumed buddies who run to higher-ups with private information to garner favour. They learn to keep their true thoughts to themselves to avoid scrutiny or risk being outed as a malcontent.

We cannot forget that the military is also a highly competitive system, so members learn political astuteness pretty quickly. They also learn the difficult lesson that some people cannot be trusted despite wearing the same uniform. Many people do not have this experience, but many others have told me about the level of emotional exhaustion that comes from 'playing the game' while remaining committed to doing their best. This means that what a person truly feels or believes is dependent and limited by the context of the moment.

In recent years, these limitations have also extended to social media where members have been cautioned that things said or even 'liked' on social media can present difficulties in their relationships at work. A common response to legitimate complaints by members can be remarkably flippant: "If you don't like it, then get out. You knew what you were getting into."

But this is not particularly accurate since most of us had absolutely no clue what we were getting into—we were just swept along as it unfolded in front of our eyes.

As I think about these issues, the things that happen before and during military service often have to be resolved even after ten, twenty, or thirty years in the military. Often, unresolved questions from early life are compounded by other military experiences. Along with thawing out emotionally and resolving the things that happen to us in the military, many people have to come to terms with things that happened in their biological families by repairing relationships with parents and biological siblings. They are faced with the challenge of relinquishing their adopted black-and-white worldview and having to learn things like forgiveness, humility, and compassion.

For many veterans, long-forgotten history stirs up intense emotions that they would prefer to forget. It is not a coincidence that the majority of military trauma cases I have treated contain early life stories of betrayal, neglect, rejection, or shame for being weak because they displayed emotion. These same problems can play themselves out in the military, but as adults they won't or can't contain their reactions in order to remain task-focused. Those people who were betrayed as children, where they had little choice or power, are often the ones who react in outrage when they experience it in the military. This reaction, in part, is because they were promised something different, and this time round they made the choice to join. In my experience, military traumas are often replays of life scripts and true recovery often means addressing these other issues as well.

Among my closest military friends, we had things in common. Many of us grew up in homes without structure, or conversely, too much structure. Many of our fathers were poor role models who were absent or drank too much or were demanding and abusive, which drove us to look for something better.

The military provided structure and direction and was not concerned with our histories or our quirks. They were only interested in how well we could meet training and operational challenges. But missing from this new family were opportunities to understand the emotional aftermath of deployments. I remember coming home after my first long deployment and the loss I felt even though we were still hundreds of miles from Halifax harbour.

Our normal routines became more relaxed as my shipmates started to talk about their excitement at the prospect of seeing wives, girlfriends, and kids. We were no longer focused on each other but on the anticipation of getting home and leaving the ship to be with families. I could feel the ship's company start to unravel. The truth was that even though I was also excited about getting home, I did not want them to leave. I did not want our closeness to disintegrate, but it did.

It would have been unimaginable to consider sharing these thoughts with any of my shipmates, for I would have been subjected to names like 'pussy', 'fag', or 'weirdo'. It would have damaged my image as a competent sailor. So I did what most of us did in those days: three weeks of drinking and carousing until people returned again and some semblance of connection, routine, and stories about the deployment started again. Some friends were gone out of my life, never to be seen again; others were gone briefly for training courses, but we would start to rekindle our closeness when our next deployment date drew closer. The same sense of familiarity and focus would re-emerge and civilian interests would decrease and disappear again as we reconstituted our military world and our home once again.

These undercurrents around connection, separation, and loss of friends continually played themselves out between us, but they could never be spoken out loud. I learned to be careful about getting too close to other people and then having to deal with missing them when they disappeared out of my life. It was just easier to be superficial with the steady stream of faces that entered and then disappeared. I don't know about the effects of instant social media these days—its effects on camaraderie or the effects of spillover between work and home. I am not suggesting that it is necessarily negative or positive but simply that this change adds a different variable into the equation of comradeship.

I think it is important to note that military brotherhood is not the same as the notion of military family. Soldiers will quickly remind me that brotherhood signifies earned trust and respect based on shared experience, adversity, and immediate commitment to each other in small groups that may exist beyond and outside the larger military family. Just because a person wears the same uniform is no assurance of being called brother. Brotherhood is more immediate, it is earned through action and a sign of respect among peers, and it can even develop as a rebellion against the larger family and the senior leadership. It can operate as a type of fringe group: "It's all bullshit, but we have each other's backs." It is common for military veterans to try to recreate these bonds by joining groups, be they social media groups, motorcycle clubs, or any manner of advocacy groups.

My wife and I both have long careers working in the health field, she much longer than me. In terms of our colleagues and workplaces, neither of us has ever used the term family to describe our relationships within our workplaces. It could be because we are accountable to our respective regulatory bodies, meaning that we are required to function independently, but more importantly the notion of unlimited liability and possible injury or death in the line of work is not expected of us. It may be this difference that highlights the importance of family and brotherhood among military and other para-military organizations. They have little choice but to band together to defend themselves and their immediate groups against external threats.

When it comes to military trauma, as a clinician, I have come to understand that a focus on particular events is only useful for its emblematic representation of larger issues experienced over a lifetime. By this I mean that particular events may crystallize struggles that members may have had for many years. For many military people, this often comes down to the fear of vulnerability and losing control.

In a well-written review of the trauma research, Dr. Peter Barglow, an American veteran and psychiatrist, highlighted some of these ongoing controversies.[11] Of particular importance is his argument that specific events are not a reliable predictor of traumatic stress reactions. My observation is that trauma reactions are not only consequential to events but also reflect other experiences—usually kept secret—that are resurrected and represented through replays of particular memories. As such, it may not be the event per se but the experience of intense emotional reactions that cannot be acknowledged that fuels ongoing traumatic reactions. The challenge may lay in fostering an institutional environment that values the role of emotionality without emasculating soldiers or raising concerns within the leadership about a weakened fighting force.

11   P. Barglow, "We can't treat soldiers' PTSD without a better diagnosis," *The Committee for Skeptical Inquiry*, 2012, 36 (3), May/June. [http://www. csicop.org/si/archive/category/ volume: 36.3].

I don't know if this is possible, but there may be particular unit-based activities within the institution to help members truly decompress and to re-orient during post-deployment phases. It would require courage from leaders to participate in forums which acknowledge unedited personal accounts from their members and where these men and women are safe from possible retaliation. If we are truly interested in helping soldiers break their silence, they need assurances that they will be protected. We also have to acknowledge that the social-relational context of deployments is quite different from post-deployment life, and often strained relationships and connections within units need to be repaired. At a skills level, one option might mean paying attention to interpersonal communication training for all members of the military.

Whether arising from a recent event or from long-forgotten neglect or abuse, reported distress often reflects the failures of avoidance, distraction, dissociation, or conscious efforts to keep prior experiences at bay. These emotionally laden memories can resurface unexpectedly and overwhelm cognitive abilities to remain focused on the present situation.[12]

One way to describe mental health problems is to view them as a consequence of disintegrated self where there is a misalignment of thoughts, emotion, and behaviour. As an example, take the fellow who is preparing supper, he experiences a sudden empty sensation in his guts, is thinking about leaving his marriage, and when asked by his wife how he is doing, he perks up with a smile and replies that he is doing great, and in that instant, he means it. In my work, the goal is often to help people understand and to process these types of disconnected experiences that can lead back to a level of re-integration or mental balance.

As it stands, military training is global in its focus on emotional toughness among its membership. The philosophy of this training is steeped in the history of the institution going back to a time before the Great Wars. But in the twenty-first century, cultural values and social expectations have changed dramatically. There may be a need to differentiate training and recognize that the skills and attributes required for deployment and combat need to be offset with specific skills training for post-deployment and in-garrison life. I believe we

12   A.N. Schore, *The Science and Art of Psychotherapy*, (New York: Norton, 2012).

can do much better than simply leaving it to individual members and their biological families to figure out. There seems to be a pressing need to unravel the contradictions and competing priorities between operational imperatives and notions of military family and brotherhood.

The family metaphor in most organizations serves primarily as a mechanism to address emotional and attachment needs of employees.[13] For military recruits, it serves to meet expectations as they are adapted to organizational aims. However, organizations are complex social structures; they are power arenas and places where conflicts arise and where discourses are built and enacted. Even then, they are not monolithic, for there are competing priorities and sometimes even blatant contradictions. For example, when it comes to looking after members, veterans often report major differences between the Navy, Air Force, and the Army. Even within each branch, there can be wide discrepancies between different units and regiments. There are places in the Army where the senior leadership vehemently defend the rights of those in their charge, and there are other places where self-interest, fear and indifference, or even harassment by the leadership means that subordinates can be left unprotected. As noted by the newly appointed Chief of the Defence Staff in 2015, harassment and abuse hurts the entire organization; people have to feel valued and safe within the organization.

Further challenging the notion of family is that behind the operational end of the system, there exists a bureaucracy that can run counter to ideals of kinship. By its nature, bureaucratic structures are meant to be logical and coldly rational, leaving little room for sentimentality. Enshrined and codified policies, procedures, and rules are meant to protect the continuity of the institution and to ensure efficient operation. Usually bureaucracies provide for consistency and fair application of rules to cover straightforward and complex situations by removing idiosyncrasies that can be introduced by human factors. A weakness of bureaucracies is that they are dependent on information that sets the machinery in motion where inadequate or incorrect information can produce flawed outcomes. This has been true in our legal system as evidenced by reports of wrongfully convicted citizens in Canada, and it has also been true in military cases.

13   O.N. Alakavuklar, "We are family - A Critical Organizational Discourse Analysis," *International Journal of Business and Management*, 2009 (1)1: 1309–1347.

I have known a former sailor for a number of years who was released administratively almost twenty years ago. His life was literally destroyed because of a bureaucratic error. He had been attending a career training course and underwent emergency stomach surgery and subsequently placed on medical leave from the course. His training instructor ignored the medical directive and ordered him to complete the final course exams. Unsurprisingly, he failed these exams. The instructor and his supervisor made an immediate recommendation for this member's release from the military for failing the course. When he was released, due to an administrative error, sexual improprieties were the official rationale for his termination. This mistake had devastating effects on his personal life in terms of possible employment and the loss of involvement within his church and working with youth because of being placed on a sexual offence register. This man thoroughly enjoyed his life in the Navy and remains loyal to the military despite everything that has happened to him and despite the obstinacy of the bureaucracy in correcting its mistake. Even after all these years, he still assigns personal responsibility for his life to the authority of the military.

In another example, several years ago, I saw a sailor who had been successfully treated for PTSD and cleared medically to resume operational duties. During a ship sanctioned indoctrination ceremony, he notified his superiors that he did not wish to participate. As part of his assigned work duties, he had been using a knife to open cardboard boxes when a costumed crew member came from behind startling him. During the interaction, he reflexively raised his hand and the knife nicked the chin of the other crew member— a senior non-commissioned officer who insisted that this sailor had purposely assaulted him. The sailor was subsequently charged with assaulting a senior officer, found guilty, and fined, which meant that after release, his Veterans Affairs Canada claim was denied because of this criminal charge on his record.

It took our combined efforts over several years and repeated appeals for this error to be corrected. The lingering issue for him was that coming from a family as the oldest boy where he had received special attention meant exceedingly high expectations of what he would do in life. Shortly after joining the Navy, he was subjected to a sexually loaded hazing experience that humiliated him and changed the course of his entire career. He was trapped. He could not admit failure to his family by leaving the military, he could not report his messmates without risking further retaliation from them, and he could never trust people enough to fit in even after a lengthy career.

It is incredibly challenging to reconcile these types of events with notions of brotherhood and family. In the first case, this sailor could have filed formal grievances or initiated legal action many years ago, but he did not take these steps in a somewhat distorted belief that he was protecting the Navy's reputation by remaining silent. His second reason for remaining silent was his deeply guarded secret that being victimized was familiar from his past and the belief that people in authority should be the ones to correct their mistakes—to redeem themselves. In the second case, this sailor enjoyed a privileged position among his siblings. This meant that much of his behaviour and his special status within his biological family were not addressed. He entered the military with demands for special attention that were quickly seen and managed by his peers. This experience epitomized his career in the military, but he was never able to accept that his problems in the military were also worsened by his own attitudes and behaviours.

Generally, cultural metaphors like *family* are used because they help us make sense of the world—how to think and how to behave in this new social setting. But metaphors are not value-free representations. They declare ideologies and world views; therefore, they have implications about what to think and what to have as information. The family metaphor as an organizational tool adopts some characteristics from one context (biological family) to another context (the military environment) to help members interpret the organizational realities and to create meaning, e.g. *I will follow orders and do my utmost to protect other soldiers because they are my brothers.*

At another level, organizations can be defined as consciously coordinated social entities with identifiable boundaries that function on a relatively continuous basis to achieve a common set of goals. Organizations are defined as deliberately planned groups, with specific goals, generally designed to outlive the participation of any particular individual, having a more or less well developed set of formal rules, a relatively fixed structure of authority, and roles and responsibilities that are independent of the personal characteristics of those filling the roles at any particular time.[14] This is a fitting description of our military institution.

---

14   M.J. Handel, *The Sociology of Organizations: Classic, Contemporary, and Critical Readings* (Washington, DC: Sage Publications, 2002).

It is common to hear the family metaphor being used by organizational spokespersons. While these statements are usually heartfelt, we also need to consider who stands to benefit from these statements. It can be a positive motivation for members to work in a family like environment that emotionally attaches them to the organization with a strong sense of belonging. It often advances a message that all members are equally important and any conflicts or disagreements can be solved within the family. From another vantage point, however, this family metaphor also allows for normative control. In addition to its positive images, the family narrative contains features of hierarchy, patriarchy, and outright denial of opposing realities.[15] In order to keep the notion of family intact, soldiers often have to rationalize unfair treatment of other members as a fault of their own or because they were really sub-standard soldiers.

With the help of this family metaphor, members are not just doing their jobs, they are protecting their brothers and sisters and the country. Superiors are not personnel managers because, as members of a family, higher-ranking people are somehow like older siblings and parents. Within this narrative, conflicts of interest cannot be acknowledged since all members are expected to dedicate themselves for the sake of their organization-family. And since you devote yourself to your family, unreasonable work demands or having one's leave cancelled by father-managers for the greater good of the unit do not matter. Importantly, it is not only about income or benefits, by creating a family atmosphere, organizations shape people by reforming them into new subjective identities melded to the group. Within this ideology then, it is not surprising that some members feel betrayed when they are let go by their military family.

Those soldiers who are worn down emotionally or distressed can be construed as mentally injured brothers and sisters. While this attention to individual members may end in helping them, ultimately it may also serve to hide inconsistencies and relational conflicts. The risk is that we may end in transforming soldiers once again; this time from a member of a warrior group into helpless and

---

15   S. Ainsworth and J.W. Cox, "Families divided: Culture and control in small family business," *Organization Studies* 2003 24(9): 1463–95.

permanent victims.[16] Their legitimate grievances often become lost when aired out in private therapy offices under the veil of confidentiality because, even when things are done against the interests of soldiers, they are not expected to outwardly criticize or show negativity since they are in the 'family'. They risk being regarded as a troublemaker or a betrayer by other members. We must not forget that whistle-blower protections have not been fully supported by our federal institutions or generally in Canada. When veterans speak out, they can be ostracized by their military buddies and other military veterans, challenging notions of brotherhood and family.

In our military structure, ironically, wholesale use of the family discourse can challenge the idea of professionalism since emotional aspects of families can interfere with actual operations. Instead, a professional military relies on accurate and rational decisions and excludes notions of emotionality, which is a direct conflict with affective family bonds. Leaders and career managers tasked with assigning subordinates to deployments often straddle the tension between friendly conversations to convince members to accept a new posting and, if this fails, resorting to issuing the request as an order. These types of situations are an ongoing reality for military members, but of course, *if you don't like it, then get out.*

The main conflicts seem to erupt for those people who are directed for medical release. It is often experienced as a fundamental betrayal of notions of brotherhood and family. On the one hand, without affiliation to the group, many people would simply leave for other careers, while on the other, wholesale use of family ideals provides a breeding ground for reactions of resentment and betrayal.

For many people, including myself, when we were buying into the military family we were unaware of what it was we were trading away. We may have been willing to reject civilian society and turn responsibility over to other people, or perhaps we were only loosely attached to our biological families, making us prime candidates for military socialization. Joining came with the promise of being a different version of ourselves; existing beyond the reach of parents and families and former communities across the country. We were willing participants in our metamorphosis towards a new identity.

16   Dineen, *Manufacturing Victims, 3rd edition", Robert Davies Publishing,* *Montreal (2001).*

We embraced a common identity, a shared view of the world that is paradoxically devoid of complexity where contradictions are not observable under black-and-white policies and rules. In some ways, it is a much simpler life because it bypasses the usual challenges faced by young adults to develop acceptable social skills, intellectual independence, emotional maturity, and learning the give-and-take of healthy relationships. Within the military family, often the only thing that matters is one's ability to contribute to unit or mission priorities. Ambiguity seemingly disappears.

As intentionally constructed groups, all organizations lack basic characteristics of a family such as kinship, family bonding, and intimate relationships since all human resource management practices usually operate against the nature of being a family. To be a member, you are observed and evaluated on skill levels and tested physically and mentally to ensure compliance with universality of service on a routine basis. When members of a family are upset, they expect understanding and support, advice, and direction. However, within the increasingly formalized nature of the military, voiced personal concerns can trigger administrative processes that question the member's continued acceptability as a member of the family. Liability concerns have become a necessary preoccupation.

Increasingly, reactions to issues that sound like a 'mental health problem' appear to trigger formal mechanisms within the health and casualty management systems. Given the complexities surrounding mental health, some supervisors are anxious about doing the wrong things and getting into trouble. I do sympathize with their concerns, but I also believe that they have considerable power and a responsibility to support their subordinates and possibly head-off more serious mental health issues. Unfortunately, they have been convinced that any sign of distress reported by their subordinates represents a danger that is beyond their competence to manage. In the past, I provided lectures to senior leaders about mental health issues among their subordinates. On many occasions, these supervisors complained that the rules were so complex that they simply did not want to know about their subordinate's personal issues because of fears that it could come back on them.

Changes have occurred in the once-clear authority of supervisors and the chain of command with the introduction of human rights legislation in the mid-eighties. As said to me by a number of older veterans: "The young guys are better educated. They know their rights, and they are not afraid to use them."

I am never sure if they think this a good or bad development. Likewise, I am not sure about the relationship between human rights coverage within the military and the emergence of universality of service legislation shortly thereafter—possibly a proactive step to head off anticipated liabilities and concerns over decreased operational readiness from the requirement to accommodate and retain injured personnel. It is a sore point for many people who want to continue to serve in uniform. Be that as it may, 'universality' signalled a significant change within the military and the disappearance of the once accepted practice of *caring for our own*. Practically, this often translated into 'hiding people' in suitable and meaningful roles until they reached retirement.

It comes as no surprise that in *this* family there is an absence of the maternal voice because of the nature and mandate of military organizations—the need to develop tough and rugged men and women who are mentally equipped to engage in the messy business of war. There are few places for the feminine, for those attributes associated with consensus, self-reflection, nurturing emotional well-being, compassion, and empathy have no place in the military. Conversely, these qualities and the admission of errors and mistakes continue to be associated with weakness and sub-standard leadership.

In most families, when a child is sick or infected by illness, other members will draw nearer to provide care for them until they are well again or they may be quarantined temporarily to protect other family members from becoming ill. Even so, the family is expected to be nearby and waiting for the sick one to recover and to rejoin the family. In organizations like the military, however, this is decidedly not what happens. Physically and mentally injured members are provided support and assistance, and if they recover, they can be accepted back into the family. If they do not recover, however, they are replaced and, more often than not, they are forgotten by the larger family, which has to move on. Granted, close friends and buddies may stay in contact, a few may be lifelong friends, but in most cases when the others redeploy or go off to another military exercise, those members who are not involved are forgotten despite all of the sentiments that everyone will be remembered.

In a family, when a parent or child dies, the entire structure is usually affected, often resulting in a re-organization of roles and relationships. It can take some family members years to come to terms with loss and some families never do recover. Within the military, there are well-entrenched ceremonies and rituals to bring deceased members back home to their biological families. Among the men and women I have seen, however, many of them continue to struggle with the absence of close friends and well-liked leaders—the holes left behind seem ever-present. There are few places to help them navigate ongoing emotional upset within their units, which is also true of most organizations and some families for that matter. These people are often believed to be depressed, which may also be true, but these men and women are also looking for ways to make sense of death and the loss of those people who are no longer present. They struggle to fill the gaps left by these people within their units and sometimes within their personal lives. It is a cruel reminder that all military members fill positions and ranks only temporarily.

In many family structures, there is also attention to the social. There are informal ways of enjoying each other to reconnect emotionally or simply to blow off steam, when needed. From planned family vacations, movie days, shopping trips, special meals and celebrations—all in the interests of maintaining the social bonds of the family system. In terms of the military, living together, planned physical activities and competitions, mess activities, special informal events, and formal events also serve the social needs of military members. Once events that involved alcohol or rigorous physical activities, initiation rituals, and team sports also served as safety valves to blow off steam and also as opportunities to regroup.

Beginning in the 1990s, many of these activities and outlets have been curtailed or forbidden for various reasons. As one Afghan vet lamented:

When we lost Shorty, we had a brief little ceremony and everyone just went their own way with their private thoughts. In the old days, the boys would get together over some beers, and we would do our crying and share our stories together and give them a proper send-off, but now this is all gone. There is no way for soldiers to give our brothers respect, so we're just left with it.

We may be running out of accepted rituals to restore affiliative bonds and to regroup following critical events. This example is not to argue for the use of alcohol or a return to hazing events but to emphasize the importance of accepted group rituals to perform a vital social function, namely supporting the social-relational life of the organization. While third location decompression was a wonderful step in this direction, veterans have told me repeatedly that, by the time they arrived in Cyprus, they just wanted to get home and to forget about the mission and that sometimes their stays turned into drunken brawls. In their minds, dealing with anything at that point was too far removed in time from events that had happened months previously—it was too late to open that can again.

When soldiers return home, the irony is that, in spite of being in the age of instant social media, they face a world of disconnection and isolation. Many of them have told me about the purity of combat and deployments. It is a place where pettiness, internal politics, and self-interest give way to more vital tasks. When they return home, the clarity and self-assuredness of their roles often disappears. Many have told me that this separation and their longing to be back with their guys were part of their reasons for wanting to go back to Afghanistan for a second or third time.

Within the context of their groups, they are normal again and they fit—their shared experiences are automatically understood—but when they are separated from their groups, some of these experiences can come back to haunt them. Mental-emotional isolation and the loss of self-confidence can be terrible things. Unfortunately, family members and friends often misinterpreted their decisions to redeploy as a simple search for excitement or as a way of avoiding family responsibilities.

It is probably not accidental that many social media groups of veterans have sprouted up over the past several years. Partly they are a reaction to reports of suicides among their friends and also in an effort to reconnect away from the demands of their workplace. Again, I think that many of them are searching to recreate and maintain the bond and personal identity provided through deployments. Within the notions of brotherhood and family, injured people expect to be drawn closer, but within a bureaucratic system they are often distanced and processed. Exceptions do occur in the form of military medics, padres, and military social workers where members can sometimes discuss their emotional needs in relative safety.

Many veterans are bitter and hiss at the notion of the caring family as nothing more than a recruiting slogan meant for public consumption. Another fellow who served in Afghanistan comes to mind. To this day, he remains the poster boy of a tough, confident, muscular man in his mid-thirties, a man rated as a top-notch soldier, and his qualities are obvious to any observer. He was one of those fellows who went above and beyond what was expected of him and then faced the possibility of charges for fulfilling his role to overcome the gaps in equipment and training. To ensure the safety of other soldiers, he had little choice but to break the rules and make up protocols and fabricate makeshift equipment fixes on the fly outside the wire. To him, his higher ups did not want to hear about the operational and equipment gaps that were placing other soldiers needlessly in harm's way.

> To admit to the things I was telling them would have embarrassed them or their Generals so they ignored me. To acknowledge my role and what I was actually doing out in the FOBs [forward operation bases] could have exposed my immediate superiors to questions from their superiors. So when it came time at the end of our deployment to acknowledge people within the unit, I had to be forgotten because my actual work would shine a negative light on my immediate superior who was being groomed for promotion. To keep the appearance that the system worked, they treated me like I never existed on that deployment. This drove me crazy, so they diagnosed me with PTSD. What a joke. Was it wrong for me to want to be recognized as a good soldier?

This soldier's officially diagnosed OSI stemmed from an experience of nearly killing a ten-year-old boy holding a toy gun approaching his vehicle. Not included in the diagnosis or treatment, however, was the intense sense of hypocrisy and anger he felt over being placed in a no-win situation by his chain of command and how this had clouded his decision over whether or not to pull the trigger: "It would have been a great outlet to just squeeze off that round."

It was probably predictable within the mental health world that he was diagnosed with PTSD and sent to treatment. But in all this, there was no place for his story to be told that provided the context for his reactions back home, partly because he was not officially supposed to be there in the first place. In the mental health system, because his anger bubbled up constantly and because he did not follow the standard course of PTSD treatment, he was viewed skeptically as a possible malingerer and as someone not complying with treatment, which contributed to his medical release. There was no place for his outrage to be taken seriously.

In other cases, there are senior ranking people who went out of their way to protect their subordinates. In the case of one master warrant officer, he worked tirelessly and eventually burned himself out trying to protect his subordinates from what he saw as unfairness within the system. He took the personal hits from his peers and some superiors but continued to take on the chain of command when needed to protect his men. For his efforts, however, in continually "pissing off the higher ups," he was passed over for deployments and commendations that he had earned, but in his words he "refused to lower himself to suck up to the right people."

He was also eventually released from the military because of PTSD, but he rejects this notion bitterly. For him, this strategy was just a convenient way to hide the problems within the system and to quietly get rid of him because he was a constant thorn to those people intent on business as usual. He is a bitter man, and he is not alone. His reactions seem to represent a common feature among the people who have been released because of post-traumatic stress. These stories demonstrate that discipline and rationality have to be balanced with attention to the emotional costs of life in uniform.

It has been said that no place exerts more control over a person's life than the military with the possible exception of incarceration. Generally, I would agree with this statement, but with at least three major considerations. The most obvious one is that military service is highly regarded in this country, and these men and women are seen as representing the best of us. Secondly, even though military members also exist within a hierarchical structure, they have access to power. Whether this is directly through the use of weapons, in the case of a combat soldier, operating sophisticated military equipment, or controlling the activities and movements of other military people, anyone can participate in the exercise of power. However, access to power also means submitting to rules and to other people in higher authority—a seeming contradiction.

In the case of mental health then, this also means that the range of acceptable options available to members are circumscribed by policies and power relationships—people can feel trapped and powerless. It may be difficult for readers to accept that some military members adopt a mental defeat or passive stance to avoid conflicts since it rubs directly against our belief in personal control and agency in our lives. We often miss the fact that, when people join the military, they are making a legal and personal commitment to turn full control of themselves over to other people. In contrast, when it comes to those who are traumatized, one of the key requirements is to help them to regain and take control over their lives—another contradiction.

By way of a historical example of this conundrum, in the early years of treating PTSD within our military, many soldiers underwent aggressive medical management from a treatment oversight stance. Many of those early patients were immediately placed on medical categories, separated from their workplaces, instructed to remain at home for extended periods of time, prescribed various medications, and in some cases had their driver's licenses rescinded. Looking back, I think these overreactions were driven by our own anxieties and lack of experience dealing with operational trauma. It is not surprising that a number of these men and women got much worse, growing more depressed and angrier. In our well-intentioned attempt to help, medical and mental health practitioners ended in taking more control from them. There is always a risk in a hierarchical system to manage issues by moving further into prescriptive efforts to control people who in turn react by giving up or they act out through defiant behaviours.

The final major difference between military members and incarcerated people is that the latter are controlled directly by their external physical environments, whereas military personnel are controlled for the most part internally. Through the process of indoctrination and adopting a military identity, they live by codes of conduct and discipline that controls their physical bodies and their minds— external rules and expectations are internalized. This stoicism is an essential quality, but it comes at a tremendous cost when members are affected emotionally. Many of them have never learned the skill of asserting themselves to have their needs met. At one extreme, they can be passive because of fears about adverse consequences, and at the other end, they can become aggressive, voicing negative sentiments without restraint or regard for their effect on others— wounded pride running amok.

In fact, this issue of veteran anger continues to be a hot topic in Canada. In many cases, the roots of this anger are related to their time in service where they could not or would not risk speaking up on their own behalf. Now as veterans, other people and outside agencies often feel the full brunt of their displaced anger leftover from their days in the military.

Between passivity and aggression lies the challenge of assertiveness for many people, including members of the military. Assertiveness is often confused with aggression, but the former means voicing one's thoughts and feelings, wants and needs, while at the same time showing appreciation and respect for another person's viewpoint. This is a challenge for soldiers because it means admitting to vulnerability and facing the risk of being ridiculed in front of others.

In terms of normal development, healthy children commonly display unconstrained emotions. However, for those people who grew up in a family that did not give much value to basic needs, the natural impulse to stand up for those needs is often suppressed, and in the military this message can be reinforced. I believe that this denial of basic emotional needs in the service of military ideals may provide a partial explanation for the relationship between chronic PTSD and histories of developmental abuse. Those veterans who experienced early life neglect or abuse often struggle with basic self-worth and are unaccustomed to speaking up for what they need and simply deny their experiences.[17]

In the example of the Afghanistan soldier who nearly shot the child, his powerlessness and resulting anger was displaced into thoughts of deadly violence—power over the life of someone else. He wanted the support of his immediate chain of command but did not know how to simply state his situation to them. Realistically, under wartime priorities and rules of engagement, it might not have made a difference in the outcome, but it could have served him in fulfilling his perceived responsibilities. In this case, this soldier grew up in a violent environment where he took responsibility for looking out for his older sister. After she was assaulted by a stranger, within months he decided to join the military. He had failed to protect her. When asked about this connection, he stated very clearly that he was powerless to protect her and could not face her. The easier solution was to leave without a word. Part of his problem in Afghanistan was his fear—real or perceived—that he could not protect other soldiers, the same way he had failed to protect his sister.

In the case of the master warrant, his anger towards the system was alternatively managed by passively antagonizing people around him and drawing aggressive behaviour on himself. In his case, he grew up in a strict military family, which meant being uprooted at various points in his life, and as a teenager he was subjected to

17   J.J. Whelan, "Effects of developmental abuse and symptom suppression among traumatized veterans," *Psychology* 2015 6: 540–548.

aggressive bullying that often meant being beaten up. When asked, his solution was to goad these bullies to hit him harder as a way of embarrassing them in front of other people. A very unusual strategy to gain control in the situation, but it seemed to work to end the bullying. In his words, he took the fun out of it for the bullies.

The irony was that this is pretty much the exact way he dealt with relationship conflicts within the military. The other noticeable quality about this man is that he is intensely private; from a personality view he could be called an introvert. These individuals are often reflective, inward-looking people, concerned and interested in their own mental life which is extremely challenging within a gregarious organization like the military where they often stand out as odd or peculiar. Being a quiet, unassuming figure within the military can garner unwanted negative attention unless they develop a reputation that they are not a person to be messed with. In fact, many of the people I have seen for PTSD were also diagnosed with social phobia—fear and anxiety in groups. This is often understood to be a consequence of PTSD, but many of these people had struggled with this anxiety for much of their careers. Alternatively, the soldier from Afghanistan would certainly be classed as extroverted—talkative, funny, and demonstrative around other people. They are generally concerned with stimulation from their external environments, including their social interactions. In Afghanistan, his job required him to spend most of his time alone. Two very different personality types who were diagnosed with PTSD and both seemed to revolve around powerlessness.

To be clear, the example of these two men is not meant to suggest that their upbringings caused the mental health issue that led to their release or to blame their reactions on the military. And it is not meant to discount the role of biology. In fact, the emerging research on intergenerational transmission of trauma reactions and epigenetics (genes turning on or off in response to environmental influences), which are beyond the scope here, are beginning to highlight the complex and dynamic relationships between heredity and environment.

The examples are meant to illustrate the point that the personal histories of these men had a direct impact on how they managed conflict within the organization as part of their mental declines; it was probably predictable that they would not trust their leadership to help them. This way of managing relationships and powerlessness by members in the military may also shed light on instances of violence and abusive behaviours towards each other. Members who are unable to recognize or voice their disappointments and anger over conflicting policies or towards other people in authority may take it out on other less powerful people in the system. As said to me repeatedly: "We have a pack mentality, and we will turn on the weak."

Six

They Keep Telling Me I Am a Victim

He felt nothing as he watched his children playing on the floor, glancing up at him now and again. For what? Approval maybe. Recognition. He didn't know, and it bothered him. He wondered what it was that was wrong with him. What was missing?

Danny assumed that normal fathers could just enjoy moments like this. But not Danny. He was only there *physically*. It was a duty to watch over them, and though he didn't resent it, he took no joy from it. His son would hand him toys or ask him questions that quietly annoyed him despite the smile Danny painted on his face.

The pain in his knees and back were always there, and this morning he was still stewing over another VAC letter sitting on the table in front of him. The battle with Veterans Affairs Canada had been going on now for almost three years since his release. His head injury had left him with constant headaches and a couple of seizures that meant that he could not apply for work anywhere or even drive his car for that matter. Here he was, a young father, with no job or future career, worrying about money, watching his two little boys immersed in the innocent world of play. In a way, he envied them because he could not recall ever having that luxury during his lifetime.

Danny grew up on the west coast, the younger of two children with an older sister, a stay-at-home mom, and his police officer father. As long as he could remember, Danny was afraid of his father.

He would come home from work and, without warning, would launch into angry outbursts over minor things. Usually this anger focused on his mother and sometimes on his older sister, especially once she hit puberty.

Danny's role, when he thought back about it now, was to spy for his father. His father would ask him questions about what his mother had been doing during the day—whether she had spoken to anyone on the phone, whether she had gone out of the house for any reason, or whether anybody had visited. In his sister's case, his father wanted to know whether she had anybody over to the house or in her room. He wanted to know what time she came home from school and whether she ever talked with him about drinking or using drugs. Danny, not knowing any better, would provide the answers each time because he did not want to upset his father and because he thought he had a special relationship with him.

It was only in the evenings, when his father would use this information in arguments with his mom or accused his sister of being sexually active, that Danny would feel bad. He would simply go off to this room and hope that it did not turn violent. When his father kicked his sister out of the home at sixteen, Danny had enough and stopped talking to his father entirely.

In Danny's memory, everybody outside of his home seemed to look up to his father and thought he was a great guy. To Danny, however, he was a manipulative hypocrite. As soon as he turned eighteen, he joined the military and was glad to be out of the house. He enjoyed the military and looked forward to being deployed overseas.

Afghanistan. It was the first and only time he'd ever left the country.

In an unfortunate accident, one of his closest friends was killed just outside Kandahar when their light armoured vehicle rolled over, and Danny immediately felt responsible for his death. He also suffered serious physical injuries and entered into trauma therapy for PTSD for several years, but he was never able to return to his unit or to his former role. His PTSD diagnosis eventually ended his career. Since leaving the military, whether at home or out in public, he would launch into angry tirades for no particular reason.

Any comment that questioned his behaviour was met with anger and defensiveness. Danny agreed to participate in a group with other veterans because of his problems in adjusting to post-military life, but even there, he was easily angered and stated, as a matter-of-fact, that he trusted no one.

It was not until he began talking about the need to be held responsible for what he had done that he began to make progress.

In his mind, the military leadership had whitewashed the accident to protect themselves, which meant that nobody, including him, was ever held accountable for the circumstances leading up to the death of his friend.

He rejected the idea of a mental injury as someone else just trying to give him a free pass. To him, the real victim was his dead friend. Predictably, he held himself responsible. In his mind, they were all hypocrites just like his father had been. In this case, the accident seemed to catapult Danny back to the guilt he had felt by being complicit with his father—Danny believed that he should have been held accountable just like his father should have been held accountable.

As a kid, he had betrayed his mom and his sister. In this case, the military accident seemed to be inextricably interwoven with unresolved issues from Danny's past. The only thing that seemed to help him move forward was his understanding of this connection. In the end, this appeared to provide a way to confront unresolved guilt and shame from both situations—the real roots of his anger problems.

■ ⬛

Are they all to be viewed as victims? Here is what Dr. Tana Dineen has to say on the subject of victimhood:

Victim, once a term reserved for those who suffered from a calamity of nature, of fate, or of violent crime, has become psychologized so that it can apply broadly to anyone and everyone who knowingly or unknowingly has been exposed to or experienced stress, distress, or trauma. Feelings of unhappiness, boredom, anger, sadness, and guilt can now all be interpreted as signs of prior trauma, creating victims.[18]

18   T. Dineen, *Manufacturing Victims*, , *3ʳᵈ edition*", Robert Davies Publishing, Montreal (2001).

Soldiers recoil at this notion of helplessness outright even though they often believe they are powerless to change things—they are left holding the bag. It is probably part of the reason why many of them appear angry much of the time. Military personnel exist between these extreme positions because of their legal commitment to allow other people in authority to take control and to direct their lives; they can be 'active agents' in some contexts and submissive in other contexts. When we envision the archetype of the warrior, we are presented with notions of controlled aggression, discipline, order, honour, and bravery. However, medically released veterans often reconstruct themselves as being betrayed and broken by the system; two very different narratives that they are left to reconcile.

Victim status may serve multiple roles. It allows professionals to be the ones with the answers and it also absolves organizations and the identified victims from responsibility. Absolution of guilt removes from consideration the need for soldiers or their leaders to perform tangible acts of restitution such as requests for forgiveness or taking actions to reconstitute relationships harmed by them through their reactions to their service.

The accepted assessment and therapy of focusing only on negative operational events to explain behaviours in the military workplace often superficially reconstitutes careers leaving out the many positive things and the meaning of one's investment in the military. Entire careers are re-ordered through the lens of specific bad memories in hopes that this will help them get past these things and back on track in their careers. To be clear, many people do find this approach helpful in gaining a different perspective, and they are able to resume their careers for varying periods of time. On the other end of the spectrum are clinicians, peers, and family members who convey messages to soldiers to just get over it and to move on. Both represent polar positions and reflect our general confusion about the topic of PTSD. In clinical practice, following medical release from the military, all subsequent disappointments and setbacks tend to be viewed through the lens of a PTSD diagnosis to explain all upset or misbehaviour—a complete victim with no way forward.

Those members who do not benefit from standard trauma therapy, and there are many of them, do seem to have complicated preservice histories along with military trauma.[19] They often reject the possibility that they may have been complicit in the outcomes that happened for them. They do not see how their behaviours of denying problems and working harder to overcome issues on their own might also have been the roots of their undoing. They hold tightly to the idea that their duties and the failures of other people to look out for them are the main reasons for their declines. And to be fair, this is a relatively easy mental leap within a system where members continually submit to authority in the form of written rules and policies and higher-ranked personnel. You are either good-to-go or not; a black or white decision with few grey areas. Of course, this external focus is at odds with the notion of paying attention to one's mental life, which requires introspection—a skill that is often denigrated as wasteful navel-gazing.

In Danny's case, he held an incredible level of responsibility and guilt over an accident where he had little control. The difference for Danny, which was inconsistent with his therapy, was that he *wanted* to be held accountable. In fact, he wanted everybody to be held accountable for the death of his friend. Even so, the accident itself could not explain the depth of his reactions in the form of PTSD and intense anger; it was only by understanding the effects of his early life that he could understand the intensity of his reactions more fully. In his case, facing guilt and the loss of his friend directly seemed to be the most helpful step for him.

In a counter-intuitive twist, he may have been better off mentally if he had been held responsible and charged with an offence. In his view, this would have provided him a tangible way to pay his dues. In his case, the issues with his family and with his father will probably take much longer because of his father's denial of his past behaviour. He has re-opened his relationship with his sister to repair the damage created by having to betray her trust all those years ago.

When we focus only on mental symptom checklists, we also run the risk of invalidating veterans' stories. We convince these men and women that exaggeration, emotional upset, or distortions

19   J.J. Whelan, "Exploring the relationships between untreated adverse childhood events and substance abuse, and their impact on PTSD relapse rates among Canadian military veterans," in *Beyond the line: Military and veteran health research*, eds. A.B. Aiken and A.H. Belanger (Kingston, ON: McGill-Queen's University Press, 2013), 180–195.

are inconsistent with reality, essentially meaning that their story is untrue. This initial comparison of the story with the facts can be quite helpful in helping soldiers gain an objective perspective. But at other times, their stories offer support for their reactions, leaving clinicians with few options but to focus on symptom control. In these cases, actions may be required which involve people outside of the therapy room.

The solution may require some act of repair that is tangible and goes beyond simply talking about things. These acts often involve other military members and leaders to be held accountable or to hold them accountable—actions towards reparation. I am not suggesting that clinicians need to be all things to all people, but I do believe that we have a responsibility to bear witness and not discount these stories out of our own discomfort or clinical limitations. We have to avoid communicating the message that nothing can be done about these other things—just suck it up and move on—a familiar message many military people know only too well. We risk recreating them as permanent victims of their past.

Alternatively, in my experience, the answers to PTSD are often contained within veterans' stories. They will usually tell us what needs to happen for repair and moving forward, but we need to pay attention. Most stories are often never heard for what they are because care providers edit these accounts or they are kept secret under the cloak of confidentiality. While client protections should be maintained, we need to acknowledge that this secrecy also serves to absolve clinicians from a responsibility to act in the best interests of their clients except in clear cases of mandated professional practice.

In my early days working within the military mental health system, there were few protections for a member's confidentiality, and this needed to be corrected. In this same timeframe, however, supervisors were often directly involved in aspects of care, and many times we were able to help resolve unit issues and breaches in relationships that were affecting these clients. With our attention on confidentiality and the focus on evidence-based professionalism, however, we appear to have lost the involvement of the workplace as a component of the 'care team' by excluding them entirely.

As I think about it, there could be practical ways to re-establish these relationships by designating specific leaders as care team members or as 'assisting navigators' where they adhere to confidentiality agreements just like any other provider. Where assurances are required, these agreements could be tied directly to security clearances. In my experience, workplace supervisors and the immediate chain of command are the experts on options available to their subordinates in the workplace, not clinicians.

It could also help reduce the needless but ongoing stigma surrounding mental health issues. In our present arrangements, clinicians are often left to be complicit in our silence, and by default we end up helping to maintain the status quo in terms of military relatedness and the stigma surrounding mental health. There have to be places to evaluate and catalogue common themes and issues contained in soldier trauma stories rather than simply reducing them to the fog of war and washing our hands of them.

One of the unfortunate realities of recasting heroes as mental health victims is that it amounts to a simplistic but convenient way to identify and to single out particular people. A mental health diagnosis turns soldiers into individuals once again, and in the military there is no room for individuals. I believe that many veterans have information and experiences that are vital to the most senior levels of the military. The consequences of particular missions on the military organization and issues traditionally treated as leadership problems or unit morale issues can easily by reconstructed as a by-product of mentally disordered soldiers.

Many veterans believe that the problem of operational stress is really an organizational issue. The military has had to contend with a high operational tempo and continually 'punch above its weight' over many years where allocated budgets barely met its personnel and equipment needs. I believe that the institution has also borne the brunt of exhaustion. There are increasing demands on its personnel to do more, and less tolerance or room to make exceptions for particular men and women who display the signs of emotional wear.

In this context, aggressive leadership can often translate into increased discipline and control, which can drive these men and women further underground. But, leadership in the form of consistency, trustworthiness, and a willingness to hear and take action on unedited accounts from subordinates alternatively could go a long way in heading off more serious issues. In my observations, there seems to be less room for older traditions, the niceties of mentorship, or attention to the emotional life of the organization. It has become an ever-demanding environment without the luxury of time to stop to regroup or for leaders to personally attend to the casualties.

Since the early nineties, Canada has been continually tasked to intervene in other cultures where life exists under entirely different value systems and in internal conflicts where traditional notions of combatants do not exist. Many soldiers have told me that the attention to combat strategies and drills, and the exclusion of cultural awareness often left them ill-prepared for the reality of existing in these countries where right and wrong were continually blurred, where their awareness of geopolitical issues had to be ignored, and where doing the honourable thing was often unclear.

Prior to their diagnosis, many of them had become disillusioned and believed that they were alone in the system—some simply withdrew quietly to the background. Others pushed back in their respective units, voicing anger because they believed they were being treated unfairly, drinking or becoming violent or insolent because they had lost their tolerance for pettiness, refusing duties, or voicing their outrage over deployment events. They pointed their fingers towards specific supervisors and the organization. And these emotional people are always at risk of being called mentally unstable. It is extremely challenging to consider that, even as they are acting out, that many of them have the best interests of the military in mind. I once treated a senior Navy NCO who told me about smoking crack cocaine on his way to work in the mornings while he looked across the harbour at his ship:

I was disgusted with them, and I just did it to show them how stupid and incompetent they were. I was right under their noses, and they could not even see that I was screwed up from our time in the Gulf. They have to wake up and see that we are hurting.

This man was eventually charged by the military police for drug possession, but before his release, he was also diagnosed with severe operational PTSD. It is not uncommon to hear that soldiers began to act out in their units on the heels of distressing events. Similar to this case, they expected other people to know their level of upset through the drastic changes in their behaviours—they place an incredible level of responsibility on other people and on their leadership over their unspoken emotional needs. At the same time, in close-knit units, one would expect that these members would be taken aside and asked how they were doing. These types of stories are incredibly disorienting in a system where stoic self-control is demanded no matter the circumstance. These mental health casualties who lose faith in the system can't or won't contain their grievances. So just like other family dynamics, these people can be scapegoated as the problem children in an otherwise well-functioning family.

The vast majority of soldiers would argue vehemently against the idea that they were affected negatively by their military service, including their deployments overseas. In fact, many of them report thriving in these environments and feel better equipped mentally and emotionally to resume their lives back home. At the same time, there are a substantial number of soldiers, estimated variously between ten and thirty percent, who seem to struggle to resume normal functioning on the heels of deployments and routine service-related stressors. They are unable to recharge following deployments.

There is an argument to be made that certain people may not be suited to the increasing mental-emotional demands of military life, but I would argue that these inadequacies cannot be determined after the experiences of training and deployments. In contrast to RCMP recruiting procedures, the military does not conduct basic psychological evaluation of enrolees to identify potential preservice issues or personalities not suited to military service. This recruiting approach seems to be based in the belief that the demands of basic training will weed out unsuitable members. It likely also reflects the military's concerns over depressed enrolment rates. Whatever the reason, in the absence of baseline ratings of mental health functioning, it is highly problematic to blame operational injuries exclusively on developmental histories.

As I have suggested, ongoing training results in an assumed and altered identity where compartmentalization and emotional avoidance are essential skills to be mastered. These are necessary skills. It may be the case that additional skills are also required to compensate for the over-reliance on these abilities; those members who do not have the ability to process emotional reactions or place trust in supportive relationships seem to be those at high risk for lingering problems. Within the mental health world, we are simply not at a point where we can predict with any certainty the people who will successfully negotiate military deployments. In fact, when it comes to human behaviour, prediction models are notoriously inaccurate and require multivariate and ongoing considerations of risk models. And the reality is that, in many cases, those people with the most troubled preservice histories turn out to be stellar leaders within the military.

Over the years, I have heard experts say that part of the reason for increased research attention to PTSD was because it was a 'sexy' issue for real science. Contextual issues like workplace environments, emotional burnout, or alcohol use in the military were considered much less important. In recent years, PTSD has also become a rallying cry and the quintessential term to describe distress of all types among this generation of military and other first-responders, and as such, an increasing number of people are receiving this diagnosis.

The latest CAF statistics estimates a threefold increase in this particular diagnosis since 2007. The reasons for these increases are unclear. Members may be more willing to disclose war-related trauma experiences because of new mental health initiatives. Perhaps it is due to the fact that the official DSM-5 criteria were substantially lowered several years ago or because PTSD has become the socially accepted way to describe military distress of all types. Alternatively, these men and women may be the canaries in the coalmine signalling dangers within an exhausted organization and the need for some form of reconciliation. In any event, despite these reported increases, many soldiers and veterans tell me that mental health efforts are simply scratching the surface of the full extent of mental issues facing soldiers. What does seem clear is that interventions to address military PTSD over the past twenty years in Canada have produced mixed results. Some members are able to return to their units following treatment, but the majority are eventually released.

Up until recently, traumatic stress reactions were characterized as a medical disease process resulting from biological anomalies that pre-ordained some people to experience adverse stress reactions. This research agenda continues with exciting but, as of yet, unproven possibilities. In a recent cutting-edge Canadian study, MEG (magnetoencephalography: a neuroimaging technique for mapping brain activity) was used to identify specific neural pathways linked with chronic PTSD.[20] The findings were somewhat surprising.

While soldiers from Afghanistan diagnosed with chronic PTSD showed persistently heightened neural activity linked with distress, other non-traumatized soldiers also showed this same hyperactivity pattern when presented with combat reminders. All of them had lingering effects from combat, but some members were still able to function effectively. This finding may reflect a skill deficit among chronically traumatized people such that they are unable to effectively manage strong emotions related to their memories. It could

---

20   B.T. Dunkley et al., "Resting-state hippocampal connectivity correlates with symptom severity in post-traumatic stress disorder," *Neuro Image: Clinical* 5 (2014): 377–384.

be the case that their efforts to avoid unresolved emotions from the past, combined with the emotional demands of deployments, wear them down.

To fully understand the effects of military deployments, in my mind, we would likely require these types of neurobiological data to be collected when people join, upon completion of basic training, and upon completion of deployments. It is the only way to truly understand the relevance of post-deployment changes. In 2012, Emily Badger reported that basic military training appears to produce strong and lingering changes in personality that last years afterwards, particularly when it comes to aggression, which is often confused with PTSD.[21] In fact, there has been a quiet shift in the trauma world in the past few years with much more attention to this issue of emotional dysregulation (the inability to properly modulate one's emotional responses) as a core feature of PTSD.

This shift has also meant a resurrection of Dr. John Bowlby's earlier work on attachment relationships.[22] In essence, the theory hinges on the belief that one's current functioning can be dictated in large part by our earliest relationships. This refocus is not necessarily a rejection of neurological phenomena, but it does move the focus away from critical military events as the central explanation of ongoing distress. I think this is a good development, but there are risks.

In the ongoing search to understand PTSD, it would be enticing to simply blame these cases on childhood issues. Several years ago, Dr. Peter Barglow argued that the relatively simplistic and unproven view of PTSD removes complexity and the context of individual cases.[23] Instead, he and many others raise the possibility that we may have misunderstood the problem by excluding the social and relational context from consideration. Consequently, in the absence of a sound theoretical basis, many clinicians were left to review autobiographical accounts about the past to decide whether this information fit within established criteria for PTSD or other mental health disorders.

---

21   E. Badger, "How the military can change personalities, slightly," *Nature & Technology*, 2012 33.

22   J. Bowlby, *Attachment and Loss*, Vol. 1, (New York: Basic Books, 1969).

23   Barglow, "We can't treat soldiers' PTSD without a better diagnosis."

In practice, however, our mental health assessments do not record all experiences including developmental history. It can be argued that our efforts involve a rewriting of history focusing on negative aspects of veterans' operational duties and more recently on negative childhood events. Other information outside of diagnostic criteria has to be ignored or retranslated. For example, information about pre-or-post deployment functioning within a soldier's unit has to be ignored because it is not considered to be relevant in determining medical diagnoses. However, the evidence suggests that what happens to a soldier in terms of actual support during the six-month period following a critical event may be the deciding factor in determining recovery or chronic distress.[24]

We focus on key events that are believed to have created a mental injury. This is a well-intentioned way to try to validate the distress reported by men and women in uniform, especially since most other western militaries are doing this same thing. I am not sure if this is the only way to understand or to acknowledge distress among soldiers and veterans. As I have suggested earlier, the downside of this approach is that we risk creating a class of permanently disabled young men and women—veterans as hero victims. In an odd manifestation, for some people, this PTSD tag forms the basis of a new identity.

By contrast, my attention to a social-relational understanding of military trauma is meant to include another perspective, based in the direct experiences of veterans, which may offer us additional ways to move forward. The standing account of trauma is based on a belief that impaired brain chemistry predisposes particular people to PTSD but, at the same time, that exposure to distressing events causes impaired brain chemistry in some people; a circular theory.

The real problems arise for those people who cannot resolve their particular issues, and their diagnoses end up trapping them as permanent victims. Some readers may ask why we need theories in the first place. Why not just do what works? The truth is that we all have theories; soldiers are taught theories about combat tactics that are practiced until they become routine; clinicians have theories

---

24   A.C. McFarlene and B.A. van der Kolk, "Trauma and its challenge to society," in *Traumatic Stress: The effects of overwhelming experience on mind, body, and society,* eds. B.A. van der Kolk, A.C. McFarlane, and L. Weisaeth (New York: Guilford Press, 2007) 24–46.

that guide their efforts to help until they become second nature. Implicit theories are often out of conscious awareness until there are problems.

We should not forget that it was not so long ago that women were theorized to be childlike and incapable of rational decisions as part of political processes, and that it took many decades for them to win their fight for the right to vote in Canada. When theories do not reflect actual experience, we all need reference points to decide appropriate course of actions. If there are disagreements between observed facts and our theories, or if the theory is only vaguely outlined, then people are left to interpret actions arbitrarily.

When it comes to the standing theory about PTSD, then, it can be at odds with the actual experiences of veterans. Common among traumatized men and women who ask for help are reactions of identity confusion, upset, and mental and emotional exhaustion. They often describe conflicted workplace relationships, a loss of interest in their work and family lives, an inability to sleep because they replay events, and an inability to incorporate their experiences into their lives back home. As a result of all of this, they are worn down and disoriented. They often drink or engage in risky activities to feel some things emotionally, and they can't seem to find a way to reset themselves. They are quick tempered, self-absorbed, irritable, and content to be by themselves. In other words, a tired and pissed-off group of people who were trained to do things that have little value in civilian life or within their home units. This is especially true for reservists and other augmentees (soldiers who are temporarily assigned to a unit) who have deployed during various missions. It is as if they lose much of their established worth and identity at the main gate when they leave for the last time: "They take our commitment and loyalty and squander them like commodities, and when we have nothing left to give, we have to go." They describe this experience as leaving parts of themselves behind.

Excluding formal diagnostic considerations for a moment, many complaints appear to represent exhaustion and disillusionment with ideals of military service, but they have no ideas about how to move forward in their lives. More than anything, veterans talk about their inability to feel some things while trying to avoid feeling other things. What seems to have changed in the culture is that these men and women want reciprocated loyalty, and they are not contained by discipline, stoicism, and emotional suppression. They are re-evaluating their military careers against the backdrop of strained values and relationships, and their inability to get back to the person they were before their deployments. Many of them had looked forward to deployments as events to test them and somehow magically transform their lives—the possibility of being a part of something important for the greater good, to become heroes—instead they are disillusioned by the realities of serving overseas.

As I have suggested earlier, in our desire to help, we can end up reducing soldiers to victim status, which may serve a variety of purposes simultaneously. Things like anger, mistrust, cynicism, and a depersonalized reaction to the world can be viewed as part of operational stress injuries. However, to acknowledge the roots of these reactions could refocus attention on the context of their military training and relationships. There may be a profound state of disorientation created through the interaction of the loss of their preservice identities and disrupted attachment to their acquired military identity. In other words, soldiers cannot undo the effects of training on their own—there is no going back—and when they lose connection to the larger institution, there is no going forward either. They exist in a sort of interpersonal limbo.

Many veterans were seeking attention and recognition within their units when they were upset or disappointed; very human reactions that they refuse to admit publicly. And when they did verbalize their concerns, they often felt dismissed. In my mind, the benefits of care and attention would be better served if received from members of their units—from the people who mattered to them—and without the price of a mental health label. If we look closely at the behaviours that constitute PTSD and other mental health issues and take the position that all behaviour is intended for some purpose, that it is social in nature, I think we need to ask what it is that these men and women are trying to communicate to people around them. Many of them have grievances and self-recriminations over personal transgressions, and they want tangible steps to correct the wrong.

Failure to live up to expectations and ideals is a negative experience for most of us and often a source of shame for proud military people. It can be described as an experience that consumes their thoughts and saps their vitality, leading to withdrawal from other people, especially those closest to them. There is a preoccupation with awful things that may have happened and their roles in these events, usually defined as flashbacks and intrusive thoughts. Contextually, shame and the risk of social disapproval are powerful motivators in general and especially relevant within the military. The opposite of this reaction is dignity and pride—most military members are intensely proud, but in the back of everyone's mind is a constant fear of failure.

In many cases, the roots of PTSD and even suicidality are rooted in perceived failures and reactions of shame—*I don't deserve to live*.[25] Suicidal thinking may also be driven by disavowed reactions like rage and helplessness, which are often redefined as depression and emotional shutdown. It is the need to do something to avoid emotional pain.

I recall seeing a soldier several years ago who had been in Srebrenica just prior to the eventual massacre. Up to the particular evening in question, there had been no overt action, and they were heading out on a routine patrol. He had taken it upon himself to disassemble and clean the carrier's mounted .50 calibre machine gun before heading out that evening. Several hours later, the Canadian patrol unexpectedly came under fire, and he froze for several seconds as rounds zipped past his head while he was setting up a tent. His buddy had taken rounds to his legs, and even though he left the tent to pull his buddy to safety, he was consumed by those few seconds.

Upon return to Canada, he turned to excessive drinking and twice attempted suicide. Now an angry and belligerent man, he was eventually released. Several years later, he was involved in a group with other veterans, including a former Warrant Officer from that deployment. He began telling his story about what he had done wrong when his former warrant spoke up:

> … hold on there, I was there that night and saw you as you put the bolt stud in that weapon even though it was not your job. Man, as I listened to the sounds of the attack on the Comms in the OP (observation post) that night, all I could think was thank Christ you took that initiative. In my mind you saved that entire patrol.

25   C. Zayfert, "Cognitive behavioral conceptualizations of retraumatization," in *Retraumatization: Assessment, Treatment, and Prevention*, eds. M.P. Duckworth, and V.M. Follette (New York: Routledge, 2012), 9–32.

I watched tears form in the younger man's eyes and the sheer relief on his face. Now five years later, he continues to do extremely well and travels across Canada and Europe as a respected member of a band. I can't help but wonder whether this conversation between these two men on the night of the patrol could have changed his career path and pre-empted his years of isolation and self-doubts. It emphasizes the power of shame and also the power of fellow military members to allay the debilitating effects from key moments. In terms of his background, this soldier grew up in an acrimonious home where there were frequent arguments between his parents. From his vantage point, his parents were so preoccupied with their own unhappiness that they neglected the children. He learned to be self-sufficient but also to be rigid and unforgiving.

There is no doubt that a substantial number of soldiers continue to bear the after-effects of their deployments, and there is a pressing need to help them resolve the impacts on their psyches. Even so, our attention on the label of PTSD to acknowledge this distress may come with unanticipated consequences, and for some people, this label defines them under a new identity—veteran as victim. As one veteran of Somalia put it:

You know, I used this PTSD label to let myself off the hook for the things I had done. I used it as a way to just give up on trying.

This soldier had finally come to understand that the PTSD label was also trapping him into a hopeless future. Other veterans feel guilty and embarrassed in front of their wives and children because they do not work or cannot participate in activities with their families. They feel misunderstood and believe they continually have to prove to themselves and people around them how they have been permanently damaged from their time in the military. I don't mean to suggest that they are pretending, I just mean that they focus on negative things consistent with what they have read or have been told about PTSD and other mental health issues. As well, for some veterans, fears about the future drive a predictable interest in financial compensation. Each 'symptom' comes to serve as evidence, amplified and focused on, while positive days or weeks have to be ignored. As countless veterans have said to me:

I feel guilty when I have a good day or a good week. Then I think there is no reason why I can't work, and then I have a bad day, and then I remind myself, see that's why I can't work.

As a clinician, I think there is also something important at play among medically released veterans that is rarely discussed. The ways in which clinicians understand PTSD often conflicts with the meanings attached to the term by veterans. For many veterans, PTSD represents bitterness over careers cut short, a reflection of disorientation and other personal costs of their deployments, and paradoxically it is a means of remaining connected to the military. In short, it is often a term that provides them an alternative version of their military identity and a direct but peculiar connection to their past.

Many of them interpret feedback that they are getting better to mean that they will have to give up this new identity; in essence that, by getting better, they may be left with no identity whatsoever. We also cannot deny the fact that proving to be chronically ill is also reinforced through interactions with bureaucracies. One of the primary mandates of Veterans Affairs Canada, which is rooted historically, is to separate fakers from legitimate claimants. As the costs of financial compensation claims and treatments increase steadily, testing and evidence requirements have become more sophisticated and expert evidence of all types is evaluated for truthfulness. There is a game that is played, and veterans have told me about the game. A retired Chief Warrant Officer put it this way:

When VAC asks you how you are doing, instead of saying that your problems are manageable on some days, you have to tell them what they need to hear, that it is severe every day or your claim will be rejected.

In sum, veterans have the understanding that there is a specific response pattern, like a code, to questions that will increase their chances of disability approval. Sometimes, case managers and other advocates have 'assisted' veterans in filling out these questionnaires. It is a terribly problematic process where the stakes seem to be forever escalating. As VAC increases evidence thresholds, veterans, their supporters, and even care providers also increase symptom severity ratings to help distressed veterans. I stopped participating in this process several years ago because I believed that it was simply too difficult to get to the truth from either side.

The belief that we have few options to direct the course of our lives in the face of external rules, laws, family, or work obligations serves to help people to avoid making tough decisions. It is easier to abdicate this responsibility. This holds true for people from all walks of life. For instance, take the example of the unhappy worker who reminds every person in the workplace about how bad it is but who, when he is asked why he does not leave for better opportunities, immediately cites a list of reasons why he is trapped and has no choice. Most people will quietly agree with him because nobody wants the argument of telling him the truth. Of course, he has choices. He might have to reorganize living expectations and search for other possibilities instead of reacting in helplessness and powerlessness. Admittedly, this can be very challenging for soldiers who have a strong sense of identification and loyalty to the military and believe that, by leaving, they are abandoning the brotherhood.

Seven

Am I a Good Man?

This was not the retirement he'd planned for. This wasn't even close. A sailor since the age of eighteen, he'd spent the last thirty-six years of his life in uniform and been all over the world. And though, over the past few years, his duties as command chief had occupied much of his days, the prospect of a life after the Navy had been something he had been looking forward to.

Finally, some time alone with Beth, he'd thought. Well, Beth and their dog (an old boxer that had long since become Beth's dog if truth be told). The kids, of course, were long gone and well into lives of their own with kids of their own; he'd missed a lot on that score. It didn't matter anymore. He and Beth were going to travel. He was finally going to build a canoe, and even before he'd pulled the pin, he had already picked up the tools and supplies he'd need and purchased a plan he liked online.

But it didn't play out that way. None of it did. Instead it had all turned to shit.

He had been out for almost six months, but all the plans he had made just seemed to wither. He did not *want* to travel anymore, he realized. How could he have not known that ahead of time? And going to the workshop each morning was daunting because being alone with his thoughts was a dark place.

Now he was preoccupied with the idea of just ending it all, thoughts that were growing more insistent with each passing day.

He tried to occupy himself by helping Beth with the gardens or spending time with the grandchildren when they were over. But nothing seemed to keep the black thoughts away.

Young faces from years past kept popping into his mind, obedient faces that looked haggard and bewildered standing in front of him. His sailors. His guts would churn at the thought of them. His chest would feel heavy. He thought mostly about Peggy's Cove and about the Gulf, times when he knew his sailors were suffering but he had to ignore what he saw in their faces and ensure they got the job done. As their Chief, he had to be tough so that they could carry on with their assigned tasks no matter how upsetting, no matter how gruesome. It was his job to see not just that the mission succeeded but that his sailors succeeded.

Now these faces were back, condemning him for his part in events that had broken a lot of them. He had pushed them, ignored the signs of break-down and their pleas for help or relief. He had been a bastard, but he had to be. Anything less would have meant letting down the Admiral and simply being replaced by someone else, somebody ready and waiting to take his seat.

Was this the price he had to pay for all those years? He was the Chief, and that meant that there was never anyone he could have trusted to talk about his stuff. Just keep pushing harder; that was all he had ever known. That was how he had gotten promoted throughout his career. Nobody could know how the loss of two divers, decades earlier, had nearly driven him mad or that years later he still felt the bitter tears of grief and guilt for not being able to protect his boys, his sailors. All those faces, those young women and men willing to do whatever he ordered, seemed adamant now that he should fry in hell. He *was* in hell, and there was no way out.

Dave had been like a tough father whose job it had been to harden and to protect them. Hell, it was a hard life they'd all signed up for—no one knew that better than he did—and he'd have been doing them no favours coddling them.

It was how he had grown up, even though in Dave's case he could find no redeeming qualities in his own father. His old man had been an angry, hateful prick who'd never once given him a break. Still, Dave had learned toughness, hadn't he? And that's what he wanted to pass on to his sailors. And not because he was a prick, but because he cared for them. When the ship was not operational, he tried to take time to talk with them and to offer advice when they had personal problems. But he could go only so far in that regard. He wanted them to know that he was tough but that he cared.

He wondered now how many of them really came away with all of that.

■ ⬛

Leaders like Dave are often required to shut down their human reactions of compassion and concern for other people in order to meet the operational requirements and expectations of their roles. They have to be tough to avoid being hesitant or indecisive. They can be caught in a real dilemma between a leadership requirement to look out for their subordinates and the need to place operational imperatives as the priority. This seems to be a contradiction that permeates the entire institution. On the one hand, there are real efforts to pay attention to the mental-emotional health of the membership while on the other hand operational necessities and bureaucratic realities means that it has to promote tough, demanding leadership. It is a contradiction that I believe the organization is trying to navigate, but in a black-and-white world, people line up on one side or the other.

Like any other organization, the military is not monolithic. There are those who believe that mental health initiatives amount to pandering to the weak, which in turn, risks degrading the operational effectiveness of the military. Conversely, there are those who believe that unit strength comes from an understanding that every soldier has to be valued and supported in good and bad times. Unfortunately, those who are medically released because of mental declines come to view these tensions as hypocrisy.

In terms of interventions, the process of having veterans think in detail about the most awful things that have ever happened to them is hypothesized to repair injuries to memory networks and even specific brain structures. Almost everybody has told me that their problems have nothing to do with memory; in fact, the problem is that it works too well. What is common is the problem of managing emotions where the skill of compartmentalization has been over-learned as the main strategy—placing these memories in metaphorical shoe boxes. Again, it is important to avoid pathologizing this ability since most healthy people also engage in this strategy to varying degrees.[26]

26   M. Goulston, "Does too much compartmentalization risk disconnecting you from people?" *Just Listen*, 26 May 2014.

Compartmentalization is what enables us to behave differently and appropriately in a variety of situations—allowing us to behave like a boss or worker on the job, a parent and/or spouse and/or grown child at home, or a teammate. The problems with this strategy begin to arise when the situations and roles are widely different. There is not much in common for a soldier serving in a warzone and days or weeks later standing in a line-up at the local coffee shop. In order to adjust to the home front, they have to package or file away the behaviours, thought processes, and events that occurred during their deployments. As a result, they learn to be highly compartmentalized.

Another way of putting this is that they are required to have extremely good boundaries so that one role does not blur or spill over into another. Depending on the duration, frequency, or intensity of deployments, these boundaries can become rigid—it all has to be packed away. If there were events that evoked strong emotional reactions, these are also packed away. Military personnel know how to stay away from emotional issues exceptionally well. As I said earlier, for soldiers, it can feel like living in two completely separated worlds.

One of the challenges for highly compartmentalized people is that, over time, they may retreat more and more into the compartments where they feel most competent and confident. For soldiers, this can mean acting stoically and emotionless in their roles as husbands and fathers where caring, empathy, and open dialogue are essential abilities. Over time, they can appear to be more like 'human doings' who don't feel particularly present as people even though they appear quite competent in their functioning. On the other hand, less compartmentalized people appear to be more present as human beings and better able to relate to other people *as people* instead of simply as functions or roles. They often have an easier time at empathizing with others.

Compartmentalization can be considered to be an over-learned, automatic mental strategy to avoid discomfort and anxiety created by conflicting values, thoughts, emotions, or beliefs. It reduces mental and emotional conflicts. For example, the fundamental belief that all life is valuable must, by obvious necessity, be carefully compartmentalized for individuals who are required on occasion to kill people or stand back and watch people be killed—or starve or any other manner of horror that takes place in war-torn areas—otherwise the rules of engagement fall apart and mission objectives become immediately untenable.

In my case, I was fascinated, and sometimes even worried, by my own mental changes as I prepared to leave home. For instance, I always grew much less talkative and much more argumentative. Much of what was a normal and expected part of life at home seemed somehow untrue or irrelevant in my military role and vice versa. It was as if I existed in two separate and disconnected worlds.

When I think about the issues facing soldiers returning from deployments, I think they also experience the same separation of identity because they have lost the context of their overseas experiences including the relevant emotional impacts. When the pressures from deployments end and the proverbial dust begins to settle, the emotional aftermath often begins to surface, which can be quite disorienting and upsetting. It becomes a case of the right emotions but the wrong context. The importance of context can offer an explanation for failures to integrate memories when they get back home, for their memories and the associated emotions have no relevance in their daily lives.

A number of years ago, research identified the phenomenon of state dependent learning. In one novel project, participants where administered alcohol during an experiment to teach them a new skill. Later they could only perform the task when alcohol was re-administered.[27] This seems to suggest that it might not be neurological anomalies that cause delayed stress reactions but the fact that elements of the experience are being recalled out of the learning context. It may be that their personal moral compass switches back on when they are back home, forcing them to re-evaluate the things they were forced to do or witness. Within formal mental health, however, this compartmentalization is usually defined as pathology, an essential feature of dissociation—a disruption of the usual connections between consciousness, memory, identity, and perception of the environment—the very core of PTSD as we conceptualize it.

An alternative to pathologizing the skill of dissociation is to view it as a form of acquired compartmentalization that allows people to manage their experiences in isolated fragments. It usually involves keeping emotional elements of these experiences at bay. These emotional avoidance skills are particularly relevant for members of the

27   G. Lowe, "Alcohol and state-dependent learning," *Substances Alcohol Actions Misuse*, 4(4) (1983): 273–282.

military given that they are honed from the first days of basic train-ing—all of us were taught the thousand-yard stare when getting jacked up by our drill instructors. So the disintegration observed by PTSD researchers may not be a result of problematic brain function at all, but instead as a product of over-learned psychological strate-gies to manage emotional intrusions.

A final component of this dissociative compartmentalization skill is an alteration of basic self-identity that is fostered through deper-sonalization (the ability to detach from one's self and to not take things personally). Military training also reinforces this skill quite effectively; if it didn't, we could not survive the demands of training or be able to place ourselves in extremely dangerous situations at a moment's notice. It allows us to follow orders, no matter the risks to ourselves or others.

Take the example of the shy, introverted soldier who uses this ability to 'assume' a different, warrior identity. The ability to shut off personal reactions and to act outside of his own body enables him to get the job done. We know that being able to distance oneself from emotions like fear or shame can allow people to develop a self-identity that carries a sense of confidence and mastery or, for a soldier like Roger, the fearlessness to walk straight into a minefield without a second thought to retrieve an injured child.

Young recruits are introduced to demanding, aggressive instructors in no-win training scenarios that create a context to disrupt their normal ways of perceiving and reacting to life. The tasks of training are aimed at focusing their attention, instilling self-discipline, relinquishing their individuality, and automati-cally submitting to authority, which can all be incredibly dis-orienting. I think that this ability to switch into auto-pilot—to ignore emotional reactions and to push one's physical and mental limits—can be defined as dissociation-in-action. It can feel like acting outside of one's own body with the ability to excel and to do the unimaginable.

As with all skills, some people seem much better suited to it than others; it may even be the case that those people who grew up in demanding developmental environments are better equipped with this ability. They may be only too willing to take on a different personal identity. So it seems crucial to keep the example of normal or adaptive dissociation in mind to understand complex stress reactions, especially in work with military clients. Remembering the adaptive uses of dissociation may also combat the tendency to pathologize dissociative symptoms and remind us that we can help people turn maladaptive use of this coping skill into adaptive capabilities.[28]

The combined psychological skill set of compartmentalization, depersonalization, and dissociation may provide the breeding ground for chronic forms of distress following ongoing or highly charged negative events. They allow people to do the unimaginable, but in my experience, these abilities can also get in the way of recovery. It is debatable whether habitual reliance on these skills contributes to the development of PTSD in the first place. Whether these strategies are viewed as psychological defences—pathological—or as acquired skills, the downside seems to be an inability to access the full range of one's emotions. In short, the very psychological skill set acquired through training may interfere with one's ability to appreciate and to process critical events and associated emotions.

For example, the opposite of dissociation is connectedness, both to internal experiences and to people around us. The goal of helping veterans to overcome trauma then, is rarely about helping them to remember what happened or even about the ability to tolerate specific feelings. The real task seems to come down to helping them understand how they adapted by using these avoidance skills to help them mentally survive unsafe environments by using their minds as a refuge—by compartmentalizing feelings, knowledge, talents, and abilities, or even parts of memories. It is an internal system that was highly adaptive in unsafe and complex environments. However, the fact that what worked overseas is different from life at home means that a system which once ran smoothly now finds itself in conflict: At one level these men and women may want to stay in mission mode, but at another level they may wish to be closer to their wives, parents, or children. Internally, they often report being intensely fearful of vulnerability and intimacy because they don't know where it may lead—they may lose control—so they run away as soon as their relationships become close.

Given that the cardinal features of post-traumatic stress reactions are emotionally loaded intrusions, it should not be a surprise that a veteran's past may be influencing his life in the present. Either he is assaulted by intrusive thoughts, feelings, images, smells, and bodily sensations, or he is disconnected, constricting his life and numbing

---

28   B. Rime, "Interpersonal emotion regulation," in *Handbook of Emotion Regulation*, ed. J.J. Gross, (New York: Guilford, 2007) 466–485.

all emotion in order to avoid these intrusions and maintain control. Typically, trauma clients interpret both sets of reactions as here-and-now reality. They make statements like "I'm never safe," indicating that the intrusion of unsafe emotions takes place across situations or they may interpret any strong emotion for that matter to alert them that they are still in danger.

In considering the broader social context, if Canadians were interested, they might hear about the outrage that veterans are left to live with because of their roles in uniform. This strain is described in this next story. This RCMP veteran struggled each day to keep from searching out and killing people on a personal hit list. Even though he had been retired for many years, he continued to be haunted by the memory of a woman who was repeatedly hospitalized because her husband would beat her during drunken fits. The most that he and the other officers could do was to visit the home and warn him to leave her alone since she was too afraid to file charges because of his treats to kill her. They were helpless to do more. This man eventually did kill his wife. Says this RCMP veteran:

I know where he lives to this day, and every morning I wake up, it takes everything I got now that I am out of uniform to stop myself from enforcing my justice on him. God-dammed uniform stopped me from doing the right thing, but not anymore.

Soldiers also live and die by professionalism and operational rules of engagement. I think often about the snipers in Bosnia who were given strict orders to hold their fire and to simply observe and report on scenes of savage rape and murder of women and young girls despite their repeated calls for permission to intervene. These men live with doubts and self-recriminations over their inability to help for which there is no outlet. In a cruel twist, their moral compasses have switched back on and their military avoidance skill set no longer works effectively. With enough time back home, they come out of adrenaline mode and the mental processes of digesting and integrating experiences takes many of them by surprise: "I look at my daughter, and it all comes back."

We all go through this process of mentally digesting experiences following serious events. We may see those people who appear to go off the rails for no reason, but if we knew their stories, we would understand that they have all the reason in the world to feel crazy and set apart from the rest of society. We ask them to do the impossible—to forget about their humanity, to hold back their instincts to help, and then ask them to simply forget about these things when they come home or retire. No wonder many of them feel divorced from the larger society.

When we try to convince soldiers that they are victims, we deny the truth by somehow trying to persuade them to feel less responsible for their roles in what may have happened or the things they could not prevent. It also takes away the meaning of their symptoms and removes from consideration the things they might want or need to do to reconcile damage caused by them. For some, continued suffering may allow them to live with the fact that they survived when their buddies did not, a type of penalty to be paid because there is no safe outlet for their grief. It may help others to avoid making tough decisions about continued military service; if they are too sick to continue, the decision is left to others to make the decision for them. It serves caregivers because it is compelling to empathize with needy people; they accept our authority as expert, our abilities, and even our values. The idea that something is wrong with the biology of certain brains also fits within the narrative that everyone is essentially a good, honourable person, and so we have veterans as *hero victims*.

When it comes to our military and RCMP veterans, this victim narrative seems to serve a purpose for the Canadian public. Let's face it, the average person does not wish to hear about the gruesome realities of life. They want to be reassured that they are safe, and only real men and women can keep us safe. I am not sure whether Canadians know how to react to stories and images of mentally wounded veterans. Scenes of physically and mentally wounded veterans, reports about police involvement and suicides, and the many stories about inadequate care seems to paint the veteran as diminished versions of strong and reliable men and women. It can stir public sympathy, which is reluctantly accepted by the veteran community.

Reports of suffering among veterans may serve to reassure us that these people are still honourable men and women despite their participation in war and death—their suffering is a sign of sacrifice that can be publicly shared. The military people who held up their part of the bargain on our behalf on the world stage, through their blood and suffering, can be seen as essentially nice sons and daughters who were up to the tasks of rugged men and women. To those people who have lost sons and daughters, brothers and sisters, hearing about the continued suffering of others reminds them that they are not alone and that they are not the only ones living with the aftermath of another all but forgotten war.

I think the notion of injured veterans also serves Canadian society insofar as it maintains the belief that our heroes are the embodiment of our progressive and humane society through our institutions. I would contend that these people are also sacrificed in order to keep our collective fears and our personal responsibility to act out of our daily awareness. We come across a house fire that is being managed by various first responders where people are hurt or destitute, and we can give it passing attention and then move on to the next thing in our awareness. We transfer authority and power to police, fire-fighters, paramedics, and military people to manage intrusions upon our need for social order so that our notions of safety are left intact. The victim metaphor also allows us to view them as self-sacrificing examples of the best that our society has to offer.

In many cases, these people epitomize the hero caricature, but other motives also drive specific people—not all heroes are good people. It is in our collective interests to ignore cases where these heroes become human and do human things. In cases that can't be ignored, they are ejected, ostracized, and erased from our public memory to keep alive our metaphors and our shared illusions.

The name of Colonel Williams is not spoken in Canada even though his history as a rising star in the military is very recent. The Canadian Airborne Regiment was banished almost immediately from the Canadian military's lexicon following Somalia—abandoning that generation of airborne soldiers. In the end, hero victims are constructed within society as innocents, which is to say passive and helpless. We expect soldiers to accept this re-creation of their identity in order for us to offer care to them. While well-meaning and probably unintentional, the results are often devastating for men and women steeped in values of strength and overcoming adversity. In her book *Manufacturing Victims*, Dr. Tana Dineen provided a scathing review of the industry of psychology—referring to talking helpers of all types as offering an empty promise to people while rendering them in the role of victims, clients, or users of services.[29]

Military spokespeople and many leaders support the belief of a caring, respectful family. But we should also acknowledge that this

---

29   T. Dineen, *Manufacturing Victims* , *3ʳᵈ edition"*, *Robert Davies Publishing,* *Montreal (2001).*

sentiment has been driven by media reports of suicides within the military—an ongoing source of concern and embarrassment for the leadership. In contrast to this notion of family, among most of the people I see exists an alternative understanding as stated by one veteran of Afghanistan:

> **You are valued and included as long as you can do what the system needs, but as soon as it becomes obvious that you have nothing left to give, you have to go.**

In terms of the system, deeming particular people mentally unfit may serve another purpose. It may provide the system legitimacy in continuing its usual way of managing its personnel as a human resource issue. Given that the majority of members do not come forward to report mental health problems, the rationale is that mental declines are issues with the members in question rather than with the system itself. And this *could* be true, but we have no way of knowing since we have never explored the question in any rigorous or independent fashion. In my world, veterans often say things like the following:

> **I wish my chain of command could be sitting here in this group to hear the stuff we talk about so that they would have to face the truth—that what they pump out to the public is crap.**

Uniformed people are separated from the larger civilian society and not only through the experiences of war. Soldiers miss community, and when something happens in this brotherhood or they come back to the mundane routines of in-garrison life, they can feel empty and alone even though they may still be with the same people. They lose their specialness, and their closeness with others just seems to evaporate. It is yet another aspect of compartmentalized life. It begins on day one of their training as one identity is rejected to be replaced by the other—the military identity that bonds us to the institution.

Maybe we came looking for this new identity in the first place, but none of us were aware of what we were trading until it came time to leave the military. We may see glimpses of the changes within ourselves upon return from training or deployments. I recognized it immediately at the end of basic training. I was different physically and mentally, and I was entirely satisfied with this metamorphosis. I was, I felt, better than my civilian friends. By the time I finished my first long deployment, any emotional ties to home or the person I thought I was before joining had been all but erased.

My father was a miner who never left my home province. As a twenty-year-old, there was no way to describe to him what I did, even excluding the limitations imposed by my security clearance obligations. There was no possibility for a conversation about what it meant for me to be continually preparing for nuclear war and to track Russian nuclear submarines sitting off the North American coast with enough fire power to obliterate the entire continent while he and the rest of my family slept oblivious to this world. He simply had no context to understand my job, so it was better for our relationship, for him especially, to believe that I was learning to be a man. Likewise, the young soldier has no way of telling his parents about the complexities of operating in a warzone, about the anguish of witnessing a sexually abused seven-year-old Afghan boy, to talk about the sights of human suffering, starvation, or the carnages of war: "Even if I could, they would not believe me."

After leaving the military, I made the mistake, during my first year of university, of answering a question from a classmate about the military. She asked what I had done, and maybe I was showing off, but I talked about a couple of things like being overseas and the exhilaration of hanging out of a helicopter over the North Atlantic and serving briefly on a Norwegian frigate (one of several types of warship of various sizes and roles) near Russian waters during the Cold War.

The incredulous look was immediate, as were the guffaws from the university jocks who thought they knew everything. I never did that again. I did talk with an ex-RCMP guy who had left the Force after ten years. I think we recognized each other by *the look*: both unsure what we were doing there among those kids or whether we would ever fit. For the most part, I just tried to forget about the military and move on. All this to say that many soldiers and veterans are alone and isolated in the civilian world and sometimes within their own organizations because they can't relate and don't share their experiences, either good or bad ones. I recently met with a senior RCMP officer who had been forced to leave his young interpreter to the Taliban when his personal security was breached in Afghanistan.

He was like a son to me, and I just abandoned him and now I can't even look my own son in the face without feeling ashamed every day. Back in my detachment, most of them don't even know that place exists, so I don't tell them that I was there.

In my mind then, traumatic stress can only be understood within the wider society of military people around them. Their experiences occur within a particular context, and the things that are difficult to understand there are near impossible to decipher when they leave that context. Collectively, professionals seem stymied by the notion of military trauma. Efforts to attribute aftereffects to aspects of a critical event, to the qualities of traumatized people including disrupted early childhoods, and more recently to errant brain functioning continue to be inadequate.

We still do not know the cause of military PTSD nor the roots and relevance of neurobiological changes, and we can't seem to agree over its designation as an illness. We still do not know why some people are negatively affected while others are seemingly unaffected. The Israeli experience may provide some clues. Israeli forces see frequent conflict and wars yet report remarkably low rates for PTSD. Some researchers speculate that it may be related to their cultural belief systems, strong social bonds, or the fact that war is part of everyday conversation affecting the entire population, military and civilian alike. Historically, there was a tradition where soldiers returning home from war were given audience and *expected* to regale those on the home front with their stories from the battlefield. During the post-WWII years, the Royal Canadian Legions served this function for many decades, but these things no longer occur in the aftermath of modern armed conflicts. Instead, stories are relegated to veterans attempting to talk to each other under cloaks of national secrecy. Many of them are people doomed to be set apart.

It is quite challenging to make generalizations about the cluster of reactions that come to be defined as PTSD. While there is general consensus in diagnosing these reactions as a mental disorder, when it comes to directions about how to resolve these issues, there is much less agreement. This lack of consensus arises from the fact that no treatment approach has been shown consistently to help the majority of people.

What does seem common to chronic trauma cases, especially among soldiers, is that quite often there is a relational aspect to its development and an issue to be resolved as part of recovery. A soldier may have been afraid in combat, which is an entirely acceptable human response to threat, but what often traps them is the belief that they let down other people or failed their training because they were weak. Those soldiers who witness atrocities or irreconcilable moral dilemmas often carry shame or outrage in silence because they were helpless or forced to betray their personal values or those of the Canadian Armed Forces.

While there are certainly times and places to *suck it up* and to get things done, there are few viable opportunities to fully decompress or to tell their stories. Their emotional wellbeing is neglected. As I discuss in subsequent stories, the difference between resolution of past events and chronic distress may come down to this issue of neglect, either real or imagined.

We are not sure about the relationship between preservice history and mental health declines among serving members. One way to understand the responses of military members is again through the lens of relationships. In terms of early attachment patterns, it may very well be that people who experience early life breaches left unresolved may be more reactive when they re-experience them as adults.[30] Developmental research has taught us that the right brain encodes early attachment patterns that might make people susceptible to deterioration when they are distressed and need assistance as adults.[31]

While the military provides soldiers with ready-made pseudo relationships developed through shared identity and struggle, these relationships are not the same as intimate, trusting relationships because they exclude vulnerability. Furthermore, there is often a level of quiet aggression in military relationships which can show itself in the blink of an eye. A compassionate ear from a buddy can quickly mutate into preachy arrogance and competition. Military relationships revolve around role personas, shared adversity, and

30   V.J. Felitti and R.F. Anda, "The relationship of adverse childhood experiences to adult health, well-being, social function, and healthcare," in *The impact of early life trauma on health and disease: The hidden epidemic*, eds. R. Lanius, E. Vermetten, and C. Pain, (Cambridge: Cambridge University Press, 2010), 77–87.

31   Schore, *The Science and Art of Psychotherapy*, New York: Norton (2012).

GHOST IN THE RANKS   113

proven worth, all of which are quite different from unconditional acceptance of oneself and others.

Those people who struggle with fundamental self-worth may be overly invested in this type of relatedness and prone to focus on roles and ranks rather than anything personal. This means that those people with troubled developmental experiences often withdraw into passivity while outwardly appearing competent and stoic, or alternatively they react in anger and retaliation in misguided attempts to maintain their image. Indeed, many traumatized veterans, at some point, just wanted somebody in authority to show genuine interest in their welfare though they were unwilling to risk losing face seeking said interest. Another seeming catch 22.

One's self-identity can be understood to be the sum product of experiences, relationships, values, interests, and ways of speaking, interacting, and being in the world. Most of us see ourselves as an individual person distinct from other people around us. In my experience, undergoing military training is no less than a direct alteration of one's core sense of self through the use of language, tasks, rewards, and punishments. It is *designed* to remake the person—a stronger, tougher version of oneself where the individual no longer exists save as a replaceable element of the group (the section, platoon, and unit).

As people undergo this process, there is a definable period of disorientation. During this time, members experience a sense of losing the familiar and taking on an altered, depersonalized sense of themselves; people become homesick for the familiar and can become anxious or passively go along with external demands.

Some people equate this process to brainwashing or cult-like indoctrination. And maybe so, but at the time, it simply feels like proving something to yourself and to other people. There are earned rewards and recognition as recruits perform as required and, more importantly, learn to not stand out. The goal is to become an unseen member of the group by acting like your fellow recruits. It does not do to look too good or too bad, for either can draw unwanted attention in front of the group.

The durability of these training effects is often under-appreciated in general society. As I mentioned earlier, Emily Badger contends that, even after basic military training, soldiers are often permanently changed. They become, as a rule, less agreeable and more aggressive—traits that do not serve them well in their future relationships. She argues that once soldiers go back in the civilian world, this aggressive style can stay with them even years after they leave the military.[32]

The new initiative of educating military populations on psychological resiliency and mental health awareness are important, recent developments for our military. Even so, the idea that resiliency is reducible to an individual skill set, or that it can be framed as a personal quality, is highly debatable. This is especially true when all related training excludes the social-relational environment.

Mental resiliency may have the potential of normalizing routine, human ways of dealing with mental stressors and serve as an alternative to compartmentalization and denial. The way it rolls out practically within units and among the membership may be a different matter, however. One outcome might be that those people who receive briefings on mental health may eventually be expected to take additional responsibility for their issues:

Man, it's everywhere. You can't say anything without somebody taking you aside and raising the *P-word*. (PTSD)

So while mental health awareness is a positive practical step, it may lead supervisors and others to become hyper-focused on signs and symptoms. Paradoxically, it could lead to undue scrutiny of relatively transitory signs of legitimate anger or frustration or low mood among specific soldiers. If this happens, it could have the effect of driving mental distress issues further underground. This is not to suggest that there is anything wrong with these initiatives, it's simply my experience that interventions usually have both intended and unintended consequences.

---

32   E. Badger, "How the military can change personalities, slightly."

Eight

Live for the Moment

The shrill *bong, bong, bong* of the ship's action alarm filled his head along with unbidden images of sailors and standby divers trying frantically to get to the two distressed divers beneath the American destroyer.

Eric had zoned out in front of the television again. He was sweating and tears were streaming down his cheeks.

It had all happened so long ago, and yet the crushing weight of the deaths fell across his chest, and it could have been yesterday. He missed Billy especially. He had taken then eighteen-year-old Eric under his wing and guided him like a younger brother during that first year in the Navy. One minute he had been joking with Billy, and barely an hour later, he had watched as they pulled his lifeless body onto the jetty.

It had been such a senseless incident. In early February of 1991, HMCS *Margaree* was in port at Madeira along with a number of ships bound for the Gulf via the Straits of Gibraltar, and all ships bound for Gibraltar had to have their hulls searched. The USS *Pharris* didn't have divers, only surface swimmers, and so divers were requested from *Margaree*. The problem was that someone fucked up, and the seawater intake for *Pharris'* engines wasn't turned off and two of the divers got pulled in. That was Billy and Cory.

Eric's life fell completely off the rails since leaving the military a year ago. He is a walking contradiction—a biker and patched club member whom all the other guys turn to for help and advice but with another darker side that is always itching for a fight:

Sometimes I just want someone to pull a knife or gun on me so that I can have an excuse to just go crazy and beat them to death, and then I snap out of it and wonder what the hell is wrong with me? I wonder if I am losing my mind.

Eric was treated and medically released in late 2014 due to an anxiety problem and physical injuries to his back and knees.

In our session, he describes the day of the drowning back in 1991 and how they were all detained aboard ship but with the bar open for everybody onboard.

We were determined to go over to the American ship and get our revenge for their stupidity... It was absolute chaos. I mean, all the rules went right out the window. Way out there, y'know? Guys drunk and crying, wanting to go home, wanting to go kill the people on the other ship. One guy broke a glass and slashed open his wrist. It just all blew me away.

In my professional life, I have seen other people also affected by this tragedy from the first Gulf War in the early 1990s. I also knew the name of one of the divers from my time in the Navy; in fact, he is buried in my hometown. In the early 1990s, there was no guidance to help the leadership know how to respond to the shock and grief among the ship's crew. Instead, Eric and everyone else were introduced to heavy drinking by the ship's senior leadership as a way to manage their distress. Operationally, given the beginning of a war campaign, the ship's deployment could not be interrupted to take care of a severely traumatized crew.

Eric came from a supportive family in a small rural community where open talks with his parents were common and where nothing out of the ordinary ever really happened.

When Billy died I thought, *man, it can come at any second.* So I just turned my back on everything my parents ever taught me and decided to live flat out, no more nice guy, just live for the moment because death can come at any second.

Eric described a career that vacillated between periods of high performance and a dark undercurrent of drunken debauchery and belligerence that lasted for nearly twenty years.

I was liked and a pretty good athlete, so they would pull me off the ships for competitions, or if it looked like I was getting in trouble, they would keep it away from me. I had a charmed life, but I really, honestly, did not give a shit about anything. They just kept promoting me and always wanted me for deployments because I took good care of the guys.

■ ⁍

What are we to make of this man's reactions?

By all accounts, Eric had been a pleasant and well-adjusted young man from a good family. He was devastated by the loss of his friend and the breakdown of military structure on his ship in the immediate aftermath of the accident. I can't help but think that this would have been a confusing and terrifying experience that left an indelible mark on him even after all these years.

He was a valued member of every crew he was part of, and when he knew that he was physically and emotionally exhausted, as a senior non-commissioned officer, he described having to demand medical treatment amid pleas from his superiors that they needed him on the ship. Eric was placed in an untenable position of having to leave his crew to take care of his own mental health—in effect abandoning them—or once again placing his own needs secondary to repeated requests from others to help them. Not surprisingly, Eric did go back to the ship temporarily, but he was simply not able to meet the physical demands any longer. He had no choice but to leave and when he did:

They completely ignored me, no calls, nothing. They threw me away when they knew I was used up.

What made matters worse in Eric's case was that, during his medical assessment, the fact that he had continued to be a high performer at work was interpreted to exclude the possibility of PTSD. It was inconceivable to this particular clinician that CAF members could hide behind 'workaholism' to distract themselves from distress. In reality, I have treated several other members of this crew who went on to complete full careers and were diagnosed, treated, and released medically because of PTSD over twenty years later. In fact, it is well known that many veterans with longstanding trauma issues continue for years as hard-driving, over-achievers within their units. Senior military personnel that I continue to treat also fit this exact description. This case raises troubling questions about the process and the role of mental health assessments for military personnel. It reinforces concerns over our lack of understanding of military trauma and its context, and PTSD generally, and the seeming arbitrariness of mental health diagnoses. I think we have to wonder whether institutional pressures are having an impact on the rates of officially recognized PTSD among military personnel or whether other characteristics of military personnel outside of official criteria warrant this particular diagnosis. For example, whether members fidget, shows signs of emotional upset, or zone out when talking about specific issues may have more impact on the eventual diagnosis compared to their answers to specific questioning. In the absence of a reliable diagnostic test then, clinicians may need to develop their own set of hidden signs of this 'disease'.

In Eric's case, he was given several other mental health diagnoses, including panic disorder that contributed to the end of his career since he did not benefit from the recommended treatment. He made only limited progress since arguably the treatment, including benzodiazepine medication, for panic symptoms did not address core historical issues. Within a year after his release, he was re-assessed and diagnosed with chronic and severe PTSD directly attributable to the diving deaths.

Once again, this story presents a significant challenge to the brotherhood narrative, and it is the cause of bitter disappointment for this man. It also highlights our continued confusion about the phenomenon of PTSD and seemingly arbitrary decisions when it comes to this diagnosis. There appears to be a misguided belief that those members experiencing chronic trauma reactions must be incompetent in some way that affects their work performance. While this is certainly true for some members, in many other cases these men and women are exceptionally adept at the skill of compartmentalization. In essence, their private emotional struggles are packaged away when it comes to their military persona and obligations.

As I have suggested, our conceptualizations of military trauma tend to focus on possible weaknesses when it comes to their abilities to fulfill military roles. We tend to focus on the characteristics of highly charged operational events and downplay the range of strategies that these members will engage in to maintain emotional control. This includes their reactions to the phenomenon of traumatic grief (reactions from the unexpected loss of loved ones in catastrophic circumstances) which is often missed when it comes to the diagnosis of operational PTSD. Eric and I spent a lot of time talking about his relationship with Billy and the lingering hole left behind by the death of this man. He had been left frozen in time because of the unexpected loss of this man.

We talked about an upcoming motorcycle road-trip he was planning. Eric quickly accepted my suggestion that he swing by Billy's hometown. In the past few days, I received a picture from Eric standing at Billy's headstone and a simple text: "It went well." As I told him, I was relieved and proud that he could muster the courage to finally face a terrible event head-on and to honour a man that meant so much to him all those years ago. It is difficult to know for certain the effects that his act of respect will have on his future mental health, but I can say that he will have less baggage to carry going forward. I look forward to seeing him again in group in the near future.

Nine

It Would Be Easier to Just Be Crazy

It's four in the morning. Paul wakes in full panic mode, sweat-soaked, his chest tight. He is struggling to breathe. The room is dark and still as a tomb. He can feel the blood rushing in his head, and when he sits up, there is a wave of dizziness that washes over him. He swears under his breath.

Got to get some air.

He pulls on the jeans and tee shirt balled on the floor and grabs the house keys from the bedside table. He knows he'll need to get out of the house and go for a walk and try to calm down. Otherwise, he'll never get back to sleep.

This has been Paul's new normal since the Peggy's Cove recovery operation following the Swissair Flight 111 disaster in September of 1998. It didn't seem to affect him right away, but after a few years, he started having problems with sleep, and between that and the panic attacks, it wore him down. Paul's job on the ship had been to operate a crane to hoist objects and bags of human debris onboard to be sorted and stored in the ship's refrigerators.

We all knew our jobs and were just going about things as we normally did, ya know... little less chatter and fewer jokes but we were managing... but when they brought the mental health people onboard, they put us

in groups and told us exactly what we were doing and that we were going to suffer mentally. Well that just blew everything apart and then we just had to go back doing the exact same job... that screwed us up.

Paul described that his way of managing was to look down from his crane position at the faces of sailors working on the deck to see how *they* were doing, which gave him a baseline to determine how *he* was doing. One face in particular served as his mental anchor during the recovery—the guy who was directing him from the deck.

I see his face whenever I have dreams. There are never any words said. It's deathly quiet, but I see his face all the time. His face was what got me through that time. I can't remember anything else, but I remember him. After the mental health briefing, I lost track of the days, and I don't know what I did. I remember that I could not look over the side of the ship anymore to see what was coming up on the hoist, and I felt like a coward. All the days just seemed to blur into each other. I had to keep looking at his face or I would have been done.

Paul was a Navy engineer who had been progressing well in his trade and enjoyed his job. He attended his TQ5 (trade qualification course) to complete his military apprenticeship following the recovery, and during the course, his infant daughter died from a serious illness, which also eventually ended his relationship with the infant's mother. During the course, he was denied compassionate leave to attend the funeral because he was not married, and not surprisingly, he failed the training.

He told me about the bouts of zoning out—dissociating—which really bothered him but, of course, he could not tell anyone then. "I didn't even know what was happening to me; I just felt guilty all the time." This problem became much worse after he was posted off the ship, and soon afterward, he began having problems with concentration and focus, losing his temper and zoning out more often at home after work, which led to many problems in his new relationship. He had no idea of how he was doing emotionally.

Paul was lucky, or so he thought. He was given a remuster to an Army trade, which meant separation from the Navy entirely. He was diagnosed with PTSD arising from the Swissair disaster and entered into treatment for several years.

> Man almost from the get-go, I started getting a hard time in my new unit because I was missing time for appointments and because of my problems with my memory and concentration. My immediate supervisor even wanted me charged for being absent without leave before even checking with me. My new MWO (Master Warrant Officer) was a real piece of work too. He was always making snide comments that PTSD was just an excuse for poor performers, but I could not say anything back to him. Nobody protected me. There was absolutely no communication between my unit and health services. I was on my own.

Paul lasted for another year in the new trade but was eventually identified for medical release. He is an incredibly angry man who grew up in a chaotic family. At first, he described his early years as normal but eventually told me the full story of his mother's temper, his parents' drinking and arguments, and about the lack of control in his home.

> I would go to other houses in the neighbourhood for some normalcy. I was the neighbourhood social butterfly.

While there were never any physical threats to him, he was on constant guard for arguments between his parents when they were drinking.

> I was always alert for anything that was going on, and if anything was about to erupt, I would get out of there in an instant. I would deal with my stuff from home by always being around other people.

■ ▙

There are a number of issues raised by Paul's story. Among other things, it emphasizes something that I think is vital in understanding trauma recovery in the military. We expect people to know the exact source of their distress and to integrate specific experiences as a private task under the umbrella of confidentiality. However, since emotional life in the military exists within the context of larger groups, which is also true for most of us, I think that there is a need for these experiences to be integrated also within the larger group. As in Paul's case, he regulated himself by observing how others were reacting and gauged his own reactions and ability to continue with his job based on how he observed others deal with the stress of the situation. This external focus to manage emotional upset was a skill he learned early in life. He had learned to take care of himself by disconnecting and daydreaming at home when he was upset emotionally and thrived outside of his home among other children.

In formal jargon, dissociation is described as form of internalization that has been related to early disorganized attachment strategies, both theoretically and empirically.[33] Disorganization in infancy is believed to increase a child's vulnerability to later problems with dissociative disorders extending into adolescence and beyond. We tend to view this ability to disconnect mentally in negative terms— as purely pathological—which means that we often miss its adaptive functions.

In fact, the ability to dissociate served to get Paul through an intense and gruesome recovery operation. His main desire, which he said repeatedly, was to be able to know what was going on in the minds of the people around him, especially for the man who served as his emotional anchor on the deck below. In his mind, he needs the larger group to help him fill in the blanks and to integrate his personal experiences. Unfortunately, and a common occurrence among veterans, he cannot muster the courage to lower his guard

33   K. Lyons-Ruth and D. Jacobvitz, "Attachment disorganization: Genetic factors, parenting contexts, and developmental transformation from infancy to adulthood," in *Handbook on Attachment: Theory, research, and clinical applications*, 2nd ed, eds. J. Cassidy and P.R Shaver (New York: Guilford, 2008), 666–697.

and talk with any former member of his crew. He is left alone with an incomplete inner experience and no realistic way of moving the experience further along. From the things he has relayed to me, I think his central questions are whether any of them felt the way he had during the operation and how they were able to put it behind them.

This story also suggests that group work—I don't mean commiseration sessions or forcing people to disclose harrowing experiences—can help members digest and reconcile their experiences through a reconstitution of the social context in which military events occur. In other words, participation with other military people may serve to engage their emotional attachment system. There is a context for the things they struggle with emotionally.

Once again, Paul's story raises the issue of preservice history when talking about military trauma. It is an issue that has gained much attention in the past several years. It is also a concern among veterans who fear that this focus on preservice history will serve as a pretext to deny operational injury claims. I believe it is important to outline some of this research and its implications for military members and veterans.

In terms of the developmental histories of those soldiers and other first responders who go on to develop chronic forms of PTSD and depression, there is an absence of information in Canada. We do not know whether those people who experience various OSIs are too highly invested in their new identities in the interests of self-worth, and we do not know the role of hyper-masculine ideals in cases of chronic PTSD.

It is quite possible that those people who invest too much in their military lives and ideals do not have a fall-back position when these things fail them. When they begin to experience any emotional-mental problems, their instinct is to ward them off to protect their self-image and to avoid the scrutiny of other people. Those people who successfully navigate various military stressors may represent a distinct population in terms of their personal investment in their military roles. In short, these healthy people may remain securely attached to outside relationships and likely do not denigrate emotional vulnerability.

I think there is an important question to be considered about first responder populations in terms of their over-investment in acquired identities to meet self-worth needs and its relationship with the phenomenon of chronic PTSD. Many young people may be attracted to these occupations because of deep-rooted needs to feel valued, to stand out, or to repair damaged self-worth from earlier experiences.

Some readers may think that I am denigrating first responders or military service. Again, absolutely not true. My point is that, if we are to understand the relationships between operational stress injuries and preservice histories, we also need to be frank about the motivations for joining in the first place. Very often national pride and desires to serve the country are nothing more than clichés for soldiers; they tell me this all the time.

In studies of the US military, it has been pointed out repeatedly that today's military draws disproportionately from lower socio-economic and marginalized groups of people. In Canada, we know that recruiting is over-represented from the Maritime region and other areas which are under economic strain. We may also be drawing disproportionately from groups of people who are economically stressed and socially marginalized. For instance, in terms of military PTSD, while studies have linked increased rates with direct combat experience, recent studies of US combat soldiers from Iraq and Afghanistan found that childhood physical and sexual abuse, living with a mentally ill caregiver, or witnessing domestic violence played critical roles in the development of post-deployment depression and PTSD.[34][35]

This relationship is unclear, but it may point to the importance of perceived neglect among distressed veterans. A somewhat provocative study of veterans from the Lebanon War assessed at baseline and again at follow-up (1983 and 2002 respectively) concluded that stressful experiences during childhood played a more significant role in the development of future PTSD than events during combat.[36]

34   O.A. Cabrera et al., "Childhood adversity and combat as predictors of depression and post-traumatic stress in deployed troops," *American Journal of Preventative Medicine*, 2007 33: 77–82.

35   E.E. Van Voorhees et al., "Childhood trauma exposure in Iraq and Afghanistan war era veterans: Implications for posttraumatic stress disorder symptoms and adult functional social support," *Child Abuse & Neglect*, 2012 36 (5): 423–432.

36   Z. Solomon et al., "The contribution of stressful life events throughout the life cycle to combat-induced psychopathology," *Journal of Traumatic Stress*, 2008 21(3): 318–325.

Again the direct linkages have not been clarified, but I think we are moving past the simplistic notion that events in childhood are the root cause of mental declines for military personnel.

Ongoing research efforts are focusing on neurobiological risk factors that may predispose some people to experience extreme reactions and an inability to calm down in the aftermath. A related line of inquiry focuses on the importance of attachment relationships in understanding reactions to trauma. From a clinical viewpoint, I wonder about the importance of developmental events in terms of central themes that may play themselves out in the military. By this I mean that those people who learned early in life to be self-reliant and skilled at emotional suppression are also sought after members by the military. These same people may end in a vicious cycle following deployments such that the more they try to contain negative images and emotions, the stronger these memories become. This heightening in the intensity of negative events by trying to ignore or distract oneself has been observed repeatedly in psychological research.[37]

An additional observation is that many people only begin to report troubling memories years after they have happened or upon retirement from the military. Many of their reports of distress centre on secretly held beliefs about personal failure, institutional neglect, and betrayals by people they trusted. They are mentally driven to reconcile what happened with what *should* have happened and are consumed by this gap. They contain or 'embody'—repeatedly experience physical signs of stress and manage these reactions through compartmentalization and dissociation—guilt, shame, outrage, or unfinished life business.

The alternative to shutting down means risking vulnerability by verbalizing their concerns. I am not suggesting that we discount physical symptoms of hyperarousal or hypoarousal, but I am suggesting that we need to directly address warded-off emotional reactions as part of helping veterans move forward towards recovery. They have been taught to develop a toughened persona—their shields—where vulnerability is equated with being out of control emotionally and unmanly.

---

37   J. J. Gross, ed., *Handbook of Emotion Regulation* (New York: Guilford Press, 2007).

In terms of the official criteria, PTSD does not focus on emotions apart from managing anxiety. This is also true for the problem of depression. Other emotions, physical reactions, problems with information processing, or spiritual and existential adjustment are treated as comorbid (i.e. distinct but simultaneous) issues.[38] However, the wide range of problems that occur with PTSD do not hold together as a syndrome, and as I said earlier, clinicians were left to offer help without a conceptual framework which undermines clinical effectiveness.

Without a coherent, over-arching theory, we are left to treat symptoms in a somewhat arbitrary fashion. Clinicians may focus variously on sleep problems, physical inactivity, depression, nightmares, marital relationships, social avoidance, anger and rage, or emotional shut-down, but nothing seems to tie these reactions together. PTSD theories do not inform therapists about the focus of treatment, and it can be difficult to determine whether veterans are getting better or worse. This also means that veteran accounts of their 'injuries' usually include many problems that do not fit within our accepted view of trauma—in other words, they do not have a real say over the accounts of their experiences. Many of their stories speak of outrage over hypocrisy, harassment, or betrayals of their loyalty and commitment even as they try to maintain allegiance to the organization.

In the past several years, the trauma field has moved beyond conceptualizing PTSD primarily as a problem of fear reactions to include other strong reactions such as anger/rage, shame, and grief. One problem with the older notion of trauma is that most military veterans would never acknowledge fear; their primary learned reactions to perceived threats are anger and aggression. Even if the primary emotional reaction was one of fear, often missed is the fact that this fear was not about external things but a concern about losing emotional control—strong emotions might cause them to freeze during a key moment. The fear was centred on the risk of emotional weakness. This reaction extends directly to their experience of any strong emotion. In other words, if they risk cracking

38   J.D. Ford and C. Courtois, "Understanding complex trauma and complex traumatic stress disorders," in *Treating Complex Traumatic Stress Disorders: An Evidence-based Guide*, eds. C. Courtois and J.D. Ford (New York, Guilford Press: 2009) 13–30.

open this door, everything may come crashing in and wipe them out in front of everyone else. In cases of memories from early abuse or neglect, lowering their guards could bring these things to the surface as well—better to leave Pandora's box closed tightly. I believe that the fundamental fear rarely verbalized is that, should they admit to having serious problems and realize that nobody is there to help when they ask, then they risk truly being lost.

If we take an alternate view, namely that PTSD may reflect grievances manifested through bodily experiences, then we might view free-floating anxiety, low energy, unexplained chronic pain or even hyper-vigilance as signs of not feeling safe to risk vulnerability within the institution or reflecting psychological separation from the larger military culture. In fact, the mixed outcomes from standard PTSD interventions and the problems of relapse and symptom rebounds could be telling us that we may be trying to solve the wrong problem. We may be attempting to fix disordered people when the real patient could be person-military relationships.

It could be the case that mental distress reflects an injury to self-identity and issues around neglect, pride, shame, or disheartenment after bearing witness to brutal realities—a disruption in their social-relational contexts. While it might not be easy to do, it is relatively straightforward to convince people that they are victims of their biology. After all, this is what most people have been led to believe about mental health issues.

There is a tendency to attribute credible OSI reports to war and deployment stress, but this is not the reality for many people who are hurt mentally during their service. There are a substantial number of veterans who never deployed overseas and yet were medically released due to depression, panic, PTSD, social anxiety or drinking because of events at their home bases. For example, I have seen a number of Air Force personnel who were devastated from retrieving the remains of downed pilots on military bases across Canada.

I remember assessing a veteran who had been released from the military because of persistent stomach problems and unexplained panic episodes. Despite repeated medical investigations and years of anti-anxiety medications he was released. Only a complete review of his military files showed that his problems started almost immediately after being tasked to recover body parts of a downed pilot nearly sixteen years earlier. His physical symptoms were never connected with possible traumatic stress reactions.

Generally, I am in agreement with Dr. Bessel van der Kolk's metaphor that trauma symptoms may be a reflection of the physical body remembering.[39] When it comes to military personnel, I would also suggest that memories of particular grievances or transgressions and unspoken anger, disgust, shame, or disavowed grief can be manifested in physical signals like headaches, sleeplessness, gastrointestinal problems, low energy, and low libido. The things that cannot be spoken are nonetheless remembered.

Even among deployed personnel who come forward during their post-deployment phase, it is often their reactions to routine military life that prompts them to come forward. They are uninvolved, angry, or drinking too much and have lost their tolerance for normal routines. They may have been a key person overseas and now feel like another nobody, which represents an insult to their pride and self-image. The loss of their sense of specialness can be devastating. In essence, as long as they were in warrior mode, they were protected from the human side of the things that they did and saw overseas. Upon their return home, they may be transferred to new units or placed under leaders who never deployed. They begin to rehash the things they did or the buddies they lost, and suddenly what made sense overseas is re-evaluated and questioned—it is often described as something suddenly snapping in their heads. All the things that were experienced, now grate on them.

Since its inception, PTSD has been a contentious diagnosis. Skeptics have asserted that it lacks a conceptual foundation and may simply represent a sociopolitical construction.[40] In the absence of biological anchors for PTSD, many critics call it "faddish" by creating a medical condition out of normal distress. I agree with Barglow's observation that emotional numbness appears to be the key factor in verifying a PTSD diagnosis. I would also add that many clinicians often misunderstand the roles of compartmentalization, functional dissociation, and depersonalization and reduce these learned ways of reacting as an issue of alexithymia (inability to describe emotions in a verbal manner). Yes, we have names for just about every mental

39   B. van der Kolk, "The body keeps the score: Memory & the evolving psychobiology of post- traumatic stress," *Harvard Review of Psychiatry*, 1994, 1(5), 253–265.

40   M.P. Duckworth and V.M. Follette, *Retraumatization: Assessment, Treatment, and Prevention* (New York: Routledge, 2012).

issue. In sum, it is virtually impossible for many military personnel to describe their inner emotional states given their avoidance skill set and the requirements to focus on the external world around them.

Our newest theories about mental distress propose a combination of genes and environment—epigenetics—a theory which contradicts the basic assumption that traumatic events are the core etiological agent (which is to say root cause). In the early days, the focus was entirely on characteristics of events that overwhelmed victims. This approach changed over the years from the observation that the majority of people exposed to horrific events did not develop lingering PTSD symptoms. This led to a shift in focus on the characteristics of the person, and this research is ongoing in terms of the attention to developmental abuse and neurobiological risk factors. Alongside this research focus, the past several years has also seen the rise of an interactional approach focusing on the core issue of emotional dysregulation (inability to properly modulate emotional reactions) and its roots in early attachments.[41]

The fact that most people do not report lingering trauma reactions in the aftermath of serious events continues to create confusion. Among those who experience negative reactions, some people have immediate negative reactions and improve in a short timeframe while others will continue to have negative reactions that become chronic; others may have no reaction or a positive reaction that shifts to negative reactions over time; and still others will only recall earlier trauma when faced with another traumatic experience. PTSD has been called a disorder of non-recovery, meaning that some people engage in a host of behaviours that interferes with their ability to move on. One key observation is that those people who experience positive reactions and growth from adverse events may have emotional processing skills not present among those who develop chronic PTSD.[42]

Historically, the PTSD diagnosis as conceptualized in the 1980s arrived during the cognitive revolution that championed the belief that our thoughts control our reality, which is also related to the older notion that rationality is the master of base instincts. This era

---

41   A. Schore, *The Science and Art of Psychotherapy*, New York: Norton (2012).

42   P.A. Frewen et al., "Alexithymia in PTSD: Psychometric and fMRI Studies," *Annals of the New York Academy of Science*, 2006 1071: 397–400.

was followed by the much vaunted "decade of the brain", spanning roughly between 1995 and 2005. It heralded the appearance of innovative neuroimaging technologies and the promise of uncovering the roots of all mental illness, but over the past several years, this paradigm has been quietly displaced by a self-regulation theory.

As opposed to behavioural interventions that focused on thinking, these newer interventions seem to focus on emotionality and attachment relationships, especially in cases of psychological trauma. Dr. Allan Schore argued that cognitive science has been left to relearn forgotten understandings about the value of emotions that are quite independent, yet, easily overpower neocortical (thinking) processes.

Furthermore, this paradigm shift from behaviour, to cognition, to bodily based emotion has acted as an integrating force forging stronger connections between the disciplines of psychology, social neuroscience, and psychiatry, all of which are now focusing on affective phenomenon.[43]

In spite of this shift, last year I attended an international conference where a noted PTSD expert commented that, in order to improve the effectiveness of cognitive-behavioural therapy, the trauma field has to develop stronger techniques to deal with this problem of emotional dysregulation. The basic tenet of cognitive-behavioural therapy (or CBT) being that by consciously monitoring one's thoughts and behaviours and how they functionally relate, one can more effectively manage one's underlying emotional reactions. I recall having a conversation with a colleague about the possibility that PTSD may amount to a problem of emotions. All other observed phenomena, including the comorbid conditions may be an outcrop of this fundamental issue.

We have struggled with issues around emotionality for many hundreds of years. Emotional phenomena were linked with psychoanalysis and the humanistic therapies that were overturned in the 1970s due to a lack of evidence for their constructs and presumed benefits. This criticism was certainly true at the time. However,

---

43   A. Schore, *The Science and Art of Psychotherapy*, New York: Norton (2012) 4.

we do seem to have come full circle with the advent of therapies like ACT (acceptance and commitment therapy), EMDR (eye movement desensitization and reprocessing), yoga, trauma group therapies, mindfulness, body-focused interventions, and the use of service animals, which do not treat cognitions as a primary focus of interventions.

By contrast, under the older CBT top-down approach—thoughts control base instincts and emotions—one's history did not matter or it mattered only insofar as it influenced current thought patterns about life challenges. In essence, the problem was really a problem of perspective, usually negative, creating unwanted emotional reactions. We were taught to challenge these problems of disordered thinking, to teach skills like stress management and assertiveness, and to help people to reframe situations in a positive light.

I am a product of this tradition, but early in my academic training, I was also trained in process-group therapy, Gestalt therapy, and Transactional Analysis, which were prevalent in the military in the 1980s and 1990s. These approaches emphasized a bottom-up focus—emotional awareness and processing—where relational breaches were the main focus of treatment for members of the military. I witnessed what amounted to transformational changes among many of these people, and I have to say that I was greatly influenced by this work.

These military people returned to their jobs and others decided to leave the military in order continue with this different, emotionally connected approach to life. They could not see themselves returning to active duty without having to shut off their emotional awareness once again. These approaches were forgotten in the mainstream lexicon for many years, but their basic tenets appear to be re-emerging to influence interventions aimed at emotional regulation, especially when it comes to the treatment of trauma.

Even so, interventions centring on emotionality are still equated with self-indulgence and notions of hysteria and the feminine; and as such, as signs of personal weakness. From a research standpoint, emotionality has been viewed as a soft, unscientific concept and as such beyond the scope of rigorous inquiry. It is somewhat ironic that neurobiological inquiry has led us back to deal with this very issue.

I experienced first-hand the crisis faced by the military when soldiers began returning to Canada during the early 1990s and witnessed the shift towards evidence-based interventions. These treatments were based on training from US trauma experts, and we went about implementing and training clinicians to provide the best researched interventions at the time. Fifteen years later, we have seen the benefits and the limitations of these trauma-focused approaches.

There has been a quiet admission in recent years that many military personnel do not benefit from these interventions. When it comes to treatments, from a neurobiological perspective, I think the real question is whether the re-experiencing of intense emotions within incompatibly safe, relational contexts can serve to lead to neural changes among traumatized people. And secondly, if this is the case, what timeframes and specific ingredients are necessary to maintain these changes or improvements?

Complicated or complex trauma reactions usually arise from events involving a fundamental loss of trust in primary relationships because it is often perpetrated by someone known or related to the sufferer. These relationships are often meant to refer to parent-child interactions but I would suggest that they also apply to adult relationships within the military context. In my experience, many military people seem to experience fundamental shifts in basic identity and attachment orientations that rival the effects of preservice histories.

Many of these soldiers, turned into veterans, seem to lose the ability to see these relationships as nurturing and reliable, which contributes to other problems like affect regulation, structural dissociation, somatic problems, and disorganized attachment patterns. Over the years, I have also seen the positive results of helping veterans to reconstitute their connections and trust with other veterans. As outlined in Seymour Sarason's earlier work, they are able to re-establish a psychological sense of community.[44]

I make no secret that I am a proponent of group interventions for military personnel, and I also re-iterate, however, that they are

44   In 1974, psychologist Seymour Sarason introduced the concept of "psychological sense of community" and proposed that it become the conceptual centre for the psychology of community. He asserted that it represented one of the major bases for self-definition. His work formed the basis of what came to be known as Community Psychology. This sense of community provides members with the feeling of belonging; members matter to each other, they care, share common values, and look out for each other's welfare: http://www.wright-house.com/psychology/sense-of-community.html.

not a panacea. And I am not suggesting that the power of groups only exists in a therapy room. It just happens to be one setting where psychological and emotional safety can be ensured. A key need for military trauma survivors seems to be social reconnection of some kind. Julian Ford and colleagues have made the point that group therapy offers a direct antidote to the isolation and disengagement that characterizes PTSD and complex trauma reactions.[45]

In a group, safety, respect, honesty, privacy and dedication to recovery are norms that provide unique opportunities for trauma survivors to see and hear, and to be seen and heard by others who also struggle with anxiety, fear, shame, guilt, alienation, and sense of powerlessness and permanent damage that is profoundly demoralizing. In a group, it is possible to find one's 'authentic voice' and to reclaim one's memories and sense of self. Groups also provide a range of emotions, guidance, and role modelling to differentiate, identify, and modulate emotions as they arise.

Despite its breadth of application in treating traumatic stress, structured group work has not been subjected to randomized clinical trials. With adults, group outcomes have been reported in studies of civilian survivors of childhood trauma, with multiply traumatized women, with concurrent mental illness, domestic violence, rape, and traumatic accidents and events with military veterans. The evidence also indicates that people who engage their traumatic memories through writing or telling their narrative, show reductions in stress; whereas, those who mentally disconnect and inhibit their emotional reactions show greater risk for PTSD.[46]

Group therapy approaches have been shown to be associated with improved functioning and adaptation during follow-up lasting two years post-treatment. In a study reported last year, we noted

45   J.D. Ford, R.D. Fallot, and M. Harris, "Group therapy in treating complex traumatic stress disorders," in *Treating Complex Traumatic Stress Disorders: An Evidence-Based Guide*, eds. C. Courtois and J. Ford (New York: Guilford Press, 2009), 415–440.

46   C. Zayfert, "Cognitive Behavioral Conceptualizations of Retraumatization," in *Retraumatization: Assessment, Treatment, and Prevention*, eds. M.P. Duckworth and V.M. Follette (New York: Routledge 2012), 9–32.

improvements lasting up to three years.[47] Veterans were much less avoidant, reduced their alcohol intake, were less agitated, and made improvements in their relationships. Despite all of the concerns over contagion reactions by placing traumatized veterans in a group setting, I think the difference here is that we were directly involved in helping them to repair their interpersonal attachments and, as a result, their emotional processes.

Veterans were able to lower their emotional guards, support each other, and hold each other accountable at a level that would rival any therapist's efforts. Across populations, trauma survivors consistently report the importance of telling their full stories in respectful and validating peer groups.[48] It provides clarity, hope, empowerment, and a sense of belonging and worthiness when they are accepted by other people.

Military veterans can serve as each other's emotional containment and provide genuine feedback on verbal and non-nonverbal emotional cues. In my mind, this process allows for the re-establishment of their social-relational military context and the unspoken security which this provides them. This safe context is also expanded by helping them take this capacity to remain emotionally present to personal relationships outside the therapy room. This type of approach to trauma requires group leaders to know their participants and to take necessary steps to establish group safety and trust before exploring life events.

It also requires leaders to have the ability to contain their own strong affective reactions—or they risk derailing and possibly harming group members. They must remain attuned to group needs. Group leaders must understand the line between controlled emotional arousal and when to intervene to ground themselves and the group membership. In essence, a relational, emotional-process-centred environment

47   J.J. Whelan, "Description and treatment outcomes for the trauma relapse prevention group (TRPG) program," presented at the 2013 conference of the Canadian Institute on Military and Veteran Health Research, Edmonton, AB.

48   J. Ford, R. Fallot, and M. Harris, "Group therapy in treating complex traumatic stress disorders," in *Treating complex traumatic stress disorders: An evidence-based guide*, C. Courtois & J. Ford, eds. (Guilford Press: New York 2009), 415–440.

can directly address psychological wounding. It provides veterans the opportunity to tell their full, unedited stories as part of recovery and moving forward. This work utilizes cognitive components; cognitive disputing and reframing, perspective-taking, and intellectualizing strategies as part of grounding and consolidation of emotionally laden memories.

A primary benefit of group therapy may lie in the ability to address shame directly. Many veterans who experience this self-rejection and stigma usually revert to defensiveness and denial as their main coping strategies, and they withdraw from other people. This issue of shame seems especially important when it comes to instances of emotional isolation and suicidality. While positive social support has been shown to buffer the effects of trauma, the ways in which this support is offered to veterans appears to be crucial in terms of the aftermath of trauma. For instance, negative reactions from the support system during the immediate aftermath of critical events may produce stigma and shame that is associated with disengagement.

Ten

I Wanted to Be Special

The clock above the teacher's desk inches towards noon. Eight-year-old Andy Jones waits anxiously—would he be outside with the other kids or would this be another remedial day with Ms. Sneed?

Finally, the school bell announces lunch break.

"I don't want any roughhousing today... Andy, please stay behind," she announces.

Within minutes, Andy is alone and at her mercy again. The usual review of his workbook began and so too did the usual pinches to his ear and tugs on the fine hairs at the back of his neck. It always hurt but he said nothing except to apologize for the disorganized scribbling in his book.

"Sorry, Ms. Sneed."

The teacher is unmoved by his meek apology: "You do nothing but waste time, you have no discipline whatsoever and I am not standing for this."

Ms. Sneed led Andy to the storeroom at the back of the class-room and slammed the door behind her. What began as slaps on his bare behind progressed to one of her hands on his private parts. Whatever this was went on for what seemed like an eternity without a word. Andy's eyes never moved from the floor below him.

"Pull up your pants and go outside with the other children," she commands.

After that day, Andy never knew when the storeroom would be called for. But he knew better than to say anything to anybody. Who would believe him anyway? He was the kid always fooling around in class disrupting the other kids. He was the one who continually tested his mother trying to help him with homework. He was the one who wet his bed upsetting his father. Andy was the direct opposite of his younger sister—the smart one. So, he knew better than to start telling tales about his teacher.

Andy is busy worrying a hangnail as he tells me this story; his eyes never leave the floor in my office. He goes on to tell me about the times he wanted to disappear as a child for being a disappointment to his parents.

> Mom and Dad are good people, so they would never say this to me, but I could feel it by how they acted around me. Nobody knew that I was dyslexic until I joined the military.... They just thought I was lazy, I just thought I was a bad kid... I hated school. The only thing I was good at was running. Being nimble on my feet meant that I was a natural for soccer—everybody wanted me on their team. I think that's the only thing that got me through school and as soon as it was over I wanted out of there.

Andy's parents were surprised when he announced at eighteen that he wanted to join the military. He wanted out of there, to forget about what had happened to him and maybe also to find a way for his parents to be proud of him. Andy did well in the military after they discovered his reading problem.

> Man, it was a relief to find out that I wasn't a dummy. I did exceptionally well with the practical things in the cook trade and even won a few competitions. Before my deployment, I had even been selected for officer training.

In Afghanistan, one of Andy's civilian workers went missing for several days. He was on the patrol that eventually discovered her body. She had been raped and left in a ditch.

That really messed with me, and I could not get past it. I felt guilty and worthless all over again. All I could think was that she had been all alone with nobody to help her. Couple of weeks later, I broke my leg pretty bad and was sent home. I was diagnosed with depression, which was eventually changed to PTSD. Doesn't matter anymore, it just meant that officer training was squashed, and I was released medically... just another broken toy.

Andy has had considerable difficulty adjusting to civilian life. Despite several years of therapy focusing on the Afghanistan deployment, he struggles with a crushing sense of worthlessness.

■ ◣

In the following section, I review research that suggests that attachment relationships within the military may have considerable influence on overall mental health. At the outset, I realize that some readers may think the discussion provides too much information while others may think it is too scant a review. Such is the task of navigating a middle road between veterans' voices and the relevant research.

Attachment theory originated in the late 1960s and has seen a powerful resurgence over the past decade in both the mental health and biological sciences. It posits that real relationships made during the earliest phases of life leave an indelible mark for the remainder of the lifespan—it lies at the centre of all emotional and social functioning.

Attachment theory also suggests that trauma can be understood within the context of military relationships. To begin, it makes perfect sense that those people who experience a lack of control or connection in early life are drawn to careers that provide the promise of a greater purpose. For some people, however, a deployment exposure can approximate events from early life, reminding them of emotional vulnerabilities, and it may also prepare them to expect the same type of reactions from their military relationships.

Clinicians can react in one of two ways to this information: Either they determine that, since there is a developmental cause for patient symptoms, they have nothing to do with the military; or they can explore the present concerns in the context of military relationships to understand the particular preservice dynamics which are being replayed. As Pamela Alexander has argued, even though child abuse is linked with adult interpersonal problems, it does not automatically lead to PTSD.[49] Again, I emphasize a central argument: Relationships in the military matter tremendously. Perceived abandonment or careless inattention from important attachment figures in the aftermath of danger are often traumatizing in their own right; this is a notion captured by betrayal trauma as advanced by Dr. Jennifer Freyd.[50]

It is generally accepted that early attachment stressors are linked to the neurobiology of impaired emotional development, enduring deficits in affect dysregulation, and precursors for personality problems. Attachment experiences are thought to shape the early organization of the right brain, and many of our therapeutic interventions attempt to tap into these relationship processes; often described as therapeutic alliances. Much of what we know about attachment styles is based on the work of Mary Ainsworth, a student of John Bowlby.

She identified four organized attachment patterns: secure, avoidant, ambivalent, and disorganized. Secure attachment means that a child does not need to distort either affect or cognition to maintain access to a parent. These children seem to learn to self-soothe and develop positive expectations of themselves and others. It is characterized by a coherent, collaborative narrative with access to both positive and negative memories and a value placed on attachment relationships.

Avoidant attachment results from a parental relationship that is cold and rejecting precisely when the child is distressed or needy. As a result, children like Andy learn to suppress negative emotions that appear to drive the parent away. The child's compulsive self-reliance occurs at the expense of his ability to recognize and to modulate

49   P.C. Alexander, "Retraumatization and Revictimization: An Attachment Perspective," in *Retraumatization: Assessment, Treatment, and Prevention*, eds. M.P. Duckworth and V.M. Follette, (New York: Routledge 2012), 191–220.

50   R.L. Gobin and J.J. Freyd, "Betrayal and Revictimization: Preliminary Findings," *Psychological Trauma: Theory, Research, Practice, and Policy*, 2009 (1) 3: 242–257.

negative feelings and is often marked by observed physiological arousal in stress situations. This style appears to diminish the quality of interactions with peers; these children appear more normal than normal, but they show increased physical signs of arousal when they are asked about parental relationships and separation. Avoidantly attached adults tend to minimize the effects of early attachment relationships and deny experiences of distress, but covertly they are often hostile, lonely, and anxious.

An ambivalent attachment is another insecure attachment pattern whereby the parent is inconsistently available, combining a pattern of neglect and direct interference at other times. Because of the ongoing threat of abandonment, the child maintains access to this parent by showing increased negative emotion in order to obtain a reaction. Unfortunately, while the strategy is effective at gaining attention, it also generates parental aversion and avoidance of the child. These children are not easily soothed and are unable to rely on the parent as a secure person. They often see themselves as incompetent and helpless and may even resort to immaturity with peers to gain attention. Therefore, they may be babied, but they are often disliked.

Finally, disorganized attachment is prevalent among abused children. They show signs of contradictory approach and avoidance behaviours, dazed expressions, and apprehension of the parent's return. In essence, a child's very presence is traumatizing to the parent whose own experiences as a child may have resulted in abuse and neglect from the parent's own caregiver. The parent responds to these memories of early trauma by relying, inappropriately, upon their own children to reduce their anxiety. This parental role reversal signals to the child that a parent is not in control.

The disorganized child, therefore, finds himself in a paradoxical situation of needing to seek comfort from a parent who is also a source of fear. This 'fright without solution' predisposes these children to dissociation in adulthood.[51] An example commonly cited is that of women who were sexually abused as children by their fathers but have to find a way to separate their view of the father as extremely dangerous and also protect the relationship with their main source of safety.

51   Alexander, "Retraumatization and Revictimization: An Attachment Perspective"

Not surprisingly, disorganized children exhibit high rates of internalizing (e.g., dissociation) and externalizing (e.g., aggression and substance abuse) behaviours and major problems in managing their emotions. These people tend to be socially inhibited and unassertive, lack a sense of personal control, and are more likely to be volatile in their relationships.

Over the years, many veterans we have treated for chronic PTSD show these insecure attachment styles; like Andy, most of them would fit within the ambivalent and disorganized categories. I want to be clear that I am not saying that this history *created* their military declines but to reinforce the point that, when they become distressed as adults, they are unlikely to accept help from other people.

When it comes to the neurobiological explanations of PTSD, research suggests that mistreated children have greater HPA (hypothalamic-pituitary-adrenal stress axis) reactivity. These research efforts have found that dysregulation of the HPA-axis provides an explanation for the persistence of fear reactions among traumatized people. As well, MRI (magnetic resonance imaging) research has shown brain atrophy in maltreated as compared to non-maltreated children that have been correlated with PTSD severity and dissociation. Maltreated people seem to have considerable difficulty managing themselves emotionally. For instance, a history of physical or sexual abuse is more common among aggressive children, and histories of neglect are more common among children who exhibit social withdrawal, social rejection, and feelings of incompetence. Numerous studies have shown connections between insecure attachment in childhood and substance abuse, suggesting a persistent effect of poor parent-child attachment on HPA-axis function.

So, what do attachment theories have to do with traumatized military personnel or other people for that matter? To begin, if our brains are truly set rigidly in childhood, then there would be no possibility of change or improvement, meaning that all of the efforts of therapy are in vain. But based on the evidence, and anecdotally, we know that veterans benefit from therapy and often make life-altering improvements. We have known for some time, in fact, that psychotherapy produces observable changes in the brain—changes in regional cerebral blood flow, neurotransmitter metabolism, gene expression, and persistent modifications in synaptic plasticity. And it seems that attending to the emotional components of trauma is an integral aspect of these interventions. In fact, Dr. Edna Foa, the originator of exposure treatment for PTSD, has stated that explicitly focusing on thoughts is not necessary in helping people overcome PTSD.[52]

To me, the underlying question centres on the permanence of childhood attachment patterns in terms of brain function. In other words, are new neural networks possible? And the good news from epigenetic and psychotherapy research seems to be a resounding yes. However, this does not mean that these changes are necessarily easy.

An example from a learning perspective: I have always wanted to play the guitar, but until recently I never had the time. My initial lessons were incredibly difficult in terms of training my fingers to do things they had never done before. The simple act of pushing wires with my fingers was frustrating. As my teacher told me—a music guy no less—I had to 'lay-down' new neural circuitry so that this action could be repeated automatically. A couple of months of daily practice and the things that were nearly impossible are now second nature and producing sounds that resemble music. This same learning seems to be required for traumatized veterans to learn to recognize, accept without judgment, tolerate, and to communicate internal states to other people. The practice of putting names to body reactions and using language, gestures, and expressions to communicate these states to other people often opens up an entirely new world of experience and connection to other people.

My clinical work has also taught me that intensely experienced emotions often result in temporal disorientation. During the experience of strong emotions, people can lose track of self-referent information about time and place; in effect, the present can suddenly become the past. They can be momentarily overcome with emotion. And it is exactly at this point that veterans risk judging themselves for not being a competent man or woman—acknowledgment and expression of strong emotions flies directly in the face of their military identities. In Andy's case, it is obvious that he carries an incredible level of shame over the sexual abuse and his inability to meet the demands of school—he judged himself as worthless. It can be argued that the circumstances of the girl's death in Afghanistan reminded him once again about his earlier life eroding his established military identity. However, it is often only through the direct

52 Cited in Schore, *The Science and Art of Psychotherapy*

experience of these warded-off emotional states within safe contexts and at manageable levels that people are later able to process the significance of their military reactions.

The experience often contributes to changes in their views of themselves in relation to other people. In a sense, the only way forward is through the experience of deeply guarded emotional reactions. To be clear, the goal is not for emotional discharge; this misses the point entirely. When veterans come to understand that they can tolerate their emotional states, they become less self-judgmental and are often able to see their experiences in an entirely different light. The side effect is that they usually feel more connected to other people.

Again, one may ask how attachment is relevant to our efforts to respond to military trauma. A number of studies have shown that social support in the wake of military trauma has direct effects on treatment outcomes. When it comes to social support, securely attached people tend to seek out and use these supports in times of stress. An insecurely attached member, however, is less likely to seek out support, but when stressed they may be pragmatic enough to seek tangible resources but not emotional supports from whomever is available. Ambivalent veterans show mixed patterns of seeking support. They appear to experience intense distress but they have low expectations of getting sufficient support, resulting in dissatisfaction with the support they do receive. Veterans who show a disorganized attachment are unlikely to seek social support and are more likely to distance themselves from other people. In my experience, they are more likely to end up in medical crises or involvement with the legal system.

These effects of attachment for soldiers seem particularly important for leaders to understand. In recent studies of US combat personnel, secure attachment was related to increased hardiness—positive sense of self, strong commitment to work, increased feelings of self-control and better mental health—and lower attachment-related anxiety and lower avoidance.[53]

When looking at the effects of leadership on the mental health of soldiers, Simpson and Rholes found that avoidant attachment among leaders was linked with greater mental health declines

53   S. Escolas, H. Escolas, and P.T. Bartone, "Adult Attachment Style, Hardiness, and Mood," *Military Behavioral Health*, 2014 (2): 129–137.

among their troops following deployments.⁵⁴ Furthermore, those soldiers who were classified as highly avoidant themselves, showed poorer group cohesion and poorer mental health outcomes.

A vitally important finding was that, even though securely attached soldiers under these avoidant leaders appeared to be buffered initially, four months later, they also showed significant mental health declines. In essence, secure attachment can only protect people for limited time frames in strained relationship contexts. This finding also has implications for the notion of the permanence of attachment styles because it suggests that soldiers can shift from secure to insecure attachment under specific leaders. It suggests that attachment may be more fluid than considered previously.

It also raises the possibility of a reverse situation. Those soldiers who are insecurely attached upon entry into the military may be able to find a 'good enough' secure base under specific leaders. This outcome has been reported anecdotally to me by many people who described key supervisors early in their careers who changed their lives and their outlooks for the better. In fact, they committed to mirroring these mentors years later. Leaders have considerable power and responsibility.

Back again to those military members who mentally check out in response to stress. This ability, otherwise termed dissociation, is often defined as the bottom-line survival defence against overwhelming, unbearable emotional experience. Studies in developmental traumatology have shown that an infant's psychobiological reaction to trauma is comprised of two separate response patterns: hyperarousal and dissociation (otherwise termed hypoarousal).

In the initial hyperarousal stage, maternal safety suddenly becomes a source of threat, triggering a startle reaction in the infant's right hemisphere, the locus of both the attachment and the fear motivational systems. This stressor activates the HPA stress axis, eliciting a sudden increase in the ANS (autonomic nervous system). In turn, there is a significant elevation in heart rate, blood pressure, and respiration—the somatic expressions of a state of fright or terror. Within seconds, the reaction to relational trauma shifts to dissociation or hypoarousal whereby the infant disengages from the external stimuli in efforts to calm down. Allan Schore further argued that children

54   J.A. Simpson and W.S. Rholes, *Attachment Theory and Research: New Directions and Emerging Themes* (New York: Guilford Press, 2015).

of traumatized mothers, through attachment with the mother, mirror her dysregulated emotional states, which offers one explanation for the intergenerational transmission of attachment trauma. In Canada, we are living with these effects from the residential school systems and the ongoing struggles among our First Nation families.[55]

The majority of people will face situations that have the potential to be traumatic, but most of them will return to some normal range of behaviour within days or weeks following the events. They will resort to a range of personal and interpersonal behaviours to reduce stress-load within the body. The general rates of reactions that go on to meet official criteria can range up to thirty percent in some military combat units. What are we to make of those people who remain chronically distressed following these events?

It may be that they focus on particular aspects of the event more intensely than other people because of their developmental histories or their current life concerns. They may realize that they are distressed but believe they have no choice but to contain these reactions on their own. For example, they may be more affected by seeing a starving child beside the roadside because they recall growing up in a neglectful family or because they have a young son or daughter at home and they are worried about not being there if something was to happen; the potential of neglecting their own children.

In our efforts to generalize principles about trauma and PTSD reactions, we tend to look for neurobiological and decontextualized principles. In essence, we leave out the particular personal and social contexts to determine the flaw or inherent weakness in biological systems that can be applied to everyone.

At this point, I refer again to Bowlby's work to outline several important issues. Attachment theory asserts that an individual's sense of safety and security is derived from maintaining a bond with an accessible and responsive caregiver. First, unchallenged maintenance of attachment bonds contributes to feelings of security.[56]

55   D. Chansonneuve, *Reclaiming connections: Understanding residential school trauma among Aboriginal people* (Aboriginal Healing Foundation, 2005).

56   R. Kobak and S. Madsen, "Disruptions in attachment bonds: Implications for theory, research, and clinical intervention," in *Handbook on Attachment: Theory, Research, and Clinical Applications*, 2nd ed., eds. J. Cassidy and P.R. Shaver (New York: Guilford Press, 2008) 23–47.

Second, when an individual perceives a threat to the caregiver's availability, he will feel anxious and angry. Third, a persistent disruption of attachment bond will result in reactions of sadness and despair. Older children and adults are likely to perceive threats to a caregiver's availability when avenues of communication are disrupted by prolonged absence, emotional disengagement, or from signals of rejection or abandonment. These events often produce feelings of anxiety, anger, and sadness similar to those that have been documented in young children's reactions to physical separation. The traditional focus on the availability of attachment figures assumes that the attachment relation will always serve as a source of safety; however, when children are exposed to abuse or extreme forms of punishment they must manage a profound dilemma—that their attachment figures are also a potential source of danger. No matter the developmental history, my observation is that military group affiliation can serve as the good enough attachment replacement where secure attachment can be fostered.

In fact, secure or insecure attachment in childhood is no guarantee of adult functioning. And we also understand that personal hardiness and resilience come down to behaviours and contextual factors across situations rather than being an acquired trait. Even so, there are a number of reasons why insecure attachment may put people at risk for psychopathology. Those people with histories of disorganized attachment in childhood seem particularly prone to dissociative disorders and externalizing problems extending into late adolescence.[57] The implications of this research for screening new recruits may seem obvious. There may be utility in identifying those people who dissociate or disconnect in emotionally arousing situations since these men and women may be the ones more likely to be harmed in response to intense or contradictory situations because of an emotional processing skill deficit.

On the other end of the spectrum exists attachment security, which arguably predisposes people to seek comfort and assistance

---

57 N.S. Weinfield et al., "Individual differences in infant-caregiver attachment: Conceptual and empirical aspects of security," in *Handbook on Attachment: Theory, Research, and Clinical Applications*, 2nd ed., eds. J. Cassidy and P.R. Shaver (New York: Guilford Press, 2008) 78–101.

from formal and informal sources of support.[58] Across a variety of personal threats—missile attack, combat training, chronic pain, and specifically attachment related threats, separation from a romantic partner, interpersonal conflict, transition to parenthood—secure people report greater reliance on support seeking than insecure people. Several studies have also found that attachment security is associated with lower levels of distress during periods of extreme stress and strain whereas attachment insecurities—anxiety, avoidance or both—are associated with heightened distress and deteriorated well-being. And secure people are more likely than insecure ones to benefit from supportive interactions.

It would be interesting, I believe, to know the rate of securely attached men and women who decide to take on military and other first responder roles. When coping with stress, secure people seem to benefit even from near proximity to a close relationship partner. Overall, the evidence consistently indicates that attachment security fosters support seeking and generally does so in constructive and active ways whereas attachment insecurity inhibits or interferes with support-seeking behaviours. Avoidant individuals react internally to threats by wanting support from others, but predictably they inhibit these reactions and they usually do not show behavioural expressions of need. Instead, they associate the thought of relying on others with fears of being rejected and abandoned, and they often appear disorganized in their efforts to seek support.

When it comes to formal help, CBT conceptualizations of mental distress seem to be lacking in a fundamental way; there is a tendency to individualize problems and reduce emotions to their associated thoughts and behaviours.[59] This emphasis on cognitions and behaviours excludes an understanding of the basic ways in which people experience and respond to their emotional

58   M. Mikulincer and P.R. Shaver, "Adult attachment and affect regulation," in *Handbook on Attachment: Theory, Research, and Clinical Applications*, 2nd ed., eds. J. Cassidy and P.R. Shaver (New York: Guilford Press, 2008), 503–531.

59   L. Campbell-Sills and D. Barlow, "Incorporating emotion regulation into conceptualizations and treatment of anxiety disorders," In Handbook of Emotion Regulation, ed. J. J. Gross (New York: Guilford Press, 2007), 542–559.

experiences. Many of the issues we identify as mental disorders may represent unhelpful strategies used by people in their attempts to self-regulate their emotions.

In fact, several recent studies show that overuse of suppression to regulate emotions may be at the root of many anxiety disorders. People with panic disorder endorse more efforts to smother reactions of anger, sadness, and anxiety—the use of suppression by these people is largely ineffective. Similarly, thought suppression is most commonly associated with obsessive compulsive disorder (or OCD), but it is also quite prevalent in other mood and anxiety disorders to control unwanted thoughts. It often leads to a paradoxical increase in negative thoughts.

In the case of OCD, it is often conceptualized as emotional regulation gone awry. Certain thoughts induce intense experiences of anxiety, disgust, shame, and other negative emotions. In the case of distraction as an emotional regulator, while it can be helpful when used in moderation, over-reliance usually maintains symptoms of anxiety and mood disorders. In military populations, these strategies can be missed entirely because of the premium placed on task-focus and attention to details. One particular military senior leader comes to mind. He admits openly that he was a 'workaholic OCD' who lost his wife and kids through his efforts to keep his deployment experiences from washing in over him.

I should have been here ten years ago, and now that I sit in a big house alone with my cat and with my career winding down, I know that I am in trouble.

A second concern with CBT arises through the emphasis on situational control to regulate emotions. These strategies can become problematic because persistent avoidance of benign or even safe situations tends to maintain fear, negatively affects prosocial functioning, and diminishes quality of life. In the case of social withdrawal, it is quite possible that this behaviour represents an attempt to manage the emotion of sadness. Whereas psychologists treating adults usually see emotion regulation as an individual issue, developmental psychologists have long established the basic interpersonal nature of emotion regulation.[60] Therefore, we should be very cautious about constructing adult psychological interventions from an individualistic perspective. Considering how much we are regulated by our close relationships, we cannot expect adults to manage this entirely on their own. In terms of trauma experiences, there seems to be an overwhelming need for people to want to talk about their experiences once they are over. This social sharing of emotion is not exclusive to trauma but extends across most other positive and negative life experiences. In some cases, the phenomenon has been observed in eighty to ninety percent of studies. The more an experience is shared, the more likely it can lead to extinction over time. And interestingly, the correlation between sharing and negative emotions is often in the opposite direction than most clinicians consider; people tend to want to share negative emotions and they do not find it aversive.[61]

However, merely verbalizing a negative emotion is not sufficient for recovery even though it tends to strengthen social bonds and serves the socio-affective needs of people. As a veteran shares the depth and intensity of his story, when it is reciprocated, the experience often serves as support, comfort, consolidation, legitimization, attention, bonding, empathy, and solutions.

According to Rime:

... [the] sharing process is thus remarkably efficient to buffer destabilizing consequences of negative emotional episodes, which result from the disconfirmed expectations, models, and world views, and which manifest themselves in anxiety, insecurity, helplessness, estrangement, alienation, loss of self-esteem, and so forth.[62]

---

60   B. Rime, "Interpersonal emotion regulation," in *Handbook of Emotion Regulation*, ed. J.J. Gross, (New York: Guilford, 2007) 466–485.

61   Ibid.

62   Ibid., 480.

Even so, the remaining task of recovery means completion of cognitive work—perspective taking—which involves getting used to a new normal, setting new goals and challenging existing world views, finding new meaning, and reappraising the meaning of events. Unfortunately, many people are not open to this work in the aftermath of a negative event, especially since other people play a central role in their experience of emotional regulation.

People have always gathered in communities in the aftermath of pain to seek protection from outside challenges.[63] This emotional attachment is probably the primary protection against feelings of helplessness and meaninglessness. It is essential for the biological survival of children, and without it, existential meaning is unthinkable for adults. In fact, more terrifying threats produce stronger allegiances to the group. Under strain conditions such as war, people may go so far as to sacrifice their own lives to assure survival of the group. However, traumatized victims also speak of incredible pain from betrayal by others. For many, this realization is the most painful lesson that trauma brings; they often feel forsaken and forgotten by their fellow human beings, which results in loneliness and social disintegration. It is a persistent theme among traumatized military veterans.

This rejection of trauma survivors may be fuelled by our Western belief that we are in full control of our destiny. This societal reaction to traumatized people seems to be particularly true when it comes to the care of first responders. Paradoxically, first responders who are traumatized may serve as a mirror, reflecting human fragility and thereby threatening the larger group; one way to deal with this threat is to identify scapegoats. In efforts to regain control, the group may end up shunning victims and blaming them for what has happened to them or for their failure to recover and get back on the job. Many testimonies from trauma survivors indicate that not being supported by people around them in the crucial aftermath of distressing events produced deeper scars than the original event itself.[64]

Society can become resentful about having its sense of safety and predictability ruffled by people who remind them of how fragile life can be. I have been told many times that these reactions also

---

63   McFarlene and van der Kolk, *Trauma and its challenge to society*, 24–46.

64   Ibid.

occur within some military units—that they were just slackers trying to avoid duties. Many people are unable to communicate intense emotions and perceptions related to trauma, and this inability to communicate makes it difficult for them to articulate their needs. Society's reactions to traumatized people are driven primarily by conservative impulses to maintain the belief that the world is essentially just, that good people rise above adversity, and that bad things only happen to bad people—the just world philosophy. However, our focus on psychological trauma brings everyone face to face with human vulnerability in the natural world and forces us to face the evil that humans inflict on one another.

Contrary to popular belief, most trauma survivors quietly accept their suffering out of shame and helplessness as well as by the need to maintain self-respect and independence. General society fears that these victims may weaken the social fabric, consume social resources, and live off society. The weak are a liability, and after a period of compassion, these victims are often singled out as parasites. According to Dr. Bessel Van der Kolk, society has to come to terms with two ideas: Victims are not responsible for having been traumatized, and victims who are not helped to resolve trauma can become volatile and anxious people, unreliable workers, ineffective parents, or prone to addiction because of unbearable feelings. This means that the practice of medicine and psychology cannot continue to be divorced from the cultural context in which trauma occurs.[65]

In military settings, medical practitioners are often required to deny their empathy for individual soldiers as part of their obligations to maintain the fighting strength of the military. Clinicians often confront the impossible ethical dilemma of helping their patients while having to decide whether these soldiers are fit for combat and thus ready to lay down their lives. Even in peacetime, there is generally a profound divergence between a soldier's experience and the way healthcare providers understand his trauma reactions.

Clinicians are tasked with evaluating the soldier's fitness for duty, which means identifying possible mental symptoms that compromise his ability to function. For their part, soldiers are usually concerned with future deployability and continued service. While this may be changing, they are reluctant to disclose how they are actually

65   I. Parker, "Critical psychology: What it is and what it is not," *Social and Personality Psychology*, 2007 1(1):1–15.

doing emotionally or talk about events that may be transpiring within their units. As stated earlier, the things that occur for soldiers during the six-month, post-event period seems crucial in determining whether or not he will develop PTSD in its chronic form. There may be fundamental personal qualities and social determinants that need to be understood more fully.

Eleven

Someone's Going to Pay

I drove my Land Rover down the highway north of Kuwait City a day or two following the liberation. For seven miles there was a line of burned-out cars, trucks, and tanks, many with the charred remains of Iraqi soldiers inside. The retreating convoy had been strafed by F-16 fighter jets. Some of the 1,500 vehicles were turned in an apparent attempt to flee backwards towards the city. They have caused a massive traffic jam. The only escape was on foot. The air was pungent with the stench of rotting bodies. In the cab of one truck were the blackened remains of a soldier curled up over the steering wheel. Bits of legs and arms stuck out in strange positions from the burnt metal. Cobra helicopters hovered noisily above me.

[from War is a Force That Gives Us Meaning, Hedges, 2003] [66]

66   C. Hedges, *War is a Force That Gives Us Meaning* (New York: Anchor Book, 2003).

Cyril was an Army transport driver during Canada's involvement in the 1990–91 Gulf War campaign. He is sitting across from me stone-faced.

"I don't think you can help me," he says. "Nobody can."

Today he has brought along a thick photo album and places it on the seat beside him, but it's up to me to ask about its contents and whether he wants me to look at it.

He shrugs. "Sure, whatever."

I take a seat beside him and open the album, and in an instant, Hedges' nightmarish descriptions are brought into living colour. I am hit by a kaleidoscope of burned vehicles and close-up images of charred corpses and pieces of bodies strewn about. Cyril moves back in his seat as I land on a photograph of an anti-aircraft battery and the two blackened shapes. The body of one soldier is still at his post while a second one is nearly buried in the sand; only his head and the charred remains of the left side of his upper body are visible.

From the corner of my eye, I can see Cyril's gaze fix on the picture and blossom in an expression that I can only describe as pure hatred.

"I will never forgive them for making us drive that road after the American bombings. There was no reason for them to make us see that horror, and I can't get that stuff out of my head. It's their fault, so why should I have to do anything?"

Soon after returning to Canada, he left the Army and spent the next twenty years as a civilian driver, severing all connections with the military, wanting nothing to do with them—his trust in tatters. He tells me that the fear of having a heart attack is the only reason he is here. His wife has continually asked him to talk with somebody about his constant headaches and stomach problems. He tells me that he barely sleeps and has periods of blacking out that are a result of unstable blood pressure.

Other than that, Cyril offers few details about his life and provides only cryptic answers to any questions. I know he has two grown children and that he seems proud of the fact that they have never seen him angry or raise his voice.

"At work, they try to get me going, and I just walk away. But at night I replay every conversation, over and over."

It is only when I ask Cyril whether his time overseas could be affecting his health and his family that he shows any emotion.

"They will *never* know about this stuff, so don't even try to go there. All they need to know is that I am there for them."

I ask him why he keeps the album and how he can live with such bitterness and hatred all of the time.

"We were forbidden to take pictures," he says. "But I did so I could have the evidence."

After some prompting, he tells me about growing up with a heavy drinking and abusive father.

"He would beat me and my sister all of the time, so when he died two years ago, I didn't even go to the funeral. My sister was my only ally, and she died six years ago, so I have no reason to talk to any of the rest of them. I am done with them."

At the end of today's session, Cyril announces that he wants to take a break from therapy. I suggest that he talk with his doctor about medication that might help him, but he has no interest in drugs and does not want his doctor to know anything about this stuff from the military.

I offer him the opportunity to return at any point, but I also know that he will likely never return.

When it comes to mental health problems among soldiers, are we simply catering to their inability to manage the normal range of emotional upset and disappointments? Are we becoming a trauma-phobic society leading to the erosion of military hardiness? I think that these are reasonable questions. Much of the research on military PTSD focuses on warzone reactions, but there is also a burgeoning literature that highlights complex relationships between childhood adversity and adult-onset PTSD. However, treatment efforts typically focus on aspects of military deployments, despite evidence that up to ninety percent of military veterans report exposure to non-military trauma, including high rates of developmental abuse.[67] [68] [69]

67 Cabrera et al., "Childhood adversity and combat as predictors of depression and post-traumatic stress in deployed troops"

68 D. Forbes et al., "Impact of combat and non-military trauma exposure on symptom reduction following treatment for veterans with posttraumatic stress disorder," *Psychiatry Research*, 2013 206 (1): 33–36.

69 J.A. Schumacher, S.F. Coffey, and P.R. Stasiewicz, "Symptom severity: Alcohol craving, and age of trauma onset in childhood and adolescent trauma survivors with comorbid alcohol dependence and posttraumatic stress disorder," *American Journal on Addictions*, 2006 15: 422–425.

Prospective studies have reported direct links between developmental abuse and neglect, and subsequent military PTSD, independent of combat exposure.[70] Childhood trauma has also been linked with increased severity of military PTSD symptoms.[71] Despite the efficacy of CBT interventions, over half of the patients do not get well, especially where people report multiple problems.[72] [73] [74] In sum, it seems clear from these studies that we need to better understand possible long-term effects of developmental abuse among traumatized military personnel who present for treatment.

We focus on trauma as cause-effect relationships and define reactions in terms of symptoms. Namely, that adult reactions simply reflect unresolved developmental distress. However, it is possible that the circumstances of current events operate by surpassing the person's usual ways of managing stress-distress—something else to be hidden away and managed on their own. Maybe there needs to be venues within the institution where things can be aired out without fears of ridicule or retaliation from others.

I know a senior medic who retired recently from the CAF. He had a long career going back as far as Rwanda and multiple tours to Afghanistan. In his words, "That last one in Afghanistan did me in." It was not a particular event; it was the fact that he knew he was exhausted emotionally, even before being convinced to take on

70   A. Mikulak, "Embattled childhoods may be the real trauma for soldiers with PTSD," Retrieved from http://www.sciencedaily.com/releases/2012/11/121119140625.htm.

71   A.E. Seifert, M.A. Polusny, & M. Murdoch, "The association between childhood physical and sexual abuse and functioning and psychiatric symptoms in a sample of U.S. Army soldiers", *Military Medicine*, 2011 176(2): 176–181.

72   D.G. Baker, C.M. Nievergelt, and V.B. Risbrough, "Posttraumatic Stress Disorder: Emerging Concepts of Pharmacotherapy," *Expert Opinion Emergent Drugs*, 2009 14(2): 251–272.

73   K. Nilamadhab, "Cognitive behavioral therapy for the treatment of post-traumatic stress disorder: A review," *Neuropsychiatric Disease and Treatment*, 2011 7:167–181.

74   B.E. Wampold et al., "Determining what works in the treatment of PTSD," *Clinical Psychology Review*, 2010 30: 923–933.

another deployment. His leadership approached him several times, and stirred his sense of responsibility and even guilt: "We need you. The young kids over there will need you." He finally gave in based on their promise to post him to a stable non-operational role upon his return.

> **When I got back, they put me in a closet for an office with absolutely nobody to talk to. They sucked everything out of me, and when I was dry, they threw me away without even batting an eye.**

A common belief among veterans is that they were simply used up and then thrown away when they had nothing left to offer. Some veterans have even disclosed instances where they were not doing well mentally and so the deployment screening process was deliberately bypassed because they possessed key skills that were needed. This sense of being used up seems to be a central part of their anger and lingering mental wounding going forward in their lives—that their commitment to each other was somehow used against them. In a way, their loyalty was their Achilles heel. As one Afghanistan vet put it:

> **It is not so much the shit that you see [over there] but what is happening around you in your unit. Are you getting encouragement or a positive word from your higher ups or just left on your own? Either way, it means a lot in how you handle what is happening over there.**

The prospect of mental illness represents a loss of control over oneself. In the military, loss of control and loss of predictability can cause major disruptions to unit functioning—these instances must be corrected or ejected. Loss of control among members erodes the necessary illusion of order, and it creates uneasiness; fear in the organization and among group members. For our part, mental health clinicians attempt to control it through analyzing, dissecting, and correcting suspected flaws in the individual, but ironically it may be this exact process of scrutiny that lays the foundations for stigma. By turning soldiers into patients, they are automatically transformed back into an individual—remember there is no place for individuals within the military.

Many clinicians, including myself, know of serving members in high positions who have mental health issues but, because those issues are unknown to people in their workplaces, they are accepted; sometimes they are seen by others as controlling, self-absorbed, or even odd, but they do the job. But as soon as mental illness is disclosed or suspected, everything seems to change, and all behaviours are re-evaluated, re-analyzed through an illness lens. How is this? I believe that generally, we have an image of well-adjusted people as somehow being problem-free and people we can trust, and this is easily overturned when flaws become public—we become afraid.

Cyril's story points to a man who is stuck with a lifetime of bitter resignation. If there ever was a man consumed by hatred, he would be this example. This is a man trapped in silence; a pragmatic man uninterested in theories about trauma or the value of trusting other people to help him. What is obvious is his hatred for authority and his belief that he had been victimized both by his father and by the military. Victims have perpetrators, and some veterans believe that the CAF and VAC owe them because of their belief that their loyalty was betrayed.

Several years ago, I stopped my work conducting mental health assessments when I realized the contest between veterans who wanted acknowledgment for service-related injuries and VAC who is tasked with weeding out malingerers and determining compensation awards. From my perspective, both parties were heavily dug-in playing their respective roles. I believed that mental health clinicians were placed squarely in the crossfire. Veterans-as-victims wanted the system to pay—in some cases, whether they needed these monies or not. A number of veterans told me that they really did not need additional money but that their fights represented a struggle to regain their pride and dignity. This victim sentiment is very strong, and it is easy for clinicians to be swallowed up within it.

From a clinical standpoint, victim mentality is often learned whereby a person tends to regard him or herself as powerless in respect to the actions of others and to think, speak, and act as if this is always the case—even in the absence of clear evidence. There is an inherent risk within a hierarchical system for members to perceive things this way, especially when those who challenge the system may be tagged as troublemakers. And when it comes to mental health, pathologizing soldiers' concerns can increase their sense of powerlessness by turning normal reactions into abnormal states and emotional problems.

A central aspect of this victim-making involves looking for and emphasizing the negative and pointing to wounds, scars, weaknesses, and lasting effects. In this place, legitimate anger or appropriate guilt is diminished, and personal responsibility to engage in corrective actions becomes irrelevant. In my experience, veterans-as-victims run the risk of becoming trapped and tangled up in passivity. Convinced that they can't take care of themselves, they become dependent, needing support and protection, but they are often angry and rebellious about this dependence on others, simultaneously.

To be clear, there is little doubt that these men and women are distressed. The problem, as I see it, is that when mental functioning is subjected to scrutiny in the interests of compensation and suitability for various programs, it can be very confusing to understand the sources of distress. Military people who are released for mental health reasons are forced to face the harsh reality that they have been deemed to be no longer fit to serve. While completely unintended, the consequence for many veterans is to feel judged as being useless.

The military's main focus has been on the resilience of individual members through campaigns encouraging members to seek care along with educational programs that teach self-management skills. These efforts are based in an individual skill deficit model. Again, this is all well and good; however, these efforts do not include the effects of military life on mental health. A substantial number of military people who have never deployed have a range of mental health problems, including depression, addiction, social phobias, and PTSD. We are left to presume that the fabric of military life is a benign backdrop to the health of individuals. In other words, that the benefits of training and the nature of hierarchical relationships and interactions are simply a given.

Should problems arise, there are pragmatic, bureaucratic mechanisms in place through formal venues like remediation and grievances. Veterans often tell me that that these bureaucratic responses are often simply a tiring head game where real solutions usually do not occur in favour of the aggrieved. They are left with the impression that the system takes no responsibility for its behaviour and cannot be held accountable for its effects on members. So I guess, in one sense, mental health programs can become a fallback haven for affected members even though secrets must be kept by all concerned.

I think about the silent ghosts in the military from the legacy of the past conflicts, the continued effects upon the membership, and the changes within the institution, which have meant that it has grown a little tougher and possibly a little less human. The institution appears to have little choice but to shed itself of its history in order to keep moving forward.

Again, this is not a search for villains. There are many committed and caring people scattered throughout the institution. They work within the available system and attempt to reconcile gaps, inconsistencies, and contradictions. My point is that there are few ways to incorporate dissenting voices from the rank and file members, for the system clamps down to control outbursts of abuse and harassment. One has to wonder about the long-term effects.

Within the military and other para-military organizations, recruits continue to be taught a particular form of strength, a particular version of manhood that is pragmatic, competitive, and unemotional; a system of training that is steeped in older versions of what it means to be a strong man or woman. The focus on mental health and trauma, however, represents a direct challenge to these older notions of rationality, especially since trauma reactions seem to be inherently emotional in nature, including reactions of sadness, guilt, outrage, and grief. Even so, emotionality continues to be viewed as self-indulgent and possibly as a sign of weakness; at the very least it is inconsistent with the warrior metaphor. Somatic reactions, including sleeplessness, obsessional thinking, and unexplained anxiety can all point to disavowed emotions that wear people down. Not surprisingly, serving members and veterans often look in the wrong places to feel alive—external sources.

Interestingly, activities like yoga, mindfulness, or service animals seem to help because they force people to slow down and connect with their internal worlds; interactions with animals can stimulate the production of oxytocin (a neurotransmitter which plays a central role in intimacy, sexual reproduction, and social bonding), which is often termed the social hormone and is linked with affiliation and social attachment. It may serve the military well in teaching skills which help develop self-reflective capacity among its warriors; maybe a shift away from Spartan mythology towards that of the Samurai. Those people who devalue emotional management may be the ones who are most prone to the dehumanizing effects of training—compartmentalization, depersonalization, and dissociation.

Despite their involvement in war and combat, it is surprising that veterans have a hard time talking about the killing of other people. It takes an incredible effort to desensitize young men and women to take the lives of other people without hesitation or self-recrimination for the act of killing, cleaning up after military suicides, or witnessing the human carnage of disasters. Compartmentalization and depersonalization work particularly well in this regard—events are simply external tasks. I wonder about the efforts to re-humanize these people.

In the old days, we would have been given a bottle of rum or a few cases of beer and left to ourselves to decompress. Again, this is not an endorsement for the role of alcohol but to emphasize the need for safe venues to decompress and to re-establish bonds. These days, helping members to come back down and to re-orient themselves seems to be left to other people like family members and friends; it does not register as an issue for military personnel. Accepting death and killing as a normal part of life can become lost in sterile, academic discussion of operational stress.

Twelve

There Was No One to Protect Me

Corporal Angela Cobbs looked tough. Sitting across from me in her military combats, her back was straight, her gaze direct, and her hands held crossed on her lap. She was twenty-five. Her dark hair was cut short, and she wore no makeup; a woman comfortably devoid of feminine accent. She was muscular with strong arms, back, and legs. Every signal that she gave off suggested that she was not a person to be messed with.

She was recovering from a minor back injury the prognosis for which was, by all accounts, good. That she had recently suffered panic attacks at work, episodes of crying, and had reported disturbed sleep patterns is what had ultimately brought her to me.

When she spoke, her voice was direct, and there were no smiles or any of the social gestures one might expect during a first encounter. She did not fidget, even a little. She was, it seemed, the very personification of military professionalism. Still there was something there beneath it all. I couldn't determine whether she was anxious or simply angry at having to talk to someone like me—someone who might mess with her head.

When asked to give me some background, she did so without undue prompting. She told me about her trade as a vehicle tech and even started to go into how she had hurt her back. I could hear a tickle develop in her voice and glanced at the bottled water in front of her. She nodded, and when she reached for it, I noticed that she had the strong confident hands of a mechanic.

I had been asked to provide an outside opinion on the suitability of Corporal Cobbs for a posting to a base outside the Atlantic region. The medical system wanted an independent opinion due to their concerns that she was feigning symptoms of distress to simply avoid being posted—their onset coinciding with the discussion of said posting.

During our first two meetings, it seemed that I did most of the talking as I explained my role to her. I reminded her several times that any private information we discussed would be kept confidential unless she wanted me to report these things back to her military system.

It was during our second meeting that she decided to trust me and tell me why it was that she was so nervous about her upcoming posting. Up to that point, she had only talked about her fear that her back injury would not heal and that this could end in a medical release. In her account, this was the reason for her anxiety.

Over the course of our conversation, I asked about her specific fears in regards to the new posting, suspecting already that her answers would not quite add up. I asked what it would entail in terms of physical expectations, and she seemed to have a good handle on things in this respect. I asked then whether she knew anybody at the new base—a likely possibility given our small military population. As it turned out, this question resulted in the first cracks in her otherwise flat and stoic attitude. Her right leg started to twitch slightly and it seemed as though she had something in her eye. Though she tried to hide it for a second or two, there was nothing to be done. Tears started welling up.

"I can't go there. I can't." She drew a ragged breath. "He'll be there. I… I just—"

"*Who* will be there?" I asked.

She continued without interruption, describing how she grew up in the region near the new base. Her mother had remarried when Angela was quite young but left that marriage when Angela was about fourteen years old, leaving her in the custody and care of her stepfather who was in the military. She was used to him being gruff and verbally abusive to her mother, but she had never really been the brunt of much more than comments about her appearance as she began approaching puberty. She had a few friends, and most of them were in the Cadets with her, but they were never invited to her home, for she did not want the embarrassment if he decided to be in one of his moods.

Within six months of her mother leaving, his verbal comments towards her deteriorated quickly over her ineptitude in keeping the house clean or not having food ready when he got home from work. This progressed to being hit about the back of the head or pushing her out of the way if he wanted near the kitchen sink.

One night after he had been drinking—this was in the spring shortly after her seventeenth birthday—he started his usual verbal assaults, which progressed to hitting her, but this time it went further. He pushed her to a sofa in the living room, and before she knew what was happening, he had pulled her dress up and was groping at her private parts. She started to scream but his hand was quickly over her mouth, his mood dark and threatening.

"I don't want you to utter one sound when I pull my hand away, and if you ever say anything about this I will kill you."

On that night he stopped and let her up. She ran to her room and thought about calling one of her friends or her mother, but his threat echoed in her head, for she knew he was capable of making good on his threat. She let it go.

She would not be so fortunate the next time it happened. Two months later she was raped. This time she didn't care about his threats and made the telephone call to tell her mother about what her stepfather had done. Her mother's reaction devastated her.

"Just because you have decided that you don't want to live with him is no reason for me to have to listen to this shit. Don't call me about him. I want nothing to do with him." And with that, she hung up the phone.

Angela thought about calling the police but had no confidence that they would investigate a member of the military. She took the last option she had. Packing a small knapsack, she left the house and hit the road. It was the first week of summer vacation. She never wanted to see him or think about what he had done to her ever again.

Within a week she had found her way to Toronto and the streets. She got lucky and ran into two girls who had an apartment. They seemed okay, but she quickly learned that their money was coming from turning tricks on the street. She wanted nothing to do with this, and the thought of it made her anxious. She stayed with the girls for a couple of months, and though they never pressured her, she always felt as though they were waiting for her to capitulate. She needed to make a decision, and they all knew it.

Given her cadet experience, she decided to apply to the military. She was relieved by her quick acceptance into the Army where she believed she would be safe. Angela completed her training and did well in her trade. A couple of years later she was promoted. She had stable friends, loved physical activity and sports, and as far as she was concerned, her past could be simply forgotten.

However, the prospect of the new posting brought her entire world crashing down around her ears. Her stepfather, the man who had abused her nine years earlier, was posted there as well. And the long festering memory of the earlier abuse was flooding back, pushing her out-of-control. All her efforts to get away from her abuser had ironically led her straight back to him, unwittingly at the hands of the military.

With her permission, my report to the medical system, which they immediately supported, indicated that posting to this base could cause considerable harm to her mental health including increased risks of self-harm. Unfortunately, she was adamant that the abuse and her stepfather's name not be mentioned outside of the medical system.

As a result, as far as her chain of command was concerned, there was no reason for her not to be posted—apart from a delay to allow recovery for her back injury. If the posting was to be deferred or prevented because of a change in her medical category for physical health reasons, or if she claimed mental health reasons, then she risked release from the CAF. She was posted with all of the supports we could recommend be put in place for her when she arrived at the new base.

■ ◥

One may ask about the relevance of this woman's preservice history to her military service; a legitimate question. Apart from the fact that the perpetrator in this case was a serving military member, an immediate response would suggest that this event has no bearing on the military at all. In fact, there is an argument that the issue is a matter for the civilian courts even though the issue is complicated again by the fact that they are both serving members of the military. The point to be made is that mental health issues are not restricted to things that occur strictly within the military. The question is really about how to respond when this information becomes known by medical professionals. Is there a responsibility to protect CAF members as they engage the health system, given that it is divorced from the operational end?

I fell through the cracks because my health team had absolutely no contact or communication with my unit.

[Navy member]

Actions taken for or against members by their local leadership, or by their career managers, occur independent of the goal of mental health clinicians, i.e., to protect the mental welfare of our clients. Those members who create problems or raise thorny issues risk the loss of employment for not being team players or not meeting the universality of service requirement. So who protects the CAF member when they come forward requesting help?

When they are left to their own fate, under the current policies and leadership, very often there are positive outcomes. The outcomes appear to depend on the likability of the particular person, their rank, and the personalities of their clinicians and their particular leaders. So the course of treatment and outcomes can be arbitrary. I believe that prospective military patients may need protections beyond the procedural avenues available to them.

For one, if they are experiencing PTSD or severe depression, they are often not in a mental state to protect their own best interests and are thus particularly vulnerable. This should serve as a signal that prospective patients might need to be assigned advocates who are answerable, with the patient's permission, to the senior leadership. An alternative might have to come down to an organized representational system where members have clear advocates within the institution tasked to tackle common employee issues.

In terms of Corporal Cobbs, I have not heard how she has fared in her new posting. Hers serves as a good example of the disconnection that exists between the CAF's efforts to address the mental welfare of its members while at the same allowing its leaders to remain divorced from such efforts. In fairness, if this sensitive personal information could have been managed by the 'career shop' (career management system), other alternatives might have been considered.

As it was, Corporal Cobbs was left feeling unprotected by the military system and forced to manage the stress of her new posting on her own. If she was to see this man directly, which is a distinct possibility, the likelihood of a full-blown mental health crisis might be expected. In the end, the possibility of a medical exit from the military probably still awaits her. I am left to wonder about the many efforts that support the care of military members. Many people, including myself, would argue that these efforts are much more than mere window dressing since they reflect ongoing improvements within the CAF. At the same time, this story points to the need for conversations that acknowledge the occurrence of these types of issues.

The well-intended and necessary separation of the medical and operational sides of the institution can exacerbate these issues, which means that patients often cannot find advocates. Often soldiers tell me about being caught in conflicts between medical and operational personnel. As I have suggested, there may be a need for the creation of organized advocacy and representation to ultimately address these types of instances. The present system of grievances and complaints to ombudsmen—which usually occur after-the-fact—rarely rectify the mental-emotional damage to members in the process. These administrative and quasi-legal proceedings can sometimes drag on indefinitely, even as members are moved toward medical release in the process. Often younger or lower-ranked members do not exercise their rights until it is too late in the process.

At present, mental health interventions focus on specific operational events, but the effects of multiple deployments, inconsistent leadership, harassment, or the military culture itself and their direct effects on the mental health of members are poorly understood. The consequences of routine military life are taken for granted: "Shit happens, get over it. It's nothing personal." As it stands, the ways of construing mental health issues do not involve the system itself and its potential to negatively or positively impact the psychological health of CAF members.

Angela's story also points to the issue of sexual violence. It is a problem faced by many organizations, including the military and the RCMP. These are events that often occur in secrecy between members of disparate rank or influence. In my early career, I worked with sexual offenders, including probation officers and clergy who had considerable power over their victims; this ranged from the power to cause them physical harm to the power to remove safety and resources. In some cases, they had the power to incarcerate victims if they did not comply with sexual demands.

These acts occurred under a shroud of secrecy where threats were backed up with the power to carry them out. What is scary and inconceivable for the military is the possibility that shining stars— the men and some women who are known and trusted—could be capable of these things behind closed doors. What I do know is that sexual pariahs and psychopaths make their way into the military just like they do in many other organizations. They can be charismatic, likable, outgoing, and highly intelligent, but many of them also harbour insatiable thirsts for power over other people. We need to acknowledge the level of narcissism and self-interest that can exist in a capable individual and fail to stand out in an organization like the Canadian Armed Forces or RCMP.

Angela's experience is also one of disconnection and being unprotected within the military family. Some of the people I have seen over the years were alpha males, the domineering, aggressive ones preoccupied with the need to be treated as special. Since all behaviour is instrumental, the use of dominance becomes their way of being treated with deference, respect, and specialness. Narcissism is defined as the pursuit of gratification from vanity or egotistic admiration of one's own attributes.

Except in cases of primary narcissism or healthy self-love, narcissism often creates problems in the person's relationships with other people. They are often pseudo-perfectionists and require always being the centre of attention.[75] A narcissistic leadership style is one in which the leader is only interested in self. Their priority is themselves—at the expense of their people. This leader exhibits the characteristics of arrogance, dominance, and hostility.[76] It is often driven by unyielding self-absorption and an ego-driven need for power and admiration.[77] The submissive ones also have investments in these exchanges with powerful people.

As stated by one male NCO:

I was always on the search for the ones with, you know, self-esteem issues, the ones who were only too willing to please... Nothing like being the knight in shining armour to help them. *I will help you... there, there...*

75   H. Kohut, *Thoughts on narcissism and narcissistic rage: In the search for the self* (Madison CT: International Universities Press, 1972), vol. 2: 615–658.

76   B. Sorotzkin, "The quest for perfection: Avoiding guilt or avoiding shame?" *Psychology Today*, April 2006

77   L. Neider, *The Dark Side of Management* (Charlotte, NC: Information Age Publishing, 2010).

Thirteen

It Just Came Out of Nowhere

Clouds of dust obscured the driver's vision as the convoy barrelled through the Afghan countryside. Then without warning, his LAV (light-armoured vehicle) was off the road and down over a slight embankment. So too was the last one following him; one LAV travelled around 100 metres before banging headlong into a ditch. Bobby's vehicle brought up solid on a boulder, nearly toppling it over.

And just like that, they were sitting ducks in a field. The rest of the vehicles were already out of sight down the road oblivious to their predicament. The first LAV was spewing fluids in all directions and had to be shut down. Theirs was running, but there was no way to move the heavy vehicle. They had no choice but to wait for the QRF (quick reaction force) and the mechanics to arrive. Despite seeing some of the locals off in the distance, the rules were to not leave the vehicles since it could be a mined area. They were helpless to do anything except scan the countryside for movement in their direction and a possible attack.

Bobby had all but forgotten about that day. He was on his way to a medical appointment with his wife when they hit some early morning fog on the highway. His vision obscured, he panicked bringing the car to a screeching halt, chewing up loose gravel from the shoulder as the vehicle careened to a stop.

A flash sweat prickled across his shoulders and the back of his neck. A vice had closed on his chest.

There was no way he could drive another foot, and he knew it. Bob bolted from the car and was walking down the road before he knew what was happening. Ten minutes later he was back. Melissa was waiting by the car, a grim expression of concern on her face. She hadn't run after him. She'd known not to do that.

"Bob, are you—"

"Just take the wheel," he said, his voice a dry croak. "We gotta go home. I just.... I can't."

They got in and buckled up. She didn't press him about the appointment or what he was going through.

A few minutes later, driving back in silence the way they came, images of the roundabout in Kabul popped into his head. The vice tightened again, and he let out a strange huff of breath and put his hands to the dashboard.

"Honey?"

"Fuck! Pull over," he said. "Pull the fuck over."

He was fumbling at his belt before they even came to a stop. He threw open the door and bolted out of the car. Drawing in the cool morning air, he lit a cigarette as the other vehicles zipped past them on the highway. He didn't care about them. He just found a rock and sat there for nearly half an hour this time.

His anxiety switched over to anger as he approached the car once again. When he was in this mood, it wasn't that he wanted to hurt anybody, but these thoughts went off in his head like a switch, an insistent urge to just go crazy or end it all.

Bobby was angry at everything and nothing at the same time. It had started after Afghanistan, almost as soon as he got home. It took everything he had to regain control of himself, to throttle back and forget. But the volcano in his guts would just lie dormant for a time, then it would rumble and erupt when he least expected. Sometimes he would be in tears for no reason, especially when he forgot for a minute and allowed himself to feel good about something. It didn't make any sense.

He was not sure when the thought of just ending it all first popped into his head. Probably after the bar fight. This had been about three months after Afghanistan. He had been out with the boys having some drinks, blowing off steam, and having a good time. But then it was like something threw a switch inside his head, and he felt some dark gear slip in his skull, and then he was in a different mode.

Out of nowhere, he had an overwhelming urge to hurt other people. Some guy he didn't know made a comment about

Afghanistan to his buddies—afterwards he couldn't even remember what it had been, only that he had thought it disrespectful—and the fight was on. Punching and kicking in a red deadening haze of fury. All opponents blurring into one.

This scene replayed itself many nights over the following year. The impulse to end the lives of these guys, these strangers at a bar, was so strong that it scared him. And on the heels of that fear was the impulse to end it all. Was he crazy? His drinking got worse, but increasingly these thoughts burned their way through the alcohol. The crazy adrenaline rages, the dark funks, the alcohol. This pattern kept going until he was hospitalized for a suspected stroke. Now he did not even have booze to blunt the edges of whatever was wrong.

There are various theories regarding impulses to harm oneself or others. One that is often spoken about is the need to do something to avoid overwhelming feelings of shame or outrage. It is as if the anger that cannot be directed at the source of the assault is turned onto oneself as a sort of self-mutiny versus helplessness. It is an understandable reaction, and while I certainly do not condone it, I can understand the impulse—doing anything can seem better than living in helplessness.

After a couple of sessions, I felt that I had a decent read on what Bob was wrestling with. I had also delved into his childhood and had learned that it was good. So I asked him.

"I wonder what your father would have to say about what it is you're going through if you could even talk to him about it."

"Oh, Dad and I have a great relationship," he said. "We can talk about anything. He would understand what I'm going through."

I nodded and leaned back in my chair.

"Well, I think perhaps it's time to take a trip back home and talk to him about it. Really let him know how you're doing." I smiled. "It's got to be at least as good as talking to strangers about it, right?"

Bob took this advice, and in the following months, he stopped drinking and showed much better control emotionally. Why would this be? I believe it is because he had gone back to an important relationship in his life and had re-established connection and benefited from this emotional bond with his father. So far, it seems to have made all the difference.

When they are released for PTSD and become civilians, veterans tend to view any signs of emotional distress as some aspect of their prior diagnosis. And indeed, feeling depressed, socially avoidant, or angry can all be reminiscent of PTSD from earlier events. But the point I would make here is that often unseen is the psychological strain caused by transitional distress.

There is much work to do to help veterans resolve unfinished business from the military before they are able to move on. The most common ones are damaged military identity from the stigmatization that comes with a diagnosis and their rejection of the civilian world because of their military training and ethos. Many veterans have few connections with the civilian world because of long deployments overseas and frequent disruptions from postings; many of them really do not have established social civilian networks.

Soldiers exist within a special sub-culture that is apart from general society but alongside it simultaneously. In order to take on the role of protectors of society, paradoxically, they have to first learn to stand apart from it. This seems to be a central issue facing many veterans released medically from the military. They do not see any way of fitting into a civilian world and often they do not have the skills or wherewithal to even begin this process. So they resort to isolation, or they try to reconnect with their past military friends which simply reminds them that they no longer belong.

To help them move forward, I believe they need dignified ways to deal with the emotional issues of leaving the military. Often the inability to confront the loss of their former identity, come to terms with anger or resentment, or acknowledge their lost confidence prevents them from taking any independent action.

A central issue seems to revolve around incorporating a view of themselves as a military veteran but also as a contributing member of the civilian society. This psychological transition process takes considerable time and effort. It requires an identity shift that involves much more than finding a civilian job or attending school or university. It often means that they have to come to terms with the loss of who they were and take deliberate steps towards a new identity.

When it comes to resolving lingering mental issues, in my experience, a period of three to five years seems to be the norm if they go about the work of repairing the past and engaging in the present. The worst thing for many of them is to decide that their military careers did not happen. Prior to release from the military, veterans may need opportunities for open debrief and decompression (more on this later). They may need to be taught *how* to leave the military.

Rightly or wrongly, many of the people I see are focused on rehashing their damaged military pride and identity and remain preoccupied with holding to account specific people or the military system for what was done to them. They are focused on trying to fix the past but pay little attention to engaging in their present lives.

The challenge for traumatized veterans is finding a way to accept and live with the past; whether they believe they let down the group or lost faith in their military family. This breach could be because they did something shameful—dishonourable—that they cannot face or talk about. Perhaps instead they struggle with feelings of betrayal and resentment. Any overriding preoccupation with the past means that present relationships (with family and loved ones) are ignored, leaving traumatized veterans tragically withdrawn from the very people who care about them.

Across a variety of civilian and military studies, evidence suggests that the vast majority of people who experience extreme stressors do not go on to develop mental problems. A recent mental health study of the CAF placed diagnosable mental health conditions at approximately seventeen percent or just under one-fifth of the military. The bigger concern for the military seems to centre around the issue of depression because of its presumed relationship with suicidality. Even so, this indicates that the majority of members, barring the problem of under-reporting, can be assumed to be functioning well mentally.

Of those military members who are diagnosed and treated for PTSD in the military, the popular literature indicates that between forty and sixty percent of patients are partially or fully responsive to standard treatments. I am unaware of the CAF statistics in this regard, but it has been projected that the majority of military personnel with PTSD will eventually be released medically. This projection is likely due to a combination of factors: First, the member may be successful in overcoming PTSD but because of liability concerns or administrative decisions, they are identified for medical release since the CAF does not have a duty to accommodate these people; and second, if we are left to assume that many military members do not fully recover, then from a safety perspective, and for the member's own welfare, they are not retainable within the CAF.

Those people who do not respond to interventions raise a number of questions from a treatment efficacy standpoint. The predictable and understandable next step is to investigate characteristics of these non-responders. The most common foci have been on current life instability such as divorce or financial instability or upon comorbidities such as chronic pain, depression, or problems with addictions. Treatment non-response has also raised questions about the role of developmental histories and the possibility of pre-service traumas.

In one study, I reported that approximately eighty-six percent of military veterans who did not respond to treatment in the military had experienced physical and sexual abuse before sixteen years of age. While this is a very high number, because of the study design, the issue of developmental neglect was not investigated. My reading of the literature seems to show that neglect may be the most significant after-effect from childhood abuse. This issue of neglect has also been found to be a significant predictor of adult PTSD; it has also been translated into notions of sanctuary trauma and betrayal trauma, which may be quite relevant in understanding military treatment outcomes.

Further complicating the treatment outcome picture are reports that failures to receive care and attention may contribute to another reaction, termed re-traumatization. Generally, this term was meant to refer to being flooded by older, long-forgotten memories of abuse and neglect. This can be quite confusing for clinicians and military clients alike, who are both focusing on military events. Sometimes the severity of the soldier's reactions is inconsistent with the characteristics or severity of the identified event leading to questions about preservice. But the overreaction may have little or nothing to do with childhood; instead perceptions of neglect and abandonment within their current unit may be the roots of their distress.

Again this seems to raise questions in regards to our theories of trauma and PTSD. First, the ways in which people understand their emotional problems can have a direct impact on them. As I have suggested above, the label of permanent injury changes a person's self-view and their ideas about the future. Second, for those people who work as clinicians, on the one hand, they can be entirely pragmatic and simply provide different strategies or techniques as needed with no unifying understanding, and this approach seems to work for many people, but problems arise when a specific approach does not help or alternatively when the treatment leads to increased distress. In the absence of a guiding framework, we are left to guess about the reasons why an approach is not working; maybe the client is not working hard enough, or maybe there is a need for increased medication. Ultimately, decisions about the strategy, such as whether to increase the intensity, stop the treatment, or shift approaches can become idiosyncratic.

There is an implicit understanding in our current understanding of PTSD that it is a brain disorder resulting from a specific psychological stressor. Even though this theory is probably debatable, we do not have interventions that directly address the observed changes in neurocortical functioning associated with PTSD. There are no medications that treat PTSD directly, and our talking interventions seem to be aimed primarily at increasing the person's awareness of specific troubling memories in the hopes that the memory will eventually fade.

Even here, there is no reported evidence that these strategies target or repair the presumed neurocortical dysfunction. In the end, most of our accepted interventions teach clients to better tolerate anxiety, to avoid certain situations, and to expend energy in their personal and social lives. In sum, the theory and our interventions remain disconnected, conceptually. I am not suggesting that they don't help because many people do benefit. I am saying that we are not sure why it helps or why some interventions don't help.

As I have described throughout, I am suggesting the inclusion of a social-relational perspective that is built on attachment and emotional regulation theories as a basis for understanding military trauma of all types. In my experience, military training results in the establishment of a different identity for most members. This new identity exists and is understood and maintained by a complex set of relationships with other military members and with the entire organization. In essence, much of what we understand about civilian life and civilian mental health may not apply to them.

A social-relational perspective can lead to direct interventions that flow from an attachment-emotional regulation view. In fact, therapists who have successes with their clients may already be doing some of these things. With the addition of new mental health initiatives in the military, which appear to have grown out of concerns over untreated PTSD and military suicides, there may come a time when emotional awareness and interpersonal communication skill development may become a routine part of military training and culture. It would seem to be a logical extension of the military's present efforts. Whether this will be a good or bad thing for the military will depend on how the organization negotiates the inherent challenges that will come with a more informed and possibly outspoken membership.

There are specific outcomes from military training and role expectancies that provide the groundwork for inabilities to process distressing events. One solution seems to point to a need to re-engage personal attachment processes to address the problem of emotional avoidance. There is still much that we need to understand about military attachment, PTSD, and emotional regulation. Attachment orientations may be particularly relevant in this regard.

As I have indicated, hyperactivation and deactivation strategies of the attachment system are common among insecurely attached people.[78] Furthermore, hyperactivation is common in anxious attachment—in efforts to move closer to other people. Deactivation is common among avoidantly attached people whose instinct is to move away from people to avoid dependence. In sum, the higher the level of insecure attachment, the higher the degree of problems with emotional regulation. And finally, the attachment styles of leaders seem to have a direct impact on the mental health of their subordinates particularly in the aftermath of distressing events.

As I have outlined, we do not know whether attachment style is an enduring quality regardless of adult environments or whether people can shift from insecure attachment to secure attachment through positive mentoring, strong group cohesion, or specific activities like therapy in adulthood. It can be argued that the military provides an intense attachment environment that can work to rival the effects of established attachment patterns from early development. Within a military context then, we don't know whether the loss of a buddy or the experience of an abusive supervisor can produce a negative attachment sequela (chronic pathological condition).

We are not exactly sure about the reasons for increases in the number of CAF mental health cases. On the surface, it seems straightforward to attribute these rates to the effects of deployments. Also, we may plausibly attribute higher self-identification to better mental health education. An equally plausible explanation is that society, and hence members of the military, have become more demanding of their workplace relationships.

Because of intense group solidarity and unique daily hardships brought on during deployments, many veterans feel alienated from citizens, family, and friends when they return. They often feel they have little in common with their civilian peers. It can be extremely scary for soldiers to come from a physically and emotionally safe

---

78   J. Cassidy and R.R. Kobak, "Avoidance and its relationship with other defensive processes," in *Clinical implications of attachment*, eds. J. Belsky and T. Nezwolski (Hillsdale NJ: Erlbaum, 1988) 300–323.

environment and suddenly re-enter society. I would echo Ian Parker's concerns over the risk that the practice of psychology may inadvertently normalize these conditions of social alienation. While mental health initiatives can help groups of individuals stand up for themselves, it can also serve the role of reproducing existing conditions.[79] We can never forget that all individuals are enmeshed within a social-political framework, and so too are their psychological problems.

The military is a unique environment, and personnel face physical and extraordinary emotional demands as a routine part of their work environments, including lengthy deployments, frequent postings, and ongoing training. As such, a percentage of personnel would be expected to suffer stress reactions as part of their careers. Essentially, we can take the view that all personnel are healthy initially but that stress takes a predictable toll on people. A second theory is that some people may slip through the screening process and, even though they do well during their initial indoctrination, trades training, and deployments, are not suited to military life. This may be due to personality characteristics, basic value systems, or because of priorities external to the military, such as family commitments, educational aspirations, or other career goals. These people may experience normal life in the military as a source of ongoing stress.

When it comes to personnel who present or who are identified as experiencing mental health problems, while the previous two rationales may have some relevance, within formal mental health additional theories exist. Namely, there still exists a belief that the person probably had some pre-existing deficit that became evident with the additional stress of training or deployments. The rationale is that additional stress exposes an underlying personality or neurobiological weakness that was there all along.

In medical circles, this situation would be similar to an athlete with a minor heart defect that did not create any problems in his life but which, when the additional strain of high physical performance is added, the heart muscle cannot manage; this is known as the diathesis-stress model. By extension, mental health problems may be understood to be rooted in early development or mental health problems prior to entering the military that are exacerbated by the addition

79   I. Parker, "Critical psychology: What it is and what it is not," *Social and Personality Psychology*, 2007 1(1):1–15.

of a demanding environment. This line of thinking suggests that the propensity for decline under stress may not be due to the military per se but because of these unseen mental health problems that are compounded by the stress of deployments, divorce, or financial pressures.

While these may offer partial explanations for the root causes of mental declines, in the case of PTSD, they do not seem to provide an explanation for treatment non-response or symptom relapse. Why is that so many people do not make a full recovery and resume their careers? Is this also a fault of childhood, or could it be that the civilian mental health framework is not a good fit for addressing the mental health needs of military personnel? Again echoing Parker's concerns, we may be reinforcing individualism and social isolation through the concepts, language, and prevailing method of offering help (which is to say meeting privately with clinicians to discuss emotional problems). These strategies seem to be fundamentally at odds with the experiences and expectations of military personnel.

Alternatively, it may be the case that other types of required support along the road to mental health recovery are currently not utilized within the military. For example, good mental health may mean that military personnel need to have safe venues within their units to discuss their honest thoughts and emotional baggage, to create genuine connections with other people, or require appropriate down time during deployments to remain healthy. As it stands, peer group expectations and operational requirements do not allow for this type of self-reflective living.

As I have said previously, military identity seems to be at odds with notions of introspection and emotional awareness. New members have to learn to become insensitive to comments or even insults and other efforts aimed at provoking reactions from them. Sometimes, interactions can also lead to threats and physical fights, but most of them learn the skill of depersonalizing stressful interactions. When the Swissair recovery operation occurred in Nova Scotia, many sailors who were tasked to the recovery described instances where this depersonalized stance was interrupted. The arrival of mental health teams meant that they were required to meet in groups where they were educated about the gruesome work they were doing and the possible reactions they might already be experiencing. As one Navy veteran put it:

They really messed with our heads. They put it right in our faces…

This well-meaning intervention intended as a form of inoculation had the opposite effect by breaching the shared emotional detachment that was required to focus on completing a gruesome job. This form of intervention is no longer condoned by the military especially since subsequent research has identified unintended harmful effects from eliciting high emotionality in the face of terrible circumstances.

These types of well-intended errors reflect our general misunderstanding of mental health. Within a pragmatic medical understanding, there is a clear demarcation of having an illness or being healthy. It is an either-or decision-making process—either one has cancer or you do not have the disease. When it comes to various mental 'diseases' the same logic is applied—either one is depressed or not. However, this either-or distinction seems to break down when we look closely from a diagnostic stance.

In the case of depression, for instance, a person may be diagnosed as dysthymic—low-grade depression—or report increasing symptoms that go all the way up to severe depression. In other words, the case of depression is best understood as existing along a continuum as evidenced by the graded interventions that may be applied to help. It seems to be the same case for traumatic stress reactions as well. A person may be affected temporarily and recovery spontaneously without outside help; they may have some symptoms that can persist over the long-term which are considered to be sub-threshold. This means that the person may be experiencing some level of chronic distress but is otherwise able to function relatively well. We can move along this continuum from mild, moderate, to severe symptoms and again interventions are adjusted to respond in kind.

However, when it comes to making a formal diagnosis of PTSD, people are usually left with an impression that they either have this disorder or they do not. This is unfortunate and seems to be an incoherent process. While it may serve employers and the interests of insurers in the form of compensation, it generally does not serve those affected. A number of people I have treated for traumatic stress reactions did not meet the complete range of official criteria even though they responded positively to the same types of treatments that are offered to those other members officially diagnosed.

Trauma assessment and diagnostic decisions remain arbitrary processes. An alternative position is that nearly all mental health concerns exist along a continuum. In fact, over the last several years, efforts have been underway to move away from our present dichotomies around mental health problems towards this dimensional understanding.[80] For instance, in the case of partial PTSD, which is not recognized for the purpose of veteran coverage in Canada, it is associated with substantial psychiatric and medical comorbidity. This, even though studies have reported that both PTSD and partial PTSD patients show similar patterns of electroencephalographic brain activation in response to trauma-related stimuli that differed from non-traumatized controls.

When it comes to treating military trauma and other mental health issues, the lack of attention to the social-relational context of mental issues may need to be corrected. The fact is that the military environment can be an intensely political arena. Members have to get along with peers even as they compete with them, and their need to impress bosses sometimes means withholding personal information that may look bad on them. In terms of supervisors, there can be a failure to protect subordinates by not challenging orders from above. The effects on subordinates can include disillusionment and disappointment in a system that espouses one thing, but can end up doing the opposite. All this to reiterate that there is a context for mental health in the military. It is probably not coincidental that the rates of military depression outstrip civilian numbers. While this issue is frequently attributed to the stress of deployments, separations, or family stressors—all of which are valid—these stressors represent only one aspect of a more complicated reality.

Many of the people I see report being depressed because of problems with their supervisors or because of unfair treatment within their units where they feel helpless. When it comes to education on mental health, then, the benefits of positive thinking are also limited by the social context. In reality, we need to have tangible evidence of control over our external environments; we need to have our concerns taken seriously, and actions need to be taken to correct problems.

In the military, by the time many members reach their first promotions, they have developed a protective cynicism, which is

---

80   J.R. Bullis et al., "A preliminary investigation of the long-term outcome of the unified protocol for transdiagnostic treatment of emotional disorders," *Comprehensive Psychiatry*, 2014 55(8): 1920–1927.

described as their personal shield. It allows them to keep going, to remain loyal to other people, and to deny events that challenge their beliefs in the organization:

If you are going to affect the attitudes of the young troops in a positive way, you have to get to them before they have too much time in… before they see too much and get cynical because after that it's too late. [Serving Army NCO]

I see this description of cynicism as a kind of adaptive compartmentalization. Each of us can conveniently forget or ignore facts about our workplaces that create unease or conflict. In contrast, and without trying to create some nostalgic better version of the past, there was a time in the military when leaders did seem to take time to know their subordinates and expressed interest in their personal lives and welfare. Because of the power and positions that leaders fill, I believe they have a central and powerful role in influencing how their personnel respond to specific situations.

A private word of support or a brief conversation to allow subordinates to air out their reactions to an event can have much more impact than any of us from the mental health world. A consistent message at the unit level for men and women to look out for each other and not to segregate their buddies when they are having problems can go a long way in heading off deeper issues. Conversely, many veterans, especially the combat arms guys, talk about being singled out in front of their peers when they have to go to the mental health folks for care or being given menial jobs when they were diagnosed with a mental health problem. I don't think these responses help people recover. These ways of being treated often produce lingering effects long after official release dates, sometimes decades later.

An understandable fear among military personnel who present with operational stress issues is that, if they disclose preservice histories of physical, sexual, or mental abuse, their claims will be discounted. This is unfortunately a legitimate concern given the tendency for insurance companies to distinguish between pre-existing injuries and those claims warranting financial compensation due to the workplace. Even so, the downside for members who do not disclose these issues is that standard interventions are less effective and can produce harm because clinicians end up trying to solve the wrong problems.

Standard PTSD treatment require capacities that abused veterans may not have (e.g., emotional tolerance) which may further erode their existing coping strategies (e.g., dissociative behaviours). Clinicians and those clients who focus only on military trauma can become frustrated when treatments produce only minimal improvements or cycle between stability and crisis. The typical reaction is to increase the intensity of the treatment or question the soldier's motivation for change. In the meantime, paranoia, fears of losing emotional control, and fears of betrayal and abandonment are not addressed as these are deemed to be issues outside of the purview of the treatment context.

In my experience, preservice histories often have an influence on treatment outcomes for military PTSD cases. Does this mean then, that their military trauma is reducible to preservice events? Not surprisingly, the answer to this question requires close examination of the broader picture.

Firstly, since we do not know the percentage of people in the military who have experienced developmental abuse or neglect, we have no way of rating the specific risk load from preservice experiences. For example, we do not know the percentage of people in the military with developmental adversities who do not experience or report mental health issues. Of the reported PTSD cases in the military, we do not have data on the number of people who also report developmental adversity. The more appropriate question might mean considering whether certain soldiers with certain developmental experiences can experience specific events as traumatizing within specific military contexts.

Admittedly, this is a complex portrayal of operational trauma, but it is one that seems consistent with the available research. For example, take the solider who grew up in an emotionally volatile household where he was powerless to help his siblings can be faced with a similar scenario that results in operational PTSD. His duties may require him to witness women and children being harmed or killed while under strict orders not to intervene, and this can re-ignite older reactions of shame and helplessness.

Likewise, we are not sure whether a history of developmental abuse matters at all or whether it is simply the legacy of toughness and emotional suppression that determines the veteran's response to care. People who survive abuse often learn to be tough, they avoid emotions, and they rely on themselves to remain in control. They may be particularly adept at using the skill set described previously. When they face systems of care where they are required to give up control, they can revert to older retaliatory behaviours, confusing their caregivers. This may be the biggest import of developmental abuse on present day responses to trauma.

When it comes to the bottom line, at least as I see it, the practice of reducing military mental health issues to individual patients is double-edged. It provides a legitimate way to offer help by bringing issues and people under the protection of the medical envelope. At the same time, the reduction of possible systemic and organizational culture problems to genetics, biology, or preservice history also prevents a consideration of those aspects of the structure itself, in the development or persistence of soldier distress. It also removes from discussion the role of leadership in contributing to—or for that matter potentially preventing—these issues from developing in the first place.

When it comes to providing care, I am not suggesting that caregivers need to be paranoid or feel responsible for protecting their patients from the operational end of the military. At the same time, if we occupy ourselves only with symptom management and ignore the institutional context, I think we risk abdicating our professional obligations to do no harm. Whether clinicians are willing to accept it or not, our work exists within complex organizations with competing priorities. The operational end of our military institution really does seem to want to live by its espoused values and is committed to the mental welfare of its members. However, we must also acknowledge the bureaucratic component of the institution, which is tasked with maintaining the system and managing its liabilities.

Often, the health system and clinicians can be positioned squarely in the middle. The things that clinicians do and the things we write about our patients can have direct career implications. This fact cannot be ignored. By excluding unit functioning and the leadership as potential contributors to patient problems and, subsequent to that, by failing to engage the workplace as part of the solution, clinicians often fall short of their goals, as evidenced by the numbers of men and women who are being released medically. We need to understand why it is that so many people feel bitter and betrayed.

Betrayal is a devastating experience for most people. In the military, because of the high premium placed on loyalty to one another, it can represent a form of living death. It is a phrase that has been repeated over and over by veterans during their therapy. Their loss of faith in the military family meant being cut-off from all established sources of safety and direction. They become like strangers in a familiar place. It can result from following orders against one's personal or military values for the sake of mission success or from a criticism or an off-handed comment following a critical event. Soldiers can feel as if they have betrayed themselves and their comrades by their inability to just suck it up or get past something that does not make sense to them.

Those people who join the military with histories of bad things from their childhood can be particularly sensitive to future betrayals. Many of them are extremely adept at managing these things on their own—a skill that is probably learned too well. In my observation, when they become distressed, they can move into a 'symptom suppression' mode and will often turn to things within their control—like substances—to calm themselves or resort to anger when they feel threatened. Their mistrust of people tends to sharpen as they move into this self-containment mode.

An intriguing question is whether their efforts to ward-off traumatic experiences were established prior to exposure to military culture or whether the additive effects of their developmental histories and their military training produces these reactions. One indication of early life efforts to suppress emotional reactions to abuse is my observation that many who report early abuse began drinking or using drugs during their adolescence and that their drinking escalated considerably following exposure to military trauma. Likewise, substance abuse and 'checking out' mentally may be used in an alternating pattern on a day-to-day basis to help them maintain emotional control. This is in keeping with research showing that substance abuse and checking out (dissociating) mediates the relationship between childhood abuse and adult PTSD severity.

It may be the case that self-management behaviours are established as a consequence of both developmental issues and military training and only become obvious during subsequent assessment and treatment of military trauma. By that time, these strategies are no longer working to contain their distress. In terms of their interpersonal functioning, their efforts to keep bad feelings away also tends to cut them off from experiencing positive feelings and rewarding social engagement. In turn, this creates challenges for some military people and veterans in fostering or accepting social support and likely interferes with their ability to engage in therapies that require trust and a strong relationship. These men and women often resist therapy efforts aimed at disrupting over-learned containment strategies, and they interpret requirements to stop drinking or to explore emotions as intensely threatening to their sense of self-control. Indeed, veterans with abuse histories often report that they continued to use alcohol or cannabis during their treatment in the military in the interests of emotional self-regulation.

For the caregivers of trauma survivors, given what we know about emotional regulation and early attachment templates, we may not be doing what we think we are doing. Most of us have been trained to believe that trauma work comes down to discussing particular memories and teaching coping skills. This type of intervention seems to work for a substantial number of people—maybe those with a secure attachment—but it does not appear to work for a large number of others. This may reflect a failure of attachment to the caregiver. These particular veteran clients may be so anxious or ambivalent about trusting others that they evoke similar rejecting or controlling reactions from their care providers.

By attending only to techniques and failing to understand and respond to the gravity of attachment relationships, I think we miss the whole point of these encounters. In my experience, helping often comes down to the creation of a good enough secure attachment base between caregivers and veterans where emotionally salient information can be received by the veteran. It is not unusual to hear that the thing that upsets most of them was the feeling of not being cared for by important people. These men and women often fail to appreciate the role of their own behaviours in recreating reactions of neglect from others. In other words, hiding the truth from other members of their units who were genuinely concerned about them often paves the way for eventual medical release.

Fourteen

Solving the Wrong Problem

Below him, flames leap at the ladder like some rabid dog straining at a chain. Dark sooty smoke and heat billow around Jerry's insulated legs and shoulders, curling past his face mask towards the sky.

He is eighty-five feet in the air, aiming the firehose directly into the belly of this familiar foe. Up here, Jerry is in charge and fully focused. Were he to look, he would see the other rubbery-legged guys staring at him in awe from their safe perch on the ground. He is used to being the centre of attention. He is running on adrenaline and numb to all else. The fatigue, he knows, will kick in later. It'll catch up to him along with untold aches and pains sometime after his feet hit the ground once more.

Jerry was a seasoned firefighter who grew up in a military family. The younger of two boys, his father was a sailor, and his mother was a stay-at-home mom. He moved across the country several times as a kid because of his father's work—Nova Scotia to British Columbia, from there to Ontario, and finally back to Nova Scotia.

For as long as he could remember, he was afraid of his father—a strict disciplinarian and a physically active man. Jerry had been a shy kid who liked drawing and music, but his father would criticize him and push him into sports whenever he had the chance. "You need to learn to be a man," he'd say. "Not a fairy."

Of course, his father wanted him to go into the military, and after a short stint with the Cadets, Jerry realized that he had no interest in it though it did serve to get his old man off his back.

> I hated anything to do with the military because they were the ones who had taken my father away, and I got to the point where I did not even want to see him come home anymore. The drinking, partying, and women when he got home was just completely off the chart for any kid to see. Their favourite thing was to give me alcohol as a six-year-old kid and have me sing songs for them. My mother wouldn't say anything. Hell, she'd join them drinking; nobody was in control in that place. What eight-year-old kid thinks about killing himself all the time?

Indeed, Jerry had been tortured by thoughts of suicide for as long as he could remember. When he discovered marijuana at fifteen it was a game changer since it gave him a reprieve from his self-destructive impulses. Jerry was bullied in school because of his size and for always being the new kid, but he never spoke about this at home. He learned to fight as a teenager even though he did not like to fight and did not respond well to violence. When he was seventeen, his girlfriend, the only person who knew him and could relate to him, was killed in a car accident. That's when Jerry just closed down.

What struck me when I first met Jerry was just how similar he was, in many respects, to the soldiers I have seen even though he himself was never more than a cadet and that only for a couple of years. Whether he likes it or not, he has many of the same qualities. He is direct, emotionless, and tough—he talks tough and looks even tougher. He has been a firefighter for nearly twenty years and the physical toll is catching up with him. He has seen many things over the years; death and injury have become nothing special.

Jerry describes one fire he attended:

> I go into this old building that's burning, I have the two-inch hitting everything, knocking down flame as I go. I hit the third floor and I'm approaching a back room when the hose brings up solid. As I hit my radio

to call for more line, I slip and *boom* I'm on the floor... can't see anything it's so black... and then I make out this face that's staring right into my mask... Jeez, I shrieked like a little girl... I've got old 'Two-Face' from the Batman movie lying here next to me. Up I get, and on the radio again, telling them to be careful when they come to the third floor landing because we've got a juicy one just inside the door... he's been here awhile."

Jerry laughs and quickly apologizes:

Hey, I mean, don't get me wrong. I meant no disrespect for the old guy, but you see so much of that stuff that you have to do something so it is not so heavy all the time.

Despite his tough appearance and tattoos, Jerry is also driven by a desire to help people. It seems to provide meaning in his life and a way to prove something to himself. Like many military men, he has a tough time trying to figure out his relationship with his father. His emotions range from anger and disgust to sadness for the way the relationship unfolded.

Diagnostically, there was not much doubt that Jerry met all the criteria for PTSD. Equally true was the fact that he had these problems for many years; starting in his early years, worsened by the traumatic death of his girlfriend, and sealed by the many horrific things he described from the firefighting world.

Jerry's stories were nothing unusual for him. Truth be told, he thought many of them were simply funny as he described scenes of burnt bodies and others in various stages of decay. Contrary to our general thoughts about trauma, the event that drove him to the point of fearing that he was losing his mind was not a negative one. In fact, it was the opposite—he had met a woman and developed strong feelings of affection for her. He told me that this woman reminded him of when he first experienced love as a teenager and that she just seemed too good to be true:

She awoke feelings in me that I buried for decades and, right away, I had this overpowering urge to just crush her. To crush that innocence and kindness and turn her into something that I could deal with. I had to get out of there, man, and now all I can do is cry all the time. I've really lost it this time.

Similar to many military people, for Jerry, emotional vulnerability—affection and tenderness—had become a terrifying place compared to the life of rugged edginess he had honed over many years. As a general observation, when we deny or reject our own emotional needs, we tend to treat other people in this same fashion. Witnessing innocence or vulnerability in others can trigger our own disavowed and unmet needs. There is often a reflexive impulse to snuff out vulnerability in other people or, more often, to simply ignore it by checking out emotionally, rather than face the prospect of our own vulnerability. Over the years, I have had this conversation with many veterans who simply think that they are cold-hearted monsters when it comes to their children—especially their own sons. These men and women can lose the ability to be vulnerable, which means that true intimacy is lost to them.

In my mind, as Jerry described his father's behaviours and experiences in the military, there is a real possibility that his father carried the effects of his military service.

In point of fact, I knew Jerry's father from my own time in the military and knew that he was a crewmember of the ill-fated HMCS *Kootenay*. In 1969, a gear box explosion and fire killed nine members of the crew during full-power trials off the coast of England.

Jerry's father eventually stopped drinking but never broached these issues related to his military service. Jerry is unforgiving:

Now the old man has turned into this holier than thou guy who wants to be my father and save me from the evils of marijuana. Man, we are well past daddy and son days. I mean, those days are long gone.

■ ◣

For military personnel and their families, the costs of packing away these emotionally charged events can come at a tremendous cost to themselves and the people closest to them. Military personnel and first responders of all types are trained to be self-sustaining groups tasked with protecting citizens from the rawness and unpredictability of life.

In a sense, those men and women who willingly take on the role of protecting society by reinforcing notions of safety and control, bear the brunt of it. They protect society from real threats, but in this process they also reduce societal anxiety by taking care of all the things that scare the rest of us—the bogeyman is everywhere, and we need it to be eradicated. Even so, many people are drawn to rubber-necking at roadside accidents, or they remain glued to reports of bad news about other people, which paradoxically re-assures them of their own continued existence.

The problem with this arrangement, however, is that tension—being physically and emotionally aroused as part of the human condition—compels people to also seek it out to feel alive. We seek novel and creative ways to scare ourselves under controlled conditions: terror-producing theme park rides, extreme sports, and risk-taking of all types. The paradox is that we seek out excitement in order to feel alive, but we seem to need unpredictability banished by these other caretakers and watchdogs.

When it comes to the well-publicized plight of first responders, I often wonder if most people would be willing to take the time to talk with a police officer, firefighter, paramedic, or soldier and witness their devastation for having held a seriously injured child in their arms. Probably not. Even if it is a family member or well-known neighbour, most people would prefer to avoid being faced with the rawness of life and the risk of being emotionally upset.

Several months ago, I spoke with a lady following a presentation on trauma. She told me that she was concerned about her younger brother who was in the RCMP, but she did not want to upset him by asking him how he was doing. She also told me that she did not want to hear about his work because it would be too upsetting for her. I think her reaction captures a general fear of being overwhelmed or burdened by having to take time out of our lives for them.

Increasingly, the anxiety managers, the protectors—roles they willingly take on for the rest of us—are separated from their communities and from their biological families. Their workplaces necessarily become their family, and when things go wrong on this front, there is often no place for many of them to turn.

One unfortunate outcome from continual military postings and the requirements of secrecy under legal and organizational agreements is that these men and women cannot ask for help from their biological families or from their communities—there are too many secrets to be kept. We ask the policewoman or the paramedic to keep secret the fact that a neighbour or relative has a serious drug problem or was arrested for abuse of a child, and the list goes on and on. In order to manage this secrecy, first responders also compartmentalize their worlds between work and home, between us and them. I think these relationship patterns contribute to the rise of the 'disintegrated self' among first responders, which in my mind, is directly related to mental disintegration—mental health declines.

Fifteen

Who Am I Now?

Delicate orange and black wings fluttered against a sandy backdrop as a butterfly hovered over a small patch of grass at Mike's feet. He was lost in the moment, reminded of the prairies and of endless summer days spent wandering the fields behind their farm.

Well, if this is my Easter present, I'll take it, he thought.

A second later, the war was back.

"Doc! Grab your shit and saddle up. It's bad, it's real fuckin' bad!"

Minutes later, Mike and the other soldier were racing out of the little compound on their way to the wreckage of a light armoured vehicle blown apart by a roadside bomb just west of Kandahar. As it turned out, they would get no closer than half a click as the quick reaction force (or QRF) busied themselves securing the scene.

Mike could see parts of the LAV III scattered obscenely across the road. Men were running about, guns drawn. Orders being barked into headsets and responses relayed to those at the scene. There were screams too and the *thump-thump-thump* of the inbound choppers. Waiting to get the green light to go in felt like an eternity, knowing he could be helping injured soldiers who were probably dying as he sat there. The helplessness he felt was torture, but there was nothing to do but wait.

He could smell it on the breeze; it was all too familiar these days. Death.

There would be six killed that day and two more seriously injured. In fact, only two would come out of that horror show uninjured. Mike had known them all, had been friends with Donnie, the Sergeant. Some of the other guys had been in to see him just the day before.

So much for Sunday, he thought. *Means absolutely nothing in this place.*

It would go down as the worst single-day loss of life for the Canadian Forces in Afghanistan.

Whenever Mike's thoughts drifted back to these memories, his body would steel itself for the physical and emotional blowback.

Who was I back then? Where are all those people who had looked to me to take care of them? Brothers and sisters. No, they were more like sons and daughters.

He'd been the Doc, and that had meant something specific back then. Now the memories were empty wrappers of what it had held. Still, sometimes it all seemed so real that he could feel the sand under his feet again and the insufferable heat closing in on him.

It was painful to go there and then come back and look around his office.

Who am I here?

All the things that mattered to his co-workers and his wife were a chore for him, a weight to endure. There would never be a chance to go back there again and recapture what had been both the best and worst time of his life. He was not even sure if he would be retained in the military.

Mike had done two stints in the sandbox, the first at his request, the second one by decree—they were short on physician assistants, so he was tagged to go. He wondered if he was affected by his tours. Probably, but he wasn't sure if it was in a good way or bad. Maybe a bit of both. Mike had begun to doubt his medical skills; things that he could once do without a second thought now required focus. The sight of blood had become a problem, and he was second-guessing himself, which was not a good sign. He was a fish out of water here at home. He was gasping for air, and somehow, in ways he could not quite understand, the air he needed was back in the desert under the blazing sun.

If he had only been given a chance, he might have saved some of his guys that day. It replayed endlessly in his head.

∎ ⬛

Military medics are described as a special breed of men and women. They are a combination of soldier and trained caregiver all rolled up in one. They stand beside other soldiers in the thick of things and often risk their own lives to get to those who are injured. They are also a confidante and counsellor at other times because the Doc is their link to being cared for in awful places. They have incredible responsibilities, which also come with a lot of authority.

They are the eyes and ears of the chain of command in terms of troop fitness, and they have the power to say who stays and who should go home. Soldiers trust them and will often tell the Doc things they would never tell anybody else. They get to know the soldiers intimately. This means that PAs (physician assistants) and Medics have additional pressures when it comes to their own mental health.

As Mike said to me many times: "I was the Doc, I couldn't have problems. My job was to take care of *other* people's problems."

Medical and mental health personnel are saddled with a belief that we should not have problems. Somehow our training in detached caring is considered, by our teachers, to be good enough to protect us from the struggles of people around us. Put simply, we are not supposed to have problems, and if we do, it is our responsibility to recognize these problems and to do something to solve them. As Mike and other medical people have repeatedly acknowledged over the years, "We eat our own." This is peculiar, but it may also be similar to the experience of other first-responders. Maybe it is also driven by fear and a need to protect ourselves by secretly blaming other medical people for their problems. We all want to protect ourselves by keeping the bogeyman at bay.

Sixteen

The Past Never Goes Away

The tiny silvery minnows that flashed in the July sun never failed to amuse them. Jordan, the older of the two, would sing strange corrupted versions of "Under the Sea" from *The Little Mermaid* while his little sister would splash around with her yellow foam noodle in an approximation of dancing. The sound of the children giggling as they played in the water re-assured her that there was hope in the world after all. Lost in these moments with them, she forgot herself and her past and simply existed in the here and now.

When Ann left the safety of the lake, however, to go into town to the drugstore or to shop for groceries, one glance from a male and she felt condemned again. She felt simultaneously assessed and accused by the eyes scanning her body, her breasts, the curve of her hips—eyes that never met hers. She felt she could read the furtive thoughts behind these eyes, and they were always the same, filled with simple lust and unspoken privilege. A fleeting encounter in an aisle or parking lot, and she would be reduced to shame and thrown back to her past life in the military.

She didn't mind having her grandchildren for the short weeks of summer since her own daughter seemed to draw little joy from motherhood. Tori was young, of course, and resented being tied down. Ann took partial responsibility there for never holding Tori accountable for anything growing up. She'd carried around a lot of guilt for dragging Tori from base to base when she was little, and in the back of her mind there had always been the vague promise never to treat her as Ann herself had been treated as a girl.

Ann grew up in a family where both her parents drank and fought continually and where she took on the responsibility, early in life, to care for her two younger siblings. This meant making sure they were fed, had clean clothes, and that they went to school. Her father left the family when she was quite young, which was probably for the best since Ann remembered vicious drunken fights between her parents—her mother the one more likely to throw punches. Ann's mother became obscene when she drank and would call each of the children terrible names like *my little bastards* –and– *the animals*.

Her mother's favourite name for Ann was her *little slut*.

One time, she couldn't have been more than sixteen, her mother invited her along to visit a Navy ship in town for a port visit. It did not take very long, once they got there, for Ann to realize that her mother's intention was to parade her in front of these men in exchange for drinks. Ann wanted no part of it and simply walked off the ship and grabbed a taxi home.

Within a year of this, Ann had a steady boyfriend and soon thereafter was a teenaged mother. Dave was local boy and sweet, but he had no prospects whatsoever. They stayed with Dave's parents for a year, while he looked for part-time jobs, but Ann knew she had to do something.

At eighteen, she headed to the local college and worked as a bookkeeper for a short time, but she knew she had to get out of there. When she was accepted into the military, she was overjoyed that they would admit her. She and Dave promised to stay in touch, but she knew better.

Ann joined the military as an attractive single mother and was grateful for the opportunity. Fourteen years later she had achieved the rank of Warrant Officer, a testament to her abilities. For the first several years, she had put up with the relentless catcalls and groping, and sometimes even enjoyed some of the attention. However, this changed with a posting to an Army base where she served as the personal assistant to a senior ranking officer, a posting that required her to go on excursions and road trips with him.

The first trip included a lot of after-hours socializing and a great deal of drinking with the senior officer—more than she was comfortable with. On the second night he made a pass at her, and when she protested, he got angry and made abundantly clear that he expected her to participate in an ongoing sexual relationship starting that night. Drunk and cowed she submitted.

The next morning she was in shock. If he noticed, he didn't seem to care. The sense of betrayal hit her like a hammer blow. This officer was almost twenty years her senior and married with children, and in Ann's mind, he had plucked her from a fourteen-year career and turned her into his private mistress. She knew she had to keep her mouth shut though, or suffer the consequences.

This went on for some time until he was finally posted elsewhere. Her relief at the news was short-lived, for she soon found out that he had briefed his replacement and planned to hand her off as a perk of the position. The first time she met with this new officer he made no secret that he expected to step into all aspects of his predecessor's role. By this time, she had had enough and reported him to her Regimental Sergeant Major for sexual harassment. Her RSM's response shocked her:

> Are you out of your mind bringing this to me? Don't you get it? Hell, I could rape you right here in my office right now and nobody would do a god-damned thing about it.

Despite this reaction, she decided to keep pushing the issue, and her complaint eventually went all the way to the Chief of Defence Staff, the top soldier in the Canadian Armed Forces. When she was called into his office for a private meeting, she was devastated when he offered her a secret deal that also required her to drop her grievance and keep it quiet. She would be released from the military with a good package and offered financial assistance if she chose to go back to school—there would be no talk of consequences for the officers involved. Stunned, Ann made the agreement just to get out of there but regretted it almost instantly.

She made abortive attempts at more schooling but was wracked with anxiety and debilitating physical health problems that kept her from classes for weeks at a time.

Ann also had a secret story that she was never able to tell anybody. Years previously, when she was struggling within the regiment to deal with her complaint, she had been approached by a young soldier with a pregnant wife. He was distressed about his upcoming deployment and approached her for help. To Ann, this soldier was clearly not mentally ready to go overseas. She approached his chain of command and advised his superior about her concerns but was told to simply stay out of it; this was a unit matter. Given her experiences at that point, the last thing she wanted was to face her own RSM again and risk further retaliation if she pushed the issue any further.

The soldier was deployed with the battle group, but barely three weeks later the news arrived that the young soldier had killed himself overseas. Ann was devastated; she had betrayed him and failed him. In Ann's mind, she had done to him what the system had been doing to her, and she could not forgive herself for that failure.

She was diagnosed with severe depression, and behind the scenes, her drinking escalated to become a serious matter in its own right. She was recommended for release medically, even as her complaint progressed through the system—part of the deal she was offered included better terms for her release.

After leaving the military and her failed attempt to attend school, Ann was successful in getting a job working with soldiers and veterans. She worked for several years in efforts to protect young soldiers to the point where her physical and mental health lay in ruins. It was beyond her to stop trying to help these young soldiers even as she struggled with urges to end her own life.

When she approached the CAF mental health system for help, she was told that she could not be traumatized by her military experiences because she had not been in combat. All she remembered from this meeting was hearing: "Well, look at you [referring to her physical appearance] what else did you expect?"

She was devastated but said nothing and never returned—maybe she had brought all of this on herself. Maybe it was her own fault. In subsequent years, she resorted to heavy drinking, sometimes looking for relationships with men at bars, but more often than not wanting to pick fights with them. Since leaving the military, she is afraid in public around men and struggles with the memories of what she did—or more precisely what she didn't do. She blames herself for a great deal. All she wants is "to just be left alone and not have to think about any of that stuff."

■ ⬛

We are taught to be principled people. Codes, values, and traditions direct the energy of the military institution. They are meant to get difficult jobs done in a coordinated way for mission success. It's just that simple. All of the training coupled with aspirations to prove oneself and to be part of something bigger are all powerful motivations. It is a life that is focused on singular tasks amid the mundane parts of in-garrison life that are forgotten in the relative clarity of being deployed.

That does not mean that these missions are easy, it just means that day-to-day living at home and all of the complexities of daily living can be forgotten—wiping up after the dog at home or waiting for the day to end to escape some boring task on-base, these things cease to exist for a while.

But what happens to people when they begin to see that ethical imperatives do not meet their high expectations—when rules do not seem to apply to everyone, when supervisors take a personal dislike to you, when someone else takes credit for your work, when a career manager shelves a promised posting because of a personal favour to someone else, or when a request for compassionate leave is denied because a supervisor is in a foul mood on a given day? These minor hassles also represent betrayals of the value system and codes, even though they are often dismissed. "Suck it up buttercup... get over it."

What happens to people as they strive to meet their part of the bargain when they see these betrayals happen to themselves and to people around them? Some members may work harder to be the good example: "I learned everything I know about being a good leader from putting up with the bad ones all during my career." [Retired CWO]

Others become cynical. "Screw it, let's get this done." Or they become disheartened trying to pretend that the system is really okay but knowing deep down that it is not. These types of conflicts can serve as the backdrop for emotional burnout and depression—being angry or hurt within a system that provides few opportunities to speak out about what is actually going on.

When it comes to managing emotions, James Gross advanced the view that emotion regulation exists on a continuum from conscious, effortful, and controlled regulation to unconscious, effortless, and automatic regulation. He also makes no assumption that any particular emotion is good or bad. Instead, emotional reactions can be understood to be:

> [a] person-situation transaction that compels attention, has particular meaning to an individual, and gives rise to a coordinated yet flexible multisystem response to the ongoing person-situation transaction.[81]

---

81   J.J. Gross, ed., *Handbook of Emotion Regulation*.

In terms of formal research, studies have shown that initiating emotionally expressive behaviour usually increases the sensation of that emotion slightly. Interestingly, decreasing the expression of emotions tends to reduce positive feelings, but in an ironic twist, withholding negative ones tends to increase our level of activation.

Ann's story emphasizes the relationship between emotional management and attachment. When regulating their emotions, avoidant people attempt to block or inhibit emotional states associated with threat. Reactions such as sadness or shame can also activate unwanted attachment related needs, memories, and behaviours among these people. These reactions are often viewed as negative emotions and expressions of weakness or vulnerability and are incompatible with their desire to maintain their self-reliance. They block natural emotional reactions to relationship threats such as rejection, separation, and loss and they try to banish these reactions from their consciousness.

Avoidant people often cannot engage in open problem solving because this frequently requires them to review their life experiences and to admit to frustration or possible defeat. They learn to mistrust the goodness of people in the world, and they often remain anxiously hyperactive by engaging in negative appraisals of benign events. They often hold onto negative beliefs about their ability to manage stress and attribute threats to uncontrollable forces and personal inadequacies. They can also heighten their negative reactions by shifting attention to internal signs of distress.[82] Finally, they may place themselves in threatening situations or make self-defeating decisions and take courses of action that end in failure. Avoidant people also tend to deal with anger by distancing themselves and attributing hostility to the motives of other people. This often contributes to uncontrollable floods of angry feelings and preoccupation with feelings of sadness and despair following conflicts.

So why would people like Ann do things that end up harming them? At a fundamental level, avoidance developed as a protective strategy against future harm. While avoidant strategies help the person to mentally defend themselves, blocking access to emotions also impaired Ann's ability to confront and to cope effectively with other life challenges. This skill deficit is likely to show itself during prolonged, highly demanding, stressful situations when there is a

---

82   Mikulincer and Shaver, "Adult attachment and affect regulation."

requirement to actively confront problems and to seek support from external sources.

In Ann's case, experience told her that men could not be trusted and that women were even worse because they were 'master manipulators'. Among these people then, there can be a particular form of depression resulting from deactivation—shutting down—strategies characterized by perfectionism, self-punishment, and self-criticism. This pattern of silent emotional suffering is also common among other chronically traumatized veterans.

From a biological standpoint, there is substantial evidence to suggest that problems with emotional regulation are associated with problems in the prefrontal-amygdala system.[83] Specifically, the loss of top-down inhibition of the amygdala (two almond-shaped nuclei located in the brain's temporal lobes) has been associated with anxiety and mood disorders. People with PTSD show impairments in a functional network involving the amygdala and anterior cingulate cortex (ACC). Among other functions, the ACC is directly involved with emotions. These deficits in prefrontal functioning have been found for PTSD and major depression and seem to be linked to people with introverted personality traits.

Again, this research also suggests that these neuronal changes are impacted greatly from early life environments by creating permanent changes in GABA (Gamma-Aminobutyric Acid: A neurotransmitter whose principal role is reducing neuronal excitability throughout the nervous system) function in the prefrontal cortex and the amygdala. We can think of GABA as the brakes throughout the nervous system—it serves to keep the system calm.

So once again, we seem to go back to the role of early development in emotional management abilities. When a person is required to restrain strong reactions produced by chronic stress, the number and density of synaptic connections in these areas of the brain tend to decrease. These findings have led researchers to the belief that chronic stress increases the ability of the amygdala to learn and express fear while, at the same time, reducing the ability of the prefrontal cortex to control fear due to impairment of the braking system. This creates a vicious cycle where fear and

83   G.J. Quirk, "Prefrontal-Amygdala interactions in the regulation of fear," in *Handbook of Emotion regulation*, ed. J.J. Gross (New York: Guilford Press, 2007), 27–46.

anxiety lead to more stress, which leads to further dysregulation. Following the reduction of stress, prefrontal changes are reversible, but amygdala changes are not, suggesting that chronic stress may lead to permanent changes in the fear circuitry. This chronic stress seems to have negative effects on the hippocampus (a brain structure related to temporal memory such as time and place) depriving the person of contextual information to recognize when they are in safe environments.

These biological descriptions of trauma reactions and other mental disorders are very interesting, if not fascinating, but we do need to separate fascination from practical usefulness. While the research seems to confirm general biological markers associated with mental distress, it has not been helpful in the development of effective interventions. Even so, biological research has contributed to a belief that complete trauma recovery is not possible; that the best that can be anticipated for patients is situational control of triggers.

Recently, these structural explanations for the effects of trauma have been challenged through the works of a number of researchers, including Porges[84] and LeDoux.[85] These researchers and others provide convincing research and arguments for the dynamic roles of complex interacting neural networks. In essence, there are vast combinations of neural circuitry involved in human experience, making it virtually impossible to explain mental health problems in terms of one or more brain structures. Their work also highlights the roles of social relationships in understanding the role of emotional processing in understanding trauma and its recovery.

We have been led to believe that the absence of positive social interactions early in life, especially from caregivers, sets a low threshold for activating the amygdala in response to potential threats that may persist throughout the lifespan.[86] A central question is whether

84   S. Porges, *The Polyvagal Theory: Neurophysiological Foundations of Emotions, Attachment, Communication, and Self-Regulation* (New York: Norton, 2011).

85   J. LeDoux, *Anxious: Using the Brain to Understand and Treat Fear and Anxiety*, (New York: Viking, 2015).

86   K.N. Ochsner and J.J. Gross, "The neural architecture of emotion regulation," in *Handbook of Emotion Regulation*, ed. J.J. Gross (New York: Guilford Press, 2007), 87–109.

adults can overcome these early response patterns. In terms of treatment outcomes, the evidence suggests that veterans can alter and improve their attachment relationships.

As I am proposing it, within a social-relational understanding of military trauma, critical events often contain elements of a breach in trust and loss of reliance on the larger group—the generalized other—for emotional security. Either because the soldier believes he has failed the group through transgression (shame) for perceived or real failure or because of some grievance (outrage) like losing trust in a leader or the mission, frequently there is a component of struggle reflecting strained interactions with the larger group.

The implications of the work in emotional regulation is that the goal for trauma repair is not reduced to teaching people to express emotion or integrate memories but primarily to help military personnel understand and appreciate that many of their reactions represented efforts to re-establish their social-relational bonds. What I mean by this is that, whether they were showing anger at work or drinking too much, soldiers and veterans may be signalling their needs or their distress to people around them. Since all behaviour is instrumental, by extension, overt behaviour often serves some purpose for the individual above and beyond what they may actually be doing in the moment. The challenge for them, and indeed for the rest of us, is to decipher what they are wanting from the larger group. They may wish to be held accountable, to be acknowledged for their efforts, or simply to have their say about events that have transpired.

More than half of the disorders outlined in DSM-5 involve emotional dysregulation. Notably, depressed patients also show a hyperactivation of the amygdala and a hypoactivation of the left prefrontal cortex. Strikingly, this pattern is opposite to normal people who regulate themselves following reappraisal of negative emotions. For any individual who is engulfed in immediate, acute fear or panic from situations—ranging from public speaking, snakes, or even combat—the use of distraction or suppression of thoughts or feelings are often the fastest antidote.[87] Indeed, several theories of affect control suggest that people can control negative experience temporarily by willfully changing the focus of their

87   G. Loewenstein, "Affective regulation and affective forecasting," in *Handbook of Emotion Regulation*, ed. J.J. Gross (New York: Guilford Press, 2007), 180–203.

attention away from negative thoughts. However, even though suppression of negative thoughts may sometimes be successful, there is considerable research suggesting that it can also have a perverse effect by prolonging and even intensifying an individual's emotional reactions. Indeed, research subjects asked to suppress negative thoughts were found later to be entertaining more negative thoughts. This effect has not been shown for positive thoughts. Namely, that suppressing positive thoughts does not increase their intensity or duration.

Ann's experience with her RSM was a key interaction that seemed to seal her fate in terms of her career and later self-recriminations, and there are a number of aspects of his reaction that are important to discuss. The position of Regimental Sergeant Major—or a ship's Cox'n, usually a person holding the rank of Chief Warrant Officer—carries incredible responsibility and power. These people are often males who are responsible for the tone of interactions and behaviours among all of their subordinates, and often they are answerable only to the unit commanding officer. These men garner much respect and fear and are often classed as characters who are direct but benevolent father figures on the one end of the spectrum or grumpy curmudgeons on the other extreme. The things that the RSM takes seriously and the things he ignores are known among everyone within his unit, regiment, or ship's company.

In Ann's case, the RSM immediately reminded her of her powerlessness and also of the fact that he was not about to take her situation seriously. Whether this was driven by misogyny or his own veiled sexual interest in her is open to speculation, but the resulting message to her was that she was alone and that she would not receive support from anybody. When it came time to stand up for the young soldier, Ann realized that her future within the unit was at risk if she made more trouble.

When I first met Ann, she was wracked with anxiety and it took many months before she trusted me, another male, to tell me about the sexual issues in the military. It took an additional year before she was able to tell me about the young soldier. She asked to participate in a group with male veterans and to tell them her story, including her guilt over the belief that she had betrayed the young soldier. I think she was genuinely shocked to hear these ex-soldiers voice their outrage on her behalf over how she had been treated. Some of them were in disbelief that this could happen in the military while others had heard similar stories during their time in uniform. Ann was amazed to hear and see the genuine level of upset for what had happened to her. Her experience with men had been entirely different all her life, and I am not sure whether she even knew what to do with this knowledge—that all men are not the same.

When it comes to the role of alcohol, it is important to describe its importance to people like Ann, in managing trauma reactions. Often trauma therapists dismiss the use of alcohol under a vague notion of self-medication or as negative coping. Often missed is the role of alcohol in providing traumatized veterans access to emotionality—either positive or negative. In Ann's case, alcohol reduced her anxiety and provided access to anger and aggression towards men without the social expectation that women should be demure and polite.

I am not advocating for the use of alcohol, but it is important to understand that this drug also affects GABA, which may explain the sense of emotional release that is often reported. Often veterans will tell me that, despite the negative outcomes from a drinking binge, they were able to talk about things typically off limits, they cried about bad things from the past, or they voiced their affection for their buddies—and as a result, they somehow feel less pressure emotionally.

Many years ago, I treated a man for chronic depression who had been injured at work. He continually denied being frustrated by the loss of his job and despite several years of not drinking he made no improvements. He ended up on a drinking binge and brandishing a sword outside his home and was arrested. Afterward, he was predictably contrite, but he also talked about experiencing an emotional release from all of the anger he had been holding towards his employer. It may sound unusual, but this drinking episode gave him a way forward, if only from the realization of how truly angry he was over his employer's negligence. He followed through with legal action against the employer.

As a general statement, we need to also understand the role of alcohol following stressful events. During charged events, naturally occurring endorphins release into the bloodstream and help moderate reactions to traumatic events. Following resolution of the event, typically, there is a rapid decline in endorphin levels and an increase in experiences of emotional distress. Under an endorphin compensation hypothesis, people often resort to alcohol/drugs to manage this rebound dysphoria. This physiological reaction is consistent with comments by trauma survivors and patients diagnosed with PTSD that they often use alcohol, heroin, marijuana, benzodiazepines, and other depressant medications to help them to sleep, reduce irritability and hypervigilance, and to control excessive startle.[88]

Other drugs are linked with PTSD numbing symptoms (e.g., prescription depressant medications), and dependence on prescription analgesics is associated with efforts by patients to reduce intrusive memories.[89] Other research with cocaine-addicted patients has shown an absence of links with avoidance symptoms but suggests that they may use the drug to increase positive moods and increase their personal sense of worth. I have heard several accounts that cocaine use may be particularly relevant in the aftermath of the Afghanistan War. As one Warrant told me:

I walked into the junior ranks at six o'clock on a Saturday morning and here were four guys with lines of coke spread out on the table in front of them.

Everyone knows that being ramped up and in adrenaline-mode can be like a mind-altering drug in itself—we feel different, think differently, we are a different, more powerful version of ourselves. Some people do not like the experience, but many soldiers tell me that they thrive on it and seek it out. Often these people are identified as sensation-seekers. In a heightened state of arousal, events unfolding around them don't seem to bother them. The problems start to surface when soldiers start to come down from this state. While they may anticipate returning to a relaxed state, they can feel a paradoxical exhaustion combined with vigilance that can be debilitating. Old memories may start popping into their heads to be reconciled as part of this coming down.

88   P.C. Ouimette, R.H. Moos, and P.J. Brown, "Substance use disorder—posttraumatic stress disorder comorbidity: A survey of treatments and proposed practice guidelines," in *Trauma and substance abuse: Causes, consequences, and treatment of comorbid disorders*, eds. P.C. Ouimette and P.J. Brown (Washington, DC: American Psychological Association, 2003), 91–110.

89   S.H. Stewart and P.J. Conrod, "Psychosocial models of functional associations between posttraumatic stress disorder and substance use disorder," in *Trauma and substance abuse: Causes, consequences, and treatment of comorbid disorders*, eds. P.C. Ouimette and P.J. Brown (Washington, DC: American Psychological Association, 2003), 29–55.

In the absence of an understanding of what is occurring, they become disoriented, which can lead to other behaviours to get out of this state and back to the familiar. I don't know whether there are venues for these men and women to come down safely or whether they have acceptable replacements for adrenaline in order to feel alive. Exposure to warzones and military service are restricted to a very small part of the population; military life is almost completely divorced from the experience of everyday life. In other words, there are few opportunities for the experiences of military people to fit into Canadian society—they are set apart.

Once again, Ann's story is instructive. Towards the end of the group, she told me that she had the phone number of the dead soldier's daughter—now a young woman attending university in the same city where she lived. Her goal was to get up the courage to meet this young woman to talk with her about the father she had never met. I have not heard from Ann in several years, and I truly hope that her experience within the group provided some sense of hope in moving ahead in her life. Ann's case is a reminder that, when people cannot be held accountable because of concerns over the possibility of institutional embarrassment or increased scrutiny, veterans can be left with unfinished business. In this case, like many others, they become cases for other people to manage.

In the end, veteran applications for mental health injuries may serve as a mechanism to manage conflicts and contradictions left-over from the military. For our part, mental health practitioners, in a somewhat sadistic twist, treat symptoms as the problem because we do not hold power or mechanisms to explore the causes of their problems. For instance, the soldier who has a DWI is investigated for an alcohol problem, which is entirely appropriate. However, the fact that he did not drink until returning from a deployment where his rules of engagement meant that he was forced to watch people being butchered becomes a coincidental background detail. It is simply too big an issue for clinicians to consider addressing. A young Air Force Private is released because of chronic anxiety and stomach problems, but the fact that he was tasked with retrieving body parts of a downed pilot was not considered in understanding his complaints. As Parker argued, by only focussing on symptoms, clinicians may end up simply validating and reinforcing mental health stereotypes and the status quo.

When it comes to any employee, I am not sure of the responses we ought to expect from organizations. Should organizations make efforts to understand the relationships between mental health declines among employees and specific workplace practices and expectations? I am not sure of the answer, but in any case, there may be a requirement for organizations to act more responsibly when it comes to the processes of ending an employee's career. I think of the example of a middle manager of a large local utility undergoing restructuring some years ago.

He was told that he was being considered for promotion to senior management and given the task of terminating the employment of many of the people in his department. Upon completion of his work, he was summoned to a meeting with a senior manager. He assumed that the decision had been made regarding his promotion. He entered the meeting and five minutes later was handed an envelope signalling his termination and directed to leave with two security guards. He was escorted to his office to pack a small box, ushered out of the building, and handed a business card to contact the company's counselling program.

When I saw him two days later he was visibly in shock and could not fathom that this could have happened.

I thought I was on the team, but all the while I was to be thrown out so that all the bad feelings about the terminations went out the door with me.

The things that are done by organizations in the final days of an employee's career can have devastating and lasting effects. This sense of betrayal and disorientation also applies to many of the veterans who I have come to know.

When it comes to soldiers who are heading for medical release, the usual way to intervene is to 'stabilize' them through medication, teach them various relaxation skills, and then have them talk in great detail about specific events repeatedly until these events lose their power to produce flashbacks or anxiety. In some cases, technology is used to 'expose' them to specific images and events from combat, and these therapies can be very helpful.

As in Ann's case, there is often another required step that seldom occurs. Many of them want to find ways to reconcile what has happened, to be forgiven for some terrible act or failure on their part, or to hold specific people accountable for mistreating them. They want to find a way to redeem themselves among their peers. For some, it was a longing to return to Afghanistan to "get it right this time" or to finally visit the grave of a long-dead buddy half way across the country. But others feel doomed precisely because they cannot find an action to take to recover their self-image and self-respect.

In another case, I met with a female military member for drinking problems who was struggling because of ongoing harassment from her supervisor. She had been referred to me because she had made a suicide attempt. She told me that at work her supervisor would order her to his office every other day and, with the door closed, would lecture and berate her for hours about military protocols, aspects of her job duties, and tirades about anything that he deemed to be military-related.

In her mind, this man's only intention was to break her down mentally. This small-statured and pleasant woman was also stronger than she realized. She had learned it growing up in a home where she had little choice but to look out for her younger sisters. Because of her mother's drinking, even as a young girl she would buy the groceries, prepare meals, and even manage the money in the house, shouldering tremendous responsibilities.

Whether this woman's supervisor simply did not like women or whether he saw her strength as a challenge to his authority, I will never know. But the fact that she eventually had to release medically from the military, in her mind, meant that he had won. She was intensely angry over her mistreatment, but in her workplace, there was no place to voice her outrage. She attempted to file a Human Rights complaint, which was denied because she had not attempted mediation with this supervisor. For her, if she embarrassed him and was then left to work with him again, his intent to harm her would only have become worse.

This inability to be able to express intensely experienced emotional states in response to stressful things is very much related to the issues that get thrown under the umbrella of chronic post-traumatic stress reactions. There need to be times and places to allow soldiers to lower their guards, but teaching these skills to alpha-minded people would not be easy.

This applies equally to female soldiers and veterans. So when one asks why these women would not react to protect themselves from their supervisors, the quick answer is that they had learned self-reliance from an early age. Their struggle with self-worth was also evident as part of their acceptance of mistreatment. Initially, I don't think either of them saw this treatment as a betrayal of trust because this was all that they had experienced from people in authority. In both cases, their fathers had been submissive men who did not intervene to help them, and in one case the father simply abandoned the family. In Ann's case, when she was unable to help the young soldier because she needed to protect herself, this served as the breaking point because she had done the unthinkable—betrayed another powerless subordinate in the interest of self-protection. She was faced with a terrible dilemma.

I think often about the circumstances that served as a set-up for Ann to view maltreatment as somehow acceptable. The situation probably revolves around her loyalty and gratitude to the military for 'doing me a favour' by providing financial stability for her and her young child. It may seem mind-boggling to readers that Ann still regards the military as her family and that she continues to hold it in high regard despite the things that were done to her by 'bad apples'.

As others have said, these people have to be rooted out of the military just as they have to be rooted out of many other organizations. Under-assertive men or women who are willing to please others can by targeted by predators. These abusive people, usually men, exist in almost every organization, and they can thrive within hyper-masculinized cultures like the military and other first response organizations.

One may ask how bright young men and women can go along with mistreatment. First of all, most of them don't even see it coming. Betrayal and breach of trust by superiors can be rationalized as special relationships because of the attention and even protections that are provided. For those people who resist, they often can feel unsupported and fear that the organization will rally behind the perpetrators. Careers can simply vanish for those who speak up or rock the boat. In any group, the conspiracy of shared denial and silence can serve to perpetuate an existing culture, while well-meaning people play carefully around the edges—remember Col. Williams.

Seventeen

I Was Someone

Ben stirs, finally, from a dead sleep. When he forces his eyes open, the mute daylight in the room checks them. He squints at the clock radio. It's 11:25. Outside somewhere is the sound of a distant car door closing then the chirp of a car alarm being set. A dog barking. The house is quiet, the bedroom is still as a tomb, and filled with the smells of stale sweat and the cooking wine he choked back the night before. *Fuck it*, he thinks. And closes his eyes again.

At some point thereafter he finds himself in the cockpit of a Lockheed CP-140 Aurora, gliding over the Arctic ice fields from CFB Greenwood. He is at peace and feels connected to the plane through the throttle. The 14 Wing Greenwood motto drifts through his head: *Operate As One*. In a moment of semi-lucidity, he takes a deep ragged breath. "This used to be me," he says to the empty co-pilot's chair and stares at the horizon.

His heart is racing when he wakes. This time, when he opens his eyes, it is 1:42, and he tells himself that he should get up and shower before the others get home. He realizes he doesn't know what day it is, only that it must be a weekday. It is hard to move. Ben is not sure he has the energy to get out of bed let alone face what is left of another day. The sour taste in his mouth reminds him that he threw away ten years of sobriety the night before in a desperate attempt, perhaps, to remember what it felt like to enjoy something.

Retired Captain Ben Samson is thirty-six. He is married and father to a ten-year-old son with whom he has a strained relationship as of late. He served as a Navigator in the Air Force for sixteen years before being medically released in 2004 because of mental health issues. He had deployed on missions from North America to the Arctic and in and out of Western and Eastern Europe during Canada's missions during the 1990s. He loved flying and still missed it terribly.

His career had been going great when he met Angie. They fell in love, married in 1997, and a year later Jonah was born. Like any new father, he was proud but at the same time unsettled by this new responsibility. It really seemed to mess with him, and did not improve over the next six months. Ben could not hold baby Jonah without getting anxious; he was afraid that he would screw up something. He wondered if all new fathers felt this way.

He decided that he needed to talk to someone. He and Angie had already seen the base social worker to talk about the stresses of parenthood, which seemed to help her but not him. Ben was referred to a psychologist, and two visits later he was diagnosed with depression and placed on medication by a psychiatrist and immediately lost his flight status—standard flying regulations. The pills seemed to make it harder to focus, his sleep was off, and he quickly became irritable. He was posted to an administrative job on the base.

The therapy with the psychologist started off with stress management skills but quickly focused on his relationship with his own father, which continued for another year. Ben learned that his father's hot temper and criticism of him growing up had a lot to do with his fears of taking on the responsibility of fatherhood. Naturally enough, he did not want to harm his own son this way.

The therapy seemed to be helping; he and Angie were talking about things, and he felt much better around his son. He was coming to the end of a six-month medical category, which signalled a meeting with the return-to-work coordinator. At the meeting, the coordinator told Ben that it would be a good idea to ease back into operational duties—but nothing too stressful. Ben agreed, but was surprised when he received a message posting him to the Operations Centre as the CO's right-hand man.

So much for non-stressful—the centre was in full swing managing routine operations and the additional challenges from the Swissair Disaster even before the tragedy of 9/11. Twelve- and four-teen-hour days were the norm. There were many nights that Ben was simply too exhausted for the two-hour drive home. He would curl up on an office sofa or bunk down in transient quarters on the base. Ben still managed to make some of his medical appointments and increasingly told his therapist that the work pressures were getting to him. She was not convinced and suggested that work was not the problem. He deferred to her. After all, what did he know about this stuff? The real problem in her mind stemmed from the issues they had been discussing about Ben's childhood. Three months later, he was summoned to a meeting with his commanding officer.

Years later he is glassy eyed when he recalls:

> I was fired for being too abrasive. I thought I had been doing a great job in meeting all our timelines, but a couple of people had made complaints about me. That day just killed me inside.

Ben continued seeing his psychologist for an additional two years, but it did not seem to help. In fact, he felt more depressed and humiliated for having been removed from his job, but as usual, all of his problems were laid squarely on his childhood insecurities. Predictably, he received a notification that he would be released medically because of chronic depression.

> They did not even try to find me another job because they were intent on getting rid of me. I was covered by the military's insurance program for two years, but after that I was on my own. Those two years were merciless. I was a worthless failure. I couldn't even be bothered with trying to find work. The best I could do was to volunteer at a shelter one morning per week.

■ ◗

I first met Ben in 2008. By this time, he had put on an additional forty pounds and had no interest in moving ahead with work or career. He picked up with me where he had left of with the psychologist from the military hospital by talking about his preservice years and his problems relating to his son and his wife. I eventually began asking him about the effects of being dismissed from the Ops Centre.

Ben's answer was immediate:

It tore the guts out of me. This was all I had ever done, and they were not interested in giving me another chance, so it was out the door for me.

He went on to tell me that, even though he had been released medically, his application to Veterans Affairs Canada for a service-related mental health issue was denied. The rationale given to him was that all of his medical records indicated personal and preservice issues. I discussed with him whether he had been under any medical restrictions when he was posted to the Ops Centre given that, at the time, he was under the care of a psychiatrist and psychologist on the base.

Ben told me that his medical category specifically said that he was to be employed in a non-stressful setting with ready access to medical supports. Ben and I re-applied to VAC, outlining how the posting had worsened his mental health issues and, in fact, that the CAF had contravened its own rules by overriding medical directives. Ben was eventually awarded coverage by VAC enabling him access to vocational rehabilitation and some financial support. He went on to complete a therapy program with me and entered into marital counselling close to his home. He also re-engaged in a relationship with his father, became involved with an operational stress peer support program, and began working on race cars—a childhood passion.

This story emphasizes several important issues. The first is the propensity for mental health clinicians working with military personnel to portray their problems exclusively as personal issues. This is consistent with our training, but it also points to reluctance on the part of clinicians to engage the workplace directly because of dual relationships with the employer. I think this situation contributes to two important outcomes.

First of all, clients are often held solely responsible for their problems, so their stories about their workplaces are often discounted. Secondly, this individual patient focus precludes any information, even at the patient's request, from going back to their workplaces. As far as supervisors are led to believe then, mental health has nothing to do with workplace expectations or relationships. They remain in the dark. I know many supervisors who would want to know this information and would engage in reasonable and sometimes extraordinary efforts to resolve these matters within their units. Instead, clients such as Ben are left with the belief that their units did not care while, in point of fact, unit personnel often don't know why these members are so bitter and why their careers come to an end—it remains a secret.

Eighteen

Frozen in Time

It was to be another day wandering the streets. It felt important to get out. It was easier to keep moving. The illusion of direction. The casual distraction of traffic on the streets, the busy intersections, the nameless faces of people rushing past him, it was a world he moved through like a ghost. Haunting it perhaps but never really touching it. Not that Jake actually longed for its touch. He didn't. None of it mattered to him at all. The goal today was to find a coffee shop and try to sit there for ten minutes without heading back to hide in his apartment—the bunker. Avoid feeling caged. Bleed off as much energy and aggression through the soles of his shoes as possible each day. That was the trick. Become just substantial enough to order a cup of coffee or buy a pack of smokes and then evaporate again.

Maintaining invisibility had its drawbacks at times—and some days were easier than others—but it helped Jake avoid conversations with strangers, which was important. Conversations had a way of spinning out of control without warning.

He might blurt it out: "To hell with Canada" or "People like you are hypocrites preoccupied only with what you can get from other people" or "The military preys on any sheep dumb enough to sign up."

Years earlier, Jake had made the mistake of telling some of his Airborne buddies that, "It was all a crock of shit. They duped us, man, relying on loyalty they didn't deserve." They had not reacted well and had turned their backs on him.

Jake grew up the oldest son of professional parents. As a teenager, he was unprepared to make career decisions, and after a year at university, he dropped out and joined the military. From the start, he recalled knowing it was all a game and that he really did not take basic training very seriously. This all seemed to change when he was accepted for training with the Airborne. There, he learned the value of pride and honour and all the things that went with being part of the Canadian Airborne Regiment. He recalled the adrenaline rush when they were called up for deployment to Somalia in 1992, even though at the time they didn't believe they were going.

We went though, and even after several weeks on the ground, we were still joking about it. Two guys would meet, shake their heads, and put big dumb expressions on their faces. "Gosh you don't think they're really going to send us to Africa, do ya?"

We were dumb kids, but we soon realized we were stuck in this stinking shithole of a country run by warlords, and there was nothing we could do. The leadership was non-existent, and the things that were reported in the media really did happen but so did a lot of other stuff.

Man, Mefloquine Mondays[90] were just surreal, and twenty years later it's like I don't know if I was even there. Like maybe I just dreamt it all. We would get jacked up by our NCOs for orders that they had not given, and they were just as messed up as we were.

I think about all the pride and chest swelling from those days and combine that with the shame and disgrace when we returned to Canada. Man, I can't get

90   Mefloquine is an anti-malaria drug with known psychiatric side effects including nightmares, visual and auditory hallucinations, anxiety, depression, and suicidal ideations. When taken for prevention (as opposed to treatment) of malaria, a dose of Mefloquine is taken weekly. The term Mefloquine Mondays refers to the day of the week the dose was administered. Soldiers often reported psychiatric side effects around their weekly dose.

past it. Canada turned its back on us and never even asked how we were, so screw Canada and this so-called brotherhood. I was betrayed by the pride I allowed myself to feel and betrayed by this whole goddamned country. So don't ask me why I can't move forward with my life. Why should I ever believe in anything or anybody ever again?

Y'know, when I got home, I did not even speak to my parents. I just hit the road and ended up on the streets on the West Coast, doing whatever came my way and just vanishing from society. It was twenty years ago, and it may as well have been yesterday that I got off that plane.

We have rejected all those young men we sent to Somalia on our behalf. We actively forgot about them and saddled them with disgrace to absolve ourselves of the lack of preparedness for that mission. Jake's story reminds me that recovery from betrayal is an extremely difficult journey, and many veterans choose to not make efforts in this regard. For those who do begin this work to repair themselves, it can come down to a corrective experience with other veterans where trust can be regained. This is much harder than it may seem on the surface, and in many cases there is no final triumphant victory. The best that Jake can do is to come to terms with the things he did while overseas; the rest is probably out of his control. I don't believe he will ever forgive the military or the country for that matter. In his view, we are nothing more than hypocrites.

They filled our heads with this idealistic horse shit and then used it against us to keep us from speaking up when we got home, so don't tell me about brotherhood.

When it comes to some forms of trauma, social workers had a wonderful strategy of utilizing genograms (written diagrams outlining extended family histories) to understand the full context of an identified patient's concerns. They would also consider the possibility that the patient could be manifesting distress as a signal of a systemic problem within the family. In effect, patients may unwittingly take on the larger family problem through their own reactions.

For example, the nine-year-old who starts getting into trouble at school may be serving as a scapegoat by drawing attention from his parent's problems because he fears that they may be divorcing. They may even unite as a couple again when they focus on him. I believe that this 'systems approach' has implications for understanding trauma reactions generally, and it may even have implications for understanding military trauma. Members may be taking on distress or larger organizational problems that cannot be spoken or confronted directly within the system.

There is ample evidence that our veterans from Somalia still quietly carry our national shame over that mission. In the end, there are few places for open dissent in a system preoccupied with the notion of team players. What purpose does a mentally ill soldier serve to his unit? How does it serve him to remain silent and to continue to carry on with stoic toughness? In order to better understand military mental health, I think we should be considering the answers to these questions along with the standard ones.

The fact is tough men and women can be traumatized and experience things like PTSD whether or not they experienced developmental abuse. Even so, there is a risk that researchers and policymakers will latch onto a simplistic and incoherent belief that childhood abuse causes adult PTSD because of some fundamental weakness.

I think the opposite—they are too tough when it comes to their emotional lives! When tough soldiers or first responders come forward with mental health issues, they seem to have a much harder time trusting people if they experienced earlier betrayal and neglect. They have a harder time recognizing and valuing their inner emotions and are continually tempted to ignore other people and instead resort back to their early coping skills—self-reliance. Learning to trust someone to help them and to lower their emotional guards are the toughest challenges most of them will face. They have all the skills of being tough but have not learned the skill of being vulnerable—another basic part of the human condition. If we are to talk about developmental abuse and military mental health issues, we would likely be better served by discussing the legacy of developmental abuse as a skill deficit and not as a fundamental weakness.

An example of what veterans tell me: "I am trapped behind the mask, but I am something entirely different inside. I am alone, cut-off, and just tired of having to be ready for anything."

When men and women can find a place, often with their peers—the people who matter—they can learn to trust again and to lower their guards, and the real miracle I often get to witness is that they start to come back to life. This is not easy work for them, and it is work, because everyone fears being turned into bowls of mush. The lesson to them is that to be a strong man or woman means learning the balance of knowing when to draw on the tough side—the protector—and when to ask for support from others and to allow their vulnerable, human qualities to show.

In the end, there is such a thing as being worn down by being too tough, and this may be at the heart of what drives operational stress and PTSD. It can be the result of successfully internalizing the values of the larger military group and then judging themselves because of a failure to meet these expected standards and values. After all, this is the whole premise of socialization—the process of becoming accepted members of the social group. In military terms, this amounts to internalizing military values as part of indoctrination into the culture.

Along with values of strength, integrity, and dependability, the golden rule is to not stand out—to fit in with everybody else. A member's sense of competence and self-respect hinges on the views of other members of the group. The risk of being shamed in military circles is ever-present because it serves as a powerful guarantor of uniformity. The risks range from possible embarrassment or ridicule in front of one's peers to being singled out by superiors whose responsibility it is to root out suspected weak members. So soldiers face a significant dilemma—if they come forward and admit problems, they risk being treated as something less than a real soldier.

Recently, military personnel have been given the message that ignoring their problems can make them worse, which is generally quite true. There is much to be said for not judging one's reactions to stressful situations and taking actions to resolve them. However, the notion of self-stigma carries the implication that a member's self-judgment is independent of military culture and values and that it represents a failure by them to take responsibility to solve their mental health issues. Sure, ultimately we each have responsibility for our health generally, including our mental health, but a soldier's mental health is greatly influenced by group acceptance and shared values—what others think matters tremendously. Adapt, endure, overcome is a powerful mantra that is reinforced every day. It is in direct opposition to admitting to limitations and shortcomings.

How are military members to reconcile these competing messages since they cannot both be true? The reaction by members is often to judge themselves harshly or simply ignore signs of mental distress. This silence also serves to exclude from conversation possible impacts of the organizational culture upon their mental health. Everyone knows of a horror story from one of their buddies: being left off a deployment, struggles to find adequate care, premature end of careers, and protracted disputes for pension and other supports following release. The centrality of military values and the occurrence of these other issues need to be discussed openly if we are intent on encouraging people to come forward.

What if part of the solution to the issue of 'self-stigma' meant challenging core military values around uniformity, strength, and independence? I am not sure if anybody would or should tamper with the fabric of the institution, but I don't think we can avoid the fact that it also needs to be part of the discussion on military mental health. For those who decide to come forward for assistance, solutions and possible ramifications need to be spelled out if there are to be safe alternatives to private suffering. As it stands, there are incredible risks to adopted military values, self-image, and livelihood for those members who step forward and self-identify.

There needs to be parallel assurances that these risks will be minimized and that these members will be protected. Otherwise, introducing the idea of self-stigma to any first-responder group runs the risk of being just another weight for them to carry—not only do they have mental health problems, but they may also be the cause of their own distress. The functioning of organizations and the day-to-day expectations placed on these men and women are not discussed.

Part of the problem in Canada and elsewhere is the reluctance to explore social factors that may challenge institutional priorities and accepted ways of doing business as usual. My question is always the same: What if Canadians had little choice but to think seriously about the responsibilities and expectations placed on 'heroes and protectors'—the terrible things they face every day while ordinary people remain oblivious to the harsher realities of life? Maybe part of the problem is that these expectations are simply too high in the end.

Anyone who has worked with military or first-responders knows that these are a group of men and women who are exquisitely trained to maintain personal control in difficult situations. They are also trained to take charge of situations where people are disoriented or in immediate need of help: "We see them on the worst day of their lives." They know how to be in-charge when things go bad. What happens when these people are directed to get help for personal problems? Well, first of all, they usually do not like the idea that they have some personal weakness, and secondly, they recoil at the idea of having to rely on strangers to help them. The urge to increase control behaviours is very difficult to resist since this is the training paradigm for many people—try harder, focus more, lock it down. The fundamental concern among veterans is that, if they give up control, they will fall apart, and nobody will able to help hold them together. I believe this to be the fundamental unspoken dance in therapy with traumatized veterans.

For all our efforts since the nineties to understand 'mental disease' by looking at the functioning of the brain, we continue to see high rates of mental health problems and ongoing reports of suicide. I think about the possibility that mental distress reflects culturally accepted ways of manifesting and signalling one's problems. In terms of military veterans, PTSD has become the accepted formula and label for the rest of us to validate what has been asked of these men and women. And it is a way for the military bureaucracy to honourably—and some might argue *conveniently*—discharge these members from its ranks. These ways of expressing-experiencing upset are highly coordinated with our societal values and mores and hence may be considered a social behaviour.

As I have suggested earlier, the notion of the quietly suffering, mentally wounded veteran is reinforced socially, which may serve multiple constituents. The problem is that there is an incredible downside to the veteran in terms of the risks of permanent victimhood. We can easily understand the prototypical reactions to traumatic events that can last days to weeks to resolve, but we are not sure what to make of delayed onset/chronic PTSD. When I think about these questions, unresolved outrage, guilt, shame, and suppressed emotions come to mind as likely candidates for consideration. I think we might have a much harder time facing the things that veterans might have to say about their deployments and missions overseas on behalf of the country.

When it comes to addiction among traumatized first responders, a striking observation is that, in the vast majority of cases, the onset of addiction was precipitated by some major life event, often from their early life. Sometimes, these events were outright sexual or physical abuse, but more often they experienced mental abuse and neglect. In nearly every case, these experiences occurred before they started regular use of alcohol or drugs.

When it comes to treating military veterans for addiction and PTSD, the same has been true. In virtually every case, there was something about the theme of the operational injury that harkened back to some major event that had never been resolved. For some people, events that occur in the military can be a form of retraumatization. I think about one Royal Canadian Regiment veteran who, at twelve years old, watched his sixteen-year-old brother shoot himself in the stomach. The brother had made a failed attempt earlier in the evening to kill their father—a belligerent and abusive drinker. Now, put him in Somalia where he was fired upon in a chaotic ambush, and he has never been able to get past it. He drinks and uses cannabis daily, and he is consumed by the guilt over the fact that, if he had ordered another type of vehicle for the deployment, this event would not have happened. Of course, his lingering reactions also go right back to the night of the shooting where he was not safe but believed it had been his responsibility to manage the conflict between his father and his brother. The truth is that in both situations there was nobody to protect him.

The event from earlier in his life had never been discussed because, firstly, the family had lied to the police saying it was an accidental discharge from cleaning the weapon. His father's continued drinking meant that nobody could talk about the circumstances, and the fact that the brother survived but moved out and distanced himself from the family left it as an unspoken secret for decades. In Somalia, this soldier's superior officer criticized him for ordering the wrong type of vehicle, but in reality, this had nothing to do with the lack of preparedness that resulted in an ambush. Alternatively, it was likely the officer's way of managing frustrations over the mission itself.

Let's look at the case of a veteran of Bosnia: "I watched as people were slaughtered and I did nothing."

At the heart of many traumas is an internal irreconcilable conflict—a conflict based in values between what did happen and what *should* have happened. Lost in the gap is often the mental playground of *what if*, which drives many instances of lingering torment. Soldiers react by being overwhelmed mentally or shifting to not caring in order to get through a tough mission. Afterwards, they often replay these events and judge their coldness when they return home. As I have suggested before, it is only when people have reached some level of stability and safety that their moral compass switches back on and events begin to sink home. When people come down from a heightened adrenaline state and the singular focus of deployments, they are often lost, which is sometimes equated to reverse culture shock. Close relationships with their buddies while they were away begin to loosen as each person begins to go their own way in terms of courses, postings, or even release.

The fact that many military members who come forward for operational stress have troubled development does not mean that this history created the military injury. There is no evidence that these people would have gone on to develop PTSD in an otherwise normal life; I am not aware of research on this topic. In fact, it may be the case that the military environment itself ends up recreating the very dynamics around betrayal and powerlessness that these members hoped to avoid by joining the military in the first place. Military screening focuses primarily on physical health and cognitive abilities and aptitudes. Recruiters are tasked with filling occupational quotas, and there is usually a demand to have them filled. So, it seems to me that the adage of "you buy it, you own it, you break it, and it is your responsibility to fix it" applies equally to our military.

The fact that the military has not conducted comprehensive mental assessments as part of the selection process does not reduce its responsibility for not doing so in the first place, especially if the plan is to attribute military mental health problems to pre-existing injuries. Admittedly, I have come back to this point several times because it is simply too enticing for bureaucrats and politicians to use preservice factors in their attempts to reduce governmental liability. If we are to hold out the promise of a caring and respectful family, then the institution has to be judged by how it behaves and how it actually responds in the majority of cases.

At a fundamental level, in order to make room for a military identity, nothing less than a displacement of the self is needed. It often necessitates a rejection of prior social values and mores. The sense of one's personal life and relationships outside the military and those values that are at odds with the group have to be placed in the background. Military roles often require a focus on the external environment, which may also require a rejection of one's internal mental life. So if the process of becoming a military member means accommodating aspects of the group within the new constitution of the self, in reality we cannot talk about the mental health of any member without also talking about this group. In one sense they are one and the same—a soldier is a representation of the collective group and the essence of the group can be observed in any soldier. The sum of its values, experience, expectations is housed in each person, and it has to be this way. This ensures that the history, values, and culture of the military continue because people die, they leave, or they are promoted to other positions.

Leave no one behind. Anyone who wears a uniform knows the importance of this mantra. The test extends beyond deployments and the battlefield; I believe that the real test happens back home when a military brother or sister is physically or mentally injured. The most hurtful thing that veterans talk about is the feeling of being abandoned when they were down. This is often laid squarely on the chain of command and the system. And admittedly sometimes that is the case, but more often what seems to really hurt them is that those they served alongside and those they would have given their lives for, turn their backs on them. Maybe, it is because their buddies are scared by words like PTSD or depression or they are caught up in their own stuff, living by the golden rule of 'suck it up' or afraid that an OSI might be contagious.

In an environment that is focused on suspected weakness, members often treat their friends like the system treats them. They may look for problems or weakness in their friends because they cannot accept the possibility of their own fragility as human beings. Military people believe in the myth of invincibility; it allows them to do unimaginable things without a second thought, but in the end, it is simply a myth. Unfortunately, when members cannot accept their own vulnerabilities, they usually reject or judge these things in others. The point is that injured members often feel alone in a supposed brotherhood and the reaction of simply leaving friends to the system and washing their hands is not enough. Systems are systems, no matter where they exist—they can be sterile and lonely places.

As one Navy vet put it:

> **I remember being on a training course when my sister-in-law was killed in a car accident. My request for a one-day compassionate leave to attend the funeral with my wife was denied. I remember the looks from the other guys—everyone knows that look that makes you feel like an ant on the floor. One guy walked up to me, gave me a big bear hug and whispered: "I know it's a tough day for you, man." That made all the difference because I was not alone or a weirdo because I was upset that someone close to me had died.**

These gestures can make all the difference. Conversely, in the increasingly professionalized world of soldiering, elements of separation and social isolation from the broader society can take root within the military.

A common reaction among military veterans is the incredible degree of self-criticism they have for being released medically. They judge themselves without mercy, and they may also blame specific people for giving them a hard time or not supporting them. If they are sad or upset, they use words like self-pity to describe their experience—*I am just whining, I need to get a grip.* Is it possible to hold unconditional positive regard for oneself and still be a responsible person?

For Dr. Kristin Neff:

> ... having compassion for oneself is really no different than having compassion for others. To have compassion for others we must notice that they are suffering. Second, compassion involves feeling moved by another person's suffering so that we respond to their pain or we suffer with their distress. When this occurs, people feel warmth, caring, and the desire to help a suffering person. Having compassion also means offering understanding or kindness to others when they fail or make mistakes, rather than judging them harshly. Finally, when we feel compassion for another, rather than pity, it means that we realize that suffering, failure, and imperfection are part of the shared human experience. Self-compassion means acting the same way towards oneself when we are having a difficult time. Instead of just sucking it up, the challenge is to simply acknowledge distress without judgment. Perhaps most importantly, having compassion for oneself means that we honour and accept our humanness.[91]

---

91   Neff, K. [http://self-compassion.org/
the-three-elements-of-self-compassion-2/].

Alternatively, when people feel self-pity, they become immersed in their own problems and forget that others have similar problems. They ignore their connection with others and instead feel that they are the only ones in the world who are suffering. Self-pity tends to be self-consuming and focused on the extent of personal suffering.

I believe strongly that the military context and the nature of social interactions need to be included in our understanding of operational stress injuries. Attention to the social-relational environment could improve perceptions of safety to enable members to make better decisions regarding mental distress. This includes a willingness to do the things necessary to put their careers back on track or deciding to end their careers and move on. Several months ago, I met with a military veteran in his mid-sixties who just wanted to have a coffee. He told me that, after thirty-one years of service, he remembered the day fifteen years previously when he walked out the main gate for the last time and the panic he felt because he had absolutely no idea of what to do with himself. He was not released for medical problems, even though his body bears the wear and tear of physical injuries of a lifetime in uniform. He became involved as a volunteer firefighter, volunteered with the police and cadets, and continues to work as a Commissionaire:

I just have to be around uniforms, otherwise I just feel scared all the time; I don't know what's wrong with me.

I suppose this man could be diagnosed with a chronic adjustment disorder or a generalized anxiety problem. For those who remember the depiction of the Borg from the Star Trek television series, they may recall the portrayal of being in the collective—logical, somehow inhuman and practical in carrying out their orders, being of one mind and the utter disorientation and inability to act when they were separated from the larger organization. The movie scenes also showed the painstaking work by other people trying to humanize them once again. I think that this man is caught somewhere between his past in the military and his life as a civilian.

An inherent flaw in attempts to reduce issues of mental health to the behaviour of patients is that the approach excludes the context in which problems develop in the first place. From basic training onward, soldiers are steeped in high-minded codes of conduct, discipline, ethical imperatives, and a view of the military as an organization larger than life. The reality is often very different, however, for many people. The same organization can be coldly logical and arbitrary. Rules can be bent to benefit people who are liked, and these same rules can be used strategically to root out suspected problems. Reduction of possible systemic and organizational culture factors to genetics, biology, or preservice history removes from consideration the structure of the organization in the development of soldier distress and removes from discussion the role of leadership in causing or potentially preventing these issues from developing in the first place.

Otherwise, apart from coordinated and combined efforts by the military and veterans affairs systems, the best thing we can offer is to help reconnect these men and women so that they can face their losses, exorcise their demons, and back each other as they have been trained to do. Through this process, they can support one another in finding the way forward. Sometimes, the way forward for self-repair (reclaiming self-respect and dignity) may involve official grievances, litigation over mistreatment, involvement of appropriate ombudsmen, or opportunities to re-enter military deployments to finish the job. Each of them has a story to tell; stories which can be incredibly personal and painful and at the same time containing themes that are common to many veterans. Shared values, regrets, unmet goals, sadness, and hopes are universally shared by many of these men and women.

Military culture has been described as institutionalized masculinity that prizes values such as self-reliance, emotional inexpression and self-control, and risk-taking. These values and the clearly defined pathway to masculine identity may be particularly attractive to people who have experienced powerlessness and lack of purpose earlier in life. It is probable that the stigma around PTSD will likely continue within first responder populations until a different masculinity is adopted within the broader social context.

An important question is whether reactions to traumatic exposures and the reluctance to seek/accept help represent the member's adherence to acquired masculine values, or whether the aftermath of developmental abuse predicts their response to treatment. To summarize, a better understanding of the factors that challenge the course of treatment, including mistrust of care providers, lack of engagement, and emotional avoidance may help improve the lives of those members who struggle with mental distress.

Epilogue

We are confronted daily by the plight of men and women who have served Canada in uniform over the past twenty-five years. Many of their stories have been well publicized, but we seem at odds when it comes to understanding their concerns and deciding what to do to help veterans re-enter civil society. Many of these men and women continue to exist in a private, unseen brotherhood of lost sons and daughters. Having worn the same uniform a number of years ago, I understand the legacy of military identity—all we had was each other, and once the identity change from civilian to military member is complete, it is often the only place where we can truly ever fit again. It can be a profound and fundamental shift in character and outlook that few people can ever understand unless they have experienced it.

It can be challenging to steer clear of generalizations when discussing issues that affect large groups of people. One limitation in making statements about military service from the vantage point of injured men and women is that it can miss the many positive aspects of military life. At the risk of being presumptuous, my message to the military would be that the focus on identifying the broken ones and diagnosing them with permanent mental disabilities comes at considerable peril to these people and to the institution itself. For many of these men and women carry secrets, both official and personal, that can never be said out loud. I believe that these members—mostly the Corporals/Master Corporals and the Captains/Majors, the working ranks at the pointy end—have information and insights that are vital to the overall health of the military family.

I have focused my career as a psychologist on the mental health of serving members of the military and veterans. My experience and formal training leaves me with an unsettling perspective. Namely, that military training, ideals, and values can present such stark differences and fundamental changes to one's personality that we can become entirely different versions of ourselves. The number one wish I hear from veterans, including young men and women, is that they want to be the person they were before they deployed or before they joined. It is experienced as a kind of deeply felt loss that is difficult to voice—a profound sense of loss.

When it comes to post-deployment mental health, I have come to believe that the central PTSD issue of emotional avoidance is often a by-product of these military ideals and training. I believe that we need to understand why some people are negatively impacted after their deployments while others are seemingly better equipped to re-adjust to life back home in Canada. While it is tempting to attribute these differences to individual biology, my observation is that these differences are likely a reflection of complex interactions between personal histories and particular military events. In my experience, operational stress injuries usually occur at the intersection between personal histories and the military social world, and it is this intersection that prompted me to write *Ghost in the Ranks*. The social-relational context of military injuries needs to be the subject of ongoing discussions when it comes to creating more effective ways to help these men and women.

Among mentally injured men and women, discussions inevitably centre around their military relationships—the frustration of trying to do their jobs in complex and contradictory situations, how they let their buddies down, disappointing behaviours from their supervisors, or anger and loss of faith in the system. But alongside all these things is their experience of mental-emotional exhaustion—a belief that they gave everything they had to the military. It is as if they had no choice in the matter; a difficult concept for ordinary people to grasp. In their minds, they turned over responsibility for themselves to other people, and parts of their humanness got lost along the way. Their focus is usually on external demands; it is much more difficult for them to talk about their loneliness or being let down or set apart from their buddies—watching people they trusted drift away. This reality is much harder to tackle, and the easy response for many of them is simply to say, "To hell with them all anyway."

This experience of disorientation and loneliness can last for years after leaving the military. They don't realize, just as I did not realize, that during their training and deployments within the military we may have missed out on other important things like self-reflection and making room for mature emotionality in adulthood. In a sense, we remained in a state of permanent adolescence, unaware of the need to navigate the emotional complexities of adulthood.[92]

Military membership is a life-altering experience for most of us. I don't think it is an over-statement to say that we are remade into something else entirely when compared to our former civilian selves. It is unparalleled in any other arena, and the effects are lasting. This transformation also sets us apart from everyday people because of our experiences and because of the traits and values we take on during this metamorphosis. At a fundamental level then, we are bound to the institution, and we maintain aspects of this identity for the remainder of our lives.

Within this context, the real threat to the mental health of military members is not reducible to operational stressors, financial problems, or even family stressors. The real threat to the health of the institution is cynicism—when members stop believing. Cynicism tells members that it is a charade, that nobody really cares, and that they are essentially on their own. It fuels reactions of betrayal and perceptions of neglect. Its tentacles reach across the institution; it is in the ranks, and it festers quietly like an unseen cancer. These are strong statements to make, but having seen it on the faces of many veterans, I cannot discount it in good conscience. I also believe that this is correctable.

When it comes to attachment to the institution, the loss of direct connections to military values and identity can be a bewildering and crippling experience for those people fearing medical release. In our efforts to understand mental declines among military people, it is tempting to look to civilian sectors for the answers. In the process, we downplay the significance of military identity and relatedness to allow us to convert issues into their civilian equivalents. Despite

92 A. Belkin, *Bring me men: Military masculinity and the benign façade of American empire (1898–2001)*, (New York: Columbia University Press, 2012).

nearly two decades, however, we have signs that something central is being missed in our efforts to import solutions from the outside. With respect to mental health treatments, these well-intended and researched approaches seem to be missing the mark by a considerable distance. The centrality of military bonds—family and brotherhood—and the threats to basic identity seem to get forgotten in our efforts to address illness.

In terms of our many military deployments, including our recent ones to Haiti and the Persian Gulf, these places and missions have been forgotten with news updates about Iraq and Syria. All of the nationalistic pride and bumper stickers in support of the troops who fought in the Afghanistan War have faded and gone silent. In stark contrast to the reception for the veterans from World War II, there were no ticker tape parades or national holidays to welcome them home.

For veterans, victory or whether we 'cut and ran' has been difficult to determine. Instead, quietly and out of the public's eye, young men and women, our newest veterans of war and other operations, continue to be released at a steady pace because of PTSD and other OSIs. Equally forgotten are the cases of suicide among serving and retired military personnel—four have died by their own hand in this past week—the true rate of premature deaths remains an open question in Canada. Still in the prime of their lives, these newest veterans often face a monumental challenge when trading in their military membership for a spot once again in the ranks of other anonymous civilians. Alienation and estrangement can serve crushing blows. Their stories and their realities receive passing attention as the military and Canadians preoccupy themselves with moving on, focused on the newest events at home and abroad. Such is life in uniform, forever focused on the next tasking, the next mission.

Our focus on identifying the crazy ones may end in doing the military membership a disservice. Despite my professional training, an inherent flaw in attempts to reduce these issues to mental health problems among individual patients is that it excludes the context in which problems develop in the first place. From basic training onward, soldiers are steeped in high-minded codes of conduct, discipline, ethical imperatives, and a view of the military as an organization larger than life. The reality is often very different, however, for many people. The same organization can be coldly logical and arbitrary and the convenience of reducing problems to individual patients cannot be overstated.

One way to understand the military's focus on operational stress injuries is to look at its purpose for the system. Apart from providing a rationale to offer care to distressed members, which it certainly does, this approach may also serve as a mechanism to manage liability concerns and the uneasiness about mental illness—a mechanism to cleanse the system and to reset its corporate memory. These peripheral goals may function to allow the institution to maintain its needed perceptions of strength and invincibility. In a sense then, medical releases may serve as a safety valve to drain away those voices that challenge the required self-image of the CAF. The alternative might simply be unacceptable; a consideration of incorporating disavowed voices that might signal necessary changes in the ways that the military manages its human resources and its social-relational environment. As a retired Army officer put it to me, "We are terrible when it comes to managing our people."

By humanizing the military workforce—by using the power of group affiliation and providing safe venues for open dialogue within and between the lower ranks and their leaders—we may prevent many instances of mental declines. Maybe I am being naïve, but I do have faith in the power of groups to foster self-repair. Many of the veterans I have encountered carry terrible secrets and, yes, some of their stories are from their preservice past and others are restricted under non-disclosure agreements, but most are personal secrets that serve to drive mental declines.

When it comes to mental health initiatives, the military understands better than most organizations that new behaviours do not occur from education or lectures alone. Practical experience has to be repeated to ensure that reactions are automatic. In the example of combat tactics, soldiers can sit in classrooms indefinitely, but the real lessons are not learned until soldiers have the experience of being ambushed while on patrol.

This same understanding needs to be applied to mental health education efforts. Soldiers can be lectured about mental-emotional health, but without practical exercises, this information can quickly be forgotten for not being relevant. They have to see it applied practically. In terms of the emotional baggage they may be carrying, I think about practical applications within units where members and their leaders can meet to openly discuss and routinely decompress—unpack their rucks—within the spirit of honesty, mutual respect, and integrity.

As well, if members of the CAF who are being released were to undergo training to help them begin the process of relinquishing aspects of their military identity, I think we could head off the problem of transitional shock. These venues might be particularly relevant for people with physical and mental injuries who often feel shunned and excluded because of their problems. Many of them never return to their former units once they are diagnosed and treated. By contrast, an experience of being together again in a cohesive network and challenging longstanding messages about compartmentalization and emotional avoidance could be invaluable for their futures.

As it stands, we usually don't take the time to say goodbye in the military; people just disappear. Formal events that truly acknowledge and thank members for their service to Canada would likely remain with them for a long time. It might also involve a concrete process of taking off the uniform in a reverse order from what occurred during basic training. It may sound counter-intuitive to speak about teaching people to be less responsible, less shut down, and increasingly treated as a peer by instructors as they progress through retraining. Even the act of writing about their military careers and presenting these complete stories to peers and superiors could help them move into the next phase of life.

In my experience, military people may have to reconcile a number of inconsistencies and contradictions in order to address their mental health:

1   That their training will direct them to hide weaknesses and to work harder to overcome them

2   Their established identity among their peers will tell them to remain tough, self-reliant, and independent

3   That embarrassment for being a drain on the unit will be difficult to face

4   That it is an incredibly difficult challenge to learn to be selfish—to place their own needs before mission and unit

5   The myth of invincibility will tell soldiers that it can never happen to them, and when it happens to others, the instinct is to blame them

6   Soldiers who grew up in unemotional or chaotic backgrounds may find it difficult to trust other people and to risk the possibility of being vulnerable

7   Many OSIs do not arise from single events but from cumulative distress and the rejection of their humanness

8   Those people who decide to play along with therapy, drink or use drugs, and avoid close relationships will often have chronic problems

9   The paradox of group-based life in the military means that, when people are upset, they withdraw into silence

10   Learning how to put emotional experiences into words and interacting without pretence or bravado is the toughest work they will ever do

11   No one manages their emotional worlds alone—emotion is by nature meant for social interaction, part of our biological make-up

12   The military rumour mill can be destructive to people

13   Many instances of chronic PTSD involve disavowed secrets

14   As close as military bonds can be, very often these are pseudo-relationships in that they are conditional and based on military roles and proven capabilities

15   Recovery from trauma often means taking some practical action of repair—talk is not enough

16   Waiting for other people to tell you that you have a problem shifts the responsibility from where it belongs—with you.

While it may be important to account for preservice issues, my concern is that blaming problems on deficient members ultimately undermines the institution. Alternatively, it is often the things that cannot be said or taken seriously that undermines group cohesion and morale. When it comes to preservice histories, the benefits of brotherhood and military family can go a long way towards helping people to overcome their past—it has done so for generations of soldiers. I know many senior leaders who came from horrific backgrounds and yet turned out to be exemplary leaders. Almost without exception, they tell me about the one supervisor, early in their careers, who took the time to guide them. These supervisors saw qualities and potential that was nurtured, and these people responded positively and often excelled.

The effects of compartmentalization and depersonalization can be countered by paying attention to subordinates, but this also means resisting the temptation to respond as bureaucrats. I think the last thing we need is for the military to mirror the less positive aspects of civil society—in many respects it can be a fractured and lonely place. The military workplace, in my view, can be a place for members to recharge and to reconnect without eroding discipline or hampering operational effectiveness.

We all know about the importance of interpersonal distance between leaders and subordinates, e.g. respect the rank and not the person. After all, leaders may need to put people directly in harm's way and may be required to sacrifice some for the greater good. Even so, these leaders still carry tremendous responsibility and even guilt over decisions they made that cost the lives of members under their charge. As it stands, they have no choice but to keep these personal issues to themselves in order to project the image of a strong leader. But, the senior leadership has also been affected by trauma.

Once again, if there were venues where these members could decompress with other members of their units, there is a strong likelihood that improved attachment bonds could lead to improvements in unit functioning without eroding discipline. It is an important consideration in light of the focus on military mental health. We need to get past our legacy of stoicism and the ironic twists of rugged individualism. On the one hand, we train people to be a part of a family, but when it comes to personal issues, they are treated as isolated individuals and victims of their biology.

I also realize that there are two sides to every story. As I have attempted to show, mental health operates and plays itself out at the intersection between members and their social-relational contexts within the military. If we occupy ourselves with looking for the villains—whether this is the search for personal weaknesses or ineffective leaders—we miss the central features of military life. Whether we focus on preservice factors or the personalities of those who report mental declines on the one hand, or blame specific leaders or bureaucratic policies on the other, we risk missing the complexities of life in uniform. It is seductive to look for simple answers to complex issues; unfortunately as a society we do it all the time.

In the end, we all know that new recruits are often not completely honest with the military about their past, and the military, for its part, is not honest with them about the true demands of military life for fear of scaring them away. So we end up with two parties continually checking out the other to fulfill unspoken expectations. People who join the military are often looking for more than a job; many are in search of a place to belong, to be larger than life, to have control, or to forget about what happened to them before joining. The military needs people who are willing to adopt its value system and ethos in order to carry out its mandates to the government. This may require placing these men and women in situations where they will not be protected and where they will see and do things that will challenge their very notions of humanity. For the most part, none of this can be talked about openly.

The practice of looking for weakness among traumatized soldiers after-the-fact is disingenuous at best. If we truly believe that fundamental weakness is the explanation for mental declines in the military, then this work has to be done at the point of recruitment or at least during basic indoctrination into the military. This would present a major challenge to the sophistication of assessments done by the military. I would contend that the current practice of looking for preservice explanations for operational reactions after-the-fact is simply untenable. We cannot unravel preservice history from military events after the process of military identity has been established.

At the end of people's careers, there is tremendous pressure on the military health system to get it right, which is further complicated by financial incentives for those being released. There are many pressures to distort the truth—clinicians want the best for their patients, so they often overestimate the impact of military operations, while members exclude their developmental history and also overestimate how poorly they are functioning in the present in the interests of their financial futures. For their part, bureaucracies focus on managing and possibly downplaying their liabilities and responsibilities to those who have served. These are all legitimate concerns.

In these arenas, there is no room for the true story because it complicates the picture. It takes considerable efforts by clinicians and arbitrators to decide about the true severity of mental health issues related to military service and the appropriate compensation levels. I don't think we have a consensus about why we offer compensation—as a payable insurance claim for injuries sustained; as recognition for lost earning potential; as a buffer to ensure the financial future of veterans who are unable or unwilling to adjust to the realities of civilian life; or some combination of all of the above. In my view, the military has to decide whether to live up to all that goes with the family metaphor, or alternatively, if members are to be viewed as contracted employees, then the military workplace might need to be transformed into a formalized workplace. This would amount to organized worker representation. In this setting, obligations and accountability by the employer and employee would be clearly articulated with identified consequences and legal recourse for both parties.

Having worked as a psychologist with military people for nearly twenty-five years, it is striking how groups of military people are larger than the sum of individual members—their individual problems usually reflect broader issues for the group to manage. When members are not able or willing to speak up or they challenge the rules, in my view, this is a group issue signalling lack of trust in the structure and leaders for not meeting the needs of the group. Conversely, if we single out an individual member and scrutinize his behaviour as the problem, the effect on everyone else is to erode safety and cohesion within the group. I believe that this has implications for the broader military context.

Military members are gregarious, competitive, and highly social and, with the advances in social media, what happens across Canada or halfway around the world is known by others almost immediately. This is how I think about the broader management of mental health within the military. Our recent protracted war in Afghanistan affected all three elements of the military and drew heavily upon reservists to meet our operational commitments. Many of these young men and women disappeared back to their home units or to their civilian jobs with little fanfare or recognition for their efforts. Some were forgotten even before getting back home.

Involvement in combat operations meant that the mental-emotional climate within the military became necessarily more rational, focused, physically demanding, and intolerant of problems that interfered with operational tempo. This also meant that many people similar to those described above were left to resolve their problems on their own. In most cases, opportunities to interact with these men and women through tolerance and compassion by superiors were surpassed by a focused management style. In this timeframe, the mental well-being of the organization seemed to also become the exclusive constituent of the medical health system.

Whether due to their personal anxieties about the topic of mental health or complex rules, many stories reflected supervisors who decreased their mentoring role with their subordinates. In my observations, the military institution became exhausted dealing with the loss and injury to thousands of promising young men and women. I believe the institution is still struggling to come to terms with these realities, and the easiest solution is simply to try to forget and to move forward. Well-meaning mantras of punching above one's weight on the world stage and doing more with less, while bolstering soldier and leadership confidence to do their best, came at tremendous costs to the organization.

The loss of personnel and the organization's inability to regroup in the face of fiscal austerity continue to ripple through the membership. Many soldiers are bitter, disheartened, left to grieve the death of their friends and respected leaders from the early days of the war. With the passage of time, there are now very few ways to air out old and forgotten events. Other people are outraged over their treatment and the breach of their own values and military codes while they were overseas. Notions of brotherhood and family became distorted and circumscribed to being applicable only to the battlefield but not at home—they ring as hollow words for those who are medically released. Anger, frustration, disillusionment, and grief are held in check as the organization moves towards a post-war posture. Even if the military could be afforded the opportunity to regroup, there is little time or luxury to spend reconciling the effects of the war on the organization.

After all these years, I still carry the legacy of having served and still have close friends from that time in my life. I am reminded of it each time I meet with individual soldiers or groups of veterans. Just like them, my sense of belonging was earned; it was not handed out freely. Within this new family, we participated in a process that transformed us into a people who could be intensely focused, proud, gregarious, perfectionistic, coldly rational and unfeeling, and mentally equipped to destroy if directed to do so—a much tougher version of ourselves. This is not to say that the military gave us new qualities; they provided an environment and the challenge to hone particular traits while downplaying and ignoring other traits that got in the way. It was like being moved a bit or a lot further to the right, a depersonalized version of ourselves on the tougher end of the personality spectrum.

Among these new brothers and sisters, we could be intimately connected and we could also be callous and, at times, inhuman towards each other; once called hazing or induction ceremonies. Through this process of being treated and treating each other roughly in a black-and-white, 'all-in' existence, we learned to dismiss our civil selves as somehow irrelevant. These metamorphic shifts to the right starts the minute young people enter basic training. Here, the number one challenge is to understand that one's entire world can crumble through disapproving looks or comments from superiors and peers; that there is no place for individuality or personal stuff and that compliance with commands is uppermost in galvanizing members into well-functioning collectives.

The military is a world of right and wrong where ambiguities and contradictions are banished as threats to decisive action. Everyone is taught that there are clear rules for every situation and ignorance of these rules is no excuse for failure. Every military person who has ever been promoted remembers the peculiar expectation that, the very next day, you are automatically expected to know the new responsibilities and roles. Or how, returning from a trade qualification course, you are expected to know the intricacies of the new role without any experience to pull it off: "You had the training, you should know this."

By far, the primary objectives of military training are safety and skill proficiency. It focuses on what people are doing wrong in the name of safety and standards. If something is done wrong, you do it again and again until you get it right. The goal is perfection so that mistakes do not happen—we continually obsess over details. Imagine a statement to the effect:

> **Well, pretty good job, Private. I see that you are conducting some parts of your weapons drills very well. There are just a few other details that we need to focus on.**

I can hear the sarcasm and laughter as I write because this scenario between a supervisor and a subordinate would never happen. It is right or it is wrong, you fit or you don't fit.

Military people learn to overcome and ignore their doubts and private thoughts, to harness adrenaline surges to remain alert and focused, to deal with long bouts of boredom, and to control the physical body so that it reacts instinctively and instantly. As I have said repeatedly, we learn to become depersonalized versions of ourselves in a world that can be demanding and merciless, and this extends logically to the way we treat each other. I believe that the effects of repeated training and military deployments reach much deeper into our consciousness, and we learn to switch off emotionally. This emotional vacuum may also explain the value of alcohol and other substances among military personnel—it quiets the vigilant thinking brain, allowing people to move to a more emotional version of themselves, at least temporarily.

Those veterans who have lived through childhood physical and sexual abuse often report higher rates of alcohol and cannabis use, paranoia, and dissociation, but they also downplay their problems with depression and trauma.[93] However, in terms of interpersonal relationships, denying and hiding personal problems may paradoxically

93   J.J. Whelan, "Effects of developmental abuse and symptom suppression among traumatized veterans." *Psychology* 2015 6: 540–548.

contribute to difficulties with emotional and social engagement, which, in turn, creates challenges for veterans in accepting help. As outlined, there is ample evidence that traumatized military personnel with complex developmental histories may benefit from group cohesion. The military ethos of backing up one's battle buddies, mutual identification, and shared experience may help tremendously in establishing psychological safety.

Military people often internalize their experiences from around the world, and they are often unaware of the effects of what they do, see, and hear. They often have few avenues to verbalize, describe, or incorporate these new experiences. In terms of help, our responses to operational trauma should focus on talking about specific military events, shouldn't they?

Well, yes and no.

For most of the people I know, talking only about specific military events is not enough for them if they are to understand what is happening to them or deciding what to do to find enjoyment and satisfaction in their present life. However, talking about their past and present relationships, trusting others, and coming to terms with strong emotions seem to be important. These strong emotions can short-circuit rational thinking almost every time—they happen in an instant and before the thinking brain knows what is happening. That is part of the reason why much of military training is meant to teach us to react instinctively and to ignore any emotional stuff.

But it's important to recognize that those things still get filed away to be dealt with later—our emotional brains remember. When people get home and come out of adrenaline mode and think it's time to relax, this stuff can come back like a tsunami, and it freaks people out. Emotions are too strong and happen unpredictably. The old way of trying to help traumatized people was to teach them to think their way through specific memories, but this has finally been replaced by a focus on attachment and emotional regulation. Fancy words, but put simply, the things people learned early in life or in the military about managing strong emotions can have a direct impact on how they respond to them as adults.

If they learned that caregivers or leaders were not available or could not be trusted to help or listen when they were distressed, when overwhelmed by what they did overseas, they are more likely to stuff it away and tough it through—just like they always had to do before. The problem this time, is that it keeps coming back to bite them, getting triggered emotionally by all kinds of stuff and feeling like they are losing their minds. Their training and the old ways to manage do not work no matter how hard they try, but the idea of lowering their guard and to truly risk trusting somebody is foreign. Even the thought of it can panic people. How does one figure out how to talk about personal stuff, including the secret stuff that no one else on the planet knows about them?

This discussion is not intended to blame people for their deployment reactions; it does mean that, if military members are going to trust helpers, the things that are getting in the way from the past also have to be addressed. Talking with another person about what they went through and what they learned from it can truly open the door to freedom from the past and help them find hope looking forward. The past does not have to govern the present and future, but it does require courage and a willingness to give people a second chance.

As well intentioned and structured as the accepted therapies are, they often inadvertently reinforce the belief that strong emotions have to be ignored. In the past, there was no place in these therapies for the primacy of affective reactions in and of themselves. When people became upset through anger or profound sadness, therapists usually helped move them back to safe ground by interrupting these emotional states through reminders to breathe, relax, or focus on something else. For a variety of reasons, therapists were taught that strong emotions equated to retraumatization and loss of control over therapy sessions. While containing emotions can certainly serve as a safety function in some cases, the wholesale use of these strategies means that emotional states cycle repeatedly but cannot be resolved since they are avoided as unsafe states. So, therapy can exacerbate the issue of emotional dysregulation.

A concern over premature death seems to lie behind many of our efforts aimed at the mental health of first responders. The topic of suicide among first responders has caught average citizens by surprise in Canada. It has created a wave of societal concern because it raises anxieties. We have attempted strategies to control it by focusing on characteristics and possible frailties of particular people. However, the prospect that heroes may decide to end their lives because of the toll of managing society's fears and its underbelly is difficult to accept. Their decisions to end their lives may represent an accusation of the very society they served—they have seen too much.

We are reluctant to look closely at the demands placed on these people and the structure of their workplaces because it may require involvement from the larger society; the rest of us may be asked to provide a direct role in protecting them. Maybe we too would be faced with fundamental dilemmas about the meaning and value of life. It is simply too convenient to look for individual weakness as a way to explain away organizational and societal issues. Military veterans and other first responders who struggle with mental health concerns could be telling us about a fundamental emptiness of an everyday life they no longer want to be a part of.

CPSIA information can be obtained
at www.ICGtesting.com
Printed in the USA
LVOW12s0154070916
503512LV00001B/89/P